Private Money Management

Switching from Mutual Funds to Private Money Managers

Private Money Management

Switching from Mutual Funds to Private Money Managers

Julie Stone
with Larry Chambers

S^{t}L

St. Lucie Press

Boca Raton   London   New York   Washington, D.C.

Library of Congress Cataloging-in-Publication Data

Stone, Julie, 1941-
    Private money management : switching from mutual funds to private money managers /
Julie Stone and Larry Chambers.
        p.   cm.
    ISBN 1-57444-301-1 (alk. paper)
    1. Retirement income--Planning. 2. Investments. 3. Finance, Personal. 4. Financial
security. I. Chambers, Larry. II. Title.

HG179 .S8444 2001
332.024′01--dc21   2001019364

Visit the CRC Press Web site at www.crcpress.com

Dedication

To my children Corie and Jon
and
To all investors, new and old.
I hope this book assists you
in developing the wealth you desire.

Julie Stone

Contents

The Authors

Julie Stone has achieved recognition as a senior investment management consultant at a major Wall Street investment firm. She is a Certified Investment Management Analyst through the Investment Management Consultant Association (IMCA). Julie was featured in Sue Herera's book *Women of the Street* and is frequently quoted in several industry trade magazines and newspapers.

Larry Chambers writes for some of the top national investment advisors representing over 3 billion dollars in asset classes, as well as for one of the nation's leading CPA firms. He has been published by major publishing houses — including Irwin, McGraw-Hill, Random House, Times Mirror, Dow Jones, and John Wiley and Sons, as well as featured in hundreds of national investment trade magazines.

INTRODUCTION

If you knew that there were no secrets, that the mysteries could all be explained, wouldn't investing take on a whole new appearance? You wouldn't run out of patience, or feel overwhelmed and just give up and do nothing. You'd settle in and wait confidently. The ability to maintain patience during difficult times requires not only an understanding of the stock market, it also requires an understanding of your own reactions to uncertainty (risk).

And if you knew exactly how much money you would need at retirement, you could figure out how much risk you'd have to take to get there. You could stop focusing on trying to find the hot investment and set about building your overall net worth. You'd develop a plan to manage your existing assets and future resources to meet your anticipated needs.

Where do you start? You don't start by looking at mutual fund returns, but rather by looking at how long you have before you retire and how much money you're going to need when you get there. If you first determine your projected monthly retirement expenses and income, then you can easily see any "shortfall." A shortfall is the difference between what you will realistically need and what you will actually have. It's what happens when your anticipated income and other earnings do not cover all your expenses.

You can make these calculations on the back of a napkin or fill out a comprehensive financial planning form. Or, you can complete the tables below, which are somewhere between these two extremes. These tables will help you determine the amounts needed to make up for any shortfall, the rate of return you will need to achieve, and the number of dollars you need to add annually to close any gap. Just knowing that information should take some of the pressure off and make the "unknown" less mysterious.

Most investors don't bother with this step, or they approach it backwards. Total return based on historical performance has become the only financial gauge for most investors. But total return is nothing more than a visual display of the past, and only certain aspects of the past, at that. It's not an indicator of the future. Historical performance only tells a fraction of what you need to know and it can be very misleading.

Let's say you figure out that your shortfall is about $300,000 and you've got twenty years or so left before retirement. You have $50,000 from the sale of property to invest. What do most people do in a similar situation? They jump at one of the mutual fund ads in a money magazine, or seek help from a traditional stockbroker or financial advisor. But if you go for these approaches, you may still have a problem. Most investment sales organizations operate within the framework of pre-tax returns and relative performance. This gets you to focus only on the rate of return and how it has compared in the past to others. You may be shown a dollar goal projection, illustrating the magic of compounding using the historical rate of return of ten percent. At ten percent, your $50,000 grows to $336,000 in twenty years; and $872,000 in thirty years. You think, I'm there! And you invest in that fund.

But here's the danger: total return drastically overstates the purchasing power that you will have, because it ignores taxes, fees, and inflation. Together, these three asset-eroders can bring your expected return down to as little as zero. Studies show that historical after-tax, after-fee, after-inflation rate of return on corporate bonds is about zero and the return on stocks, while higher, can be as low as two percent after all expenses, including the advisor's fee, are subtracted. Sometimes experienced practitioners deduct for taxes and factor for inflation, but do not figure in the fees.

What a difference these oversights can make! If you figure your taxes at around 2.5 percent and your broker consultant's fee at 2.5 percent, our ten percent return assumption could be reduced to five percent. So after taxes and fees, your $50,000 in twenty years is not worth $336,000, but only $132,000. Subtract three percent for inflation and real dollar projections drop to $74,000. *Whoops!* You will not hit your target!

You could be short by hundreds of thousands of dollars without time to make it up. This creates frustrated investors who become, in effect, market timers — often selling an existing fund and buying a new one in hopes of gaining back lost ground. The classic buy-high, sell-low syndrome results. Investors who do this a few times become disillusioned with the never-ending process of picking new actively managed investments, and many quit investing altogether.

The point is, even if you are lucky and pick the best mutual funds, that still doesn't mean that you will meet your actual objectives. Your goal should be to focus on the dollar amount you will need and on total *after*-tax return. Total after-tax return is after fees, after expenses, after any and everything that stands in your way of achieving your goal.

You should control what you can control: understand which combinations of investments will give you the highest probability of making up any shortfalls, lower your costs — and operate your investment program fully aware of the tax consequences.

Steps to Follow

When planning for retirement, most of us quickly discover that our anticipated income and other earnings will not cover all of our expenses and we will have a shortfall. That recognition is often the beginning of putting an effective investment plan in place.

- Step one: calculate your monthly retirement expenses (Chart A). Figure out how many dollars will be required to satisfactorily meet your monthly retirement expenses. In the chart below, first estimate your current costs and those you expect to decrease when you retire, in Columns A and B. Then, in Columns C and D, record your current costs and the projected costs that may increase when you retire. The total represents your estimated annual retirement expenses.
- Step two: calculate your retirement income (Chart B). Primary sources of retirement income typically include employee-sponsored retirement plans, IRAs, Keoghs and SEP-IRAs, social security, and personal savings. Identify all the known variables that are under your control, such as time periods, tax rates, required cash flows, and fees. The focus should be on what's reliably predictable.
- Step three: calculate your annual savings requirements. Use Tables 1, 2, and 3 to help you calculate the amount of money you'll need to save for retirement. Keep adjusting the known variables. View financial goals as future liabilities that need to be met. This will help you to take the amount of risk needed, not too much or too little. You may think of yourself as a conservative investor; but if your shortfall is too large, you may have to do something different.

Costs that may be reduced at retirement	Current amount	Estimated amount
Housing	$_____	$_____
Life insurance	$_____	$_____
Transportation	$_____	$_____
Clothing & personal care	$_____	$_____
Taxes	$_____	$_____
Business travel and entertainment	$_____	$_____
Miscellaneous purchases	$_____	$_____
Loan repayments and interest	$_____	$_____
Education		
Total costs	$_____	$_____
	Column A	Column B

Costs that may be reduced at retirement	Current amount	Estimated amount
Medical *(Hospital insurance, supplemental insurance, prescriptions, dentist)*	$_____	$_____
Food	$_____	$_____
Recreation and entertainment *(Vacations, family travel, hobbies, etc.)*	$_____	$_____
Auto insurance	$_____	$_____
Other	$_____	$_____
Total costs	$_____	$_____
	Column C	Column D

- You can expect total monthly retirement expenses to be approximately 75% of your current income.
- Think about how your expenses will change at retirement and then reallocate the dollars accordingly. For example, you may not spend as much on housing and car but you may spend more on recreation, travel and medical.

Total Current Monthly Expenses
(Add column A and column C)

Total Estimated Monthly Expenses at Retirement
(Add column B and column D)

Estimated Annual Retirement Expense
(Multiply expenses by 12)

Chart A. Calculate your monthly retirement expenses.

Your Projections	**Example I: My plans to retire in 20 years**	

1. Annual retirement expenses
(From Chart A, at the bottom of the page.)

$ _____ $ 50,000   ·My estimated annual retirement expenses are $50,000

2. Retirement income

a) Social Security income

$ _____ $ 10,000

b) Other income (defined benefit plans, post-retirement income, rents, royalties)

$ _____ $ 10,000   I estimate $10,000 from Social Security. I estimate $10,000 to come from book royalties.

3. Total income
(Add lines 2a and 2b)

$ _____ $ 20,000   My total projected income is $20,000.

4. Income shortfall
(Line 1 minus line 3)

$ _____ $ 30,000   By subtracting my retirement income from my retirement expenses, I found a shortfalll of $30,000.

5. Total assets needed at retirement
(From Table 1)

$ _____ $ 657,337   I plan on retiring in 20 years, Table 1 shows that I'll need total $657,337 saved by the time I retire. Inflation is considered in this amount.

6. Amount you have saved already for retirement

a) IRAs/Keoghs

$ _____ $ 10,000   I also have saved $10,000 in my SEP IRA.

b) Employer-sponsored retirement plans

$ _____ $ 0

c) Other investments/savings (stocks, bonds, CDs, mutual funds, money market funds, etc.)

$ _____ $ 50,000   This is the value of my brokerage portfolio.

d) Equity in home (optional)

$ _____ $ 0   In my home. You've got to live some where.

7. Total amount saved
(Add lines 6a through 6d)

$ _____ $ 60,000   Combining the assets listed in line 6, I have saved this amount.

8. Value of current savings at retirement
a) Portfolio Compounding Factor
(From Table 2)

$ _____ $ 6.73   In Table 2, I have determined the factor selecting 10% as my rate of return. 6.73 times $60,000 is $403,800.

b) Multiply total from line 7 by line 8a

$ _____ $ 403,800

9. Asset shortfall at retirement
(Line 5 minus line 8b)

$ _____ $ 253,537   By subtracting $403,800 from $657,337 I estimated that is the amount I must have saved by the time I retire.

10. Annual Savings needed
(From Table 3)

$ _____ $ 4,000   In order to meet this goal, Table 3 suggests that I save approximately $4,000 per year for the next 20 years.

Chart B. Calculate your retirement income, Part 2.

The balance of this book will show you an investment strategy with the highest probability of achieving the absolute dollars you need, within your time frame, and with the appropriate level of risk — and will teach you how to apply it. Think of it this way: your investment program should be designed to overcome any shortfalls, not to beat the stock market.

Calculate Your Retirement Income and Annual Savings Goal
Use these tables to help you calculate the amount of money you'll need to save for retirement.

Table 1: Total Assets Requirement *(at retirement)*

If your income shortfall is	*Years to retirement* 5	10	15	20	25	30	35	40
$10,000	121,665	148,024	180,094	219,112	266,584	324,340	394,609	480,102
$20,000	243,331	296,049	360,189	438,225	533,167	648,680	789,218	960,204
$30,000	364,996	444,073	540,283	657,337	799,751	973,019	1,183,827	1,440,306
$50,000	608,326	740,122	900,472	1,095,562	1,332,918	1,621,699	1,973,044	2,400,510

Table 2. Portfolio Compounding Factor *(compounded annually)*

Years to your goal	*Rate of return* 8%	9%	10%
10	2.16	2.37	2.59
15	3.17	3.64	4.18
20	4.66	5.60	6.73
25	6.85	8.62	10.83
30	10.06	13.27	17.45

Assumptions:
Tax-deferred income
No depletion of principal
Annual return on assets: 8%
Annual inflation: 4%
Annual savings made at the end of each year (Table 3)

Table 3. Annual Savings Requirement *(needed to reach savings goal)*

If your income shortfall is:	5	10	15	20	25	30
$50,000	8,190	3,137	1,574	873	508	304
$100,000	16,380	6,275	3,147	1,746	1,017	608
$150,000	24,570	9,412	4,721	2,619	1,525	912
$200,000	32,759	12,549	6,295	3,492	2,034	1,216
$300,000	49,139	18,824	9,442	5,238	3,050	1,824
$500,000	81,899	31,373	15,737	8,730	5,084	3,040

INTRODUCTION

Contents

1 Investment Strategies — What Works and What Doesn't

The problem is that most investment strategies can't replicate their positive results. If they could, you'd be guaranteed to achieve the success of Peter Lynch.

We'll start by examining various investment strategies to see which are truly effective, and weed out those that have been proven to be ineffective.

About ninety-seven percent of all mutual funds use an investment management strategy called "active management." As the words accurately describe, active managers move investments around. But think of the last time you moved house — it cost you both money and time. It's the same principle in investing. We will examine many active management strategies. First, we'll look at one that involves trying to time the markets.

Market Timing

Market timing is the attempt to be in the market when it goes up and out of the market when it goes down. Market-timers have to be right twice. First, they must get out of a particular market before it declines. Then they must get back in early enough to catch the next market rise.

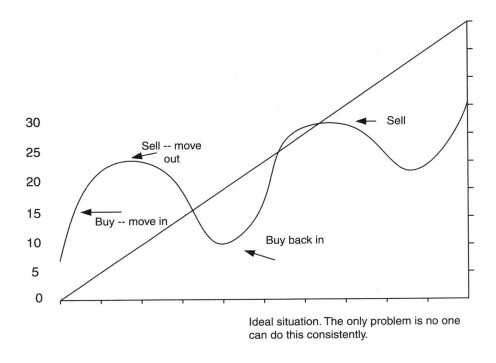

Figure 1.1 Marketing timing.

Diversification

The term *diversification* is used so often by so many people that it has lost its meaning. In the financial world, diversification means not having all your money in any one type of investment. Mutual funds, by design, are diversified. Investing in mutual funds is the first step you can take to reduce your investment risk. Your overall investment performance should be less volatile with a broad variety of investments rather than with a single type. The graphs in Figure 1.2 illustrate the importance of diversification.

These graphs illustrate the compounding growth on two $10,000 investments over a 25-year period. The $10,000 on the left assumes a single investment at an 8% return. The graph on the right assumes diversification of $10,000 into five $2,000 investments at different returns.

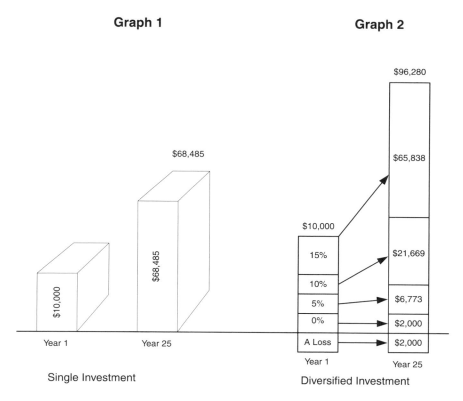

Graph 1

Graph 2

$68,485

$10,000

$68,485

Year 1   Year 25

Single Investment

$96,280

$65,838

$10,000

15% $21,669

10%

5% $6,773

0% $2,000

A Loss $2,000

Year 1   Year 25

Diversified Investment

While three of the five investments were a lower return than the single investment, the total for the diversified side was substantially higher.

Figure 1.2 Diversification.

Graph 1 illustrates a single investment of $10,000 at an eight percent return during twenty-five years. Graph 2 also illustrates diversifying the same $10,000 investment into five separate $2,000 amounts, producing various returns. Although three of the five investments showed a lower return than the single investment, the total for the diversified side was substantially higher. While it's true you would have been further ahead by being invested in just the "hot" fund, that's a matter of luck and not predictable beforehand.

Each asset responds differently to changes in the economy and investment marketplace. If you look back at the `70s and `80s, the market was down while interest rates and real estate soared. The trick is to own a variety of assets, because a short-term decline in one can be balanced by others that are stable or going up in value. The stock markets may go up one year and down the next, while other investments, such as certificates of deposit (CDs) may remain unchanged. Investors who own shares of a stock fund combined with bond funds are usually better off than those who limit themselves to stocks only.

The higher volatility of stocks means higher risk. Suppose all your money is invested in stocks and you need to sell some of your holdings to meet an emergency. If the stocks in your mutual funds are depressed when you need to sell, you could be forced to take a loss on your investment. (Forget the tax deferral for now, that's only one part of the equation.) Owning other investments would give you flexibility in liquidating investments to raise needed cash, while allowing you to hold your stocks until those prices improved. A diversified portfolio provides both liquidity and comparative stability.

During the long run, owning a wide variety of investments has proven to be the best strategy. Money market funds or cash can provide a foundation of stability and liquidity that is ideal for cash reserves. Bonds are good for steady income, and stocks have had the greatest potential for growth.

Effective and Ineffective Diversification

Diversification is a prudent method for managing certain types of investment risk. For example, unsystematic risks, those risks associated with individual securities, can be reduced through diversification. However, it doesn't work to invest all of your assets in the same market segment, or in segments that tend to move in tandem. The risk is that all your investments could decrease in value at the same time. For instance, investing in the Standard and Poor's 500 Stock Index and the Dow Jones Industrial Average would be ineffective diversification, since both tend to move in the same direction at the same time. Both are indexes composed of large capitalized companies in the U.S.

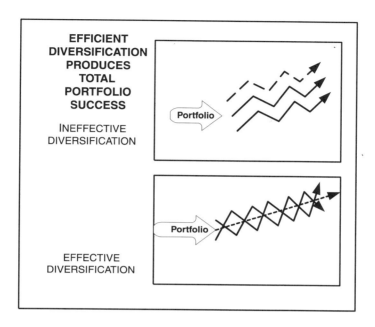

Figure 1.3 The concept of efficient diversification.

Effective diversification is having a portfolio of investments that tend to move dissimilarly. This is the premise of Harry Markowitz's Nobel Prize winning modern portfolio theory. He showed that, to the extent that securities in a portfolio do not move in concert with each other, their individual risks can be effectively diversified away. The overall risk of a portfolio is *not* the average risk of each of the investments. In fact, you can actually have a low-risk portfolio made up of high-risk assets.

This is a profound academic investment discovery that represents a dramatic breakthrough in investment methodology and the way many professional investors manage money. Many investment professionals now recognize that effective diversification reduces portfolio price changes in mutual funds and smooths out returns when coupled with investments such as bank CDs and fixed income type investments.

Combining Dissimilar Investments

Combining dissimilar investments can significantly enhance returns: if you have two investment portfolios with the same average or arithmetic return, the portfolio with less volatility will have a greater compound or geometric rate of return. For example, let's assume that you are considering two mutual funds. Both of them have an average annual expected return of ten percent. How would you determine which fund is better? If one fund is more volatile than the other, their compound return and ending values will be different.

Purchasing asset classes with a low correlation to one another is the Nobel Prize winning secret for achieving better portfolio consistency. What do I mean by "low correlation"? Technically, correlation is a statistical measure of the degree to which the movement of two variables is related.

Asset Allocation

Only a few years ago, the term *asset allocation* did not exist. Modern portfolio theory added a third dimension to the process of diversification. The shorthand definition for asset allocation is to allocate your money among various asset categories.

Determinants of Portfolio Performance

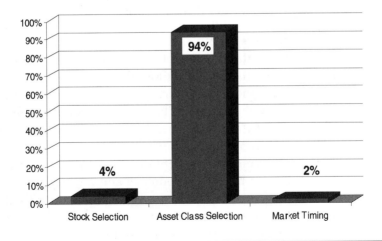

Figure 1.4 Total return variations. (Data from Brinson, B.G.P., Singer, B.D., and Beebower, G.L., *Financial Analysts Journal* (May–June):1996.)

Determining the right asset allocation can be critical to your investment success. Although the term is often used interchangeably with diversification, don't confuse the two. They are not the same thing.

Tools for asset allocation range from a pen and note pad to sophisticated software programs. Software-assisted asset allocation has become common among professional financial advisors and eliminates much of the previous guesswork in the process. This is where an investment advisor or financial planner can really earn his or her fees — by using proper asset allocation and diversification, they can outperform the major indexes over long periods of time.

Time

The last and most critical ingredient in the investment mix is *time*. This one is my favorite because it is the one *known* element in our equation — it affects us all the same — nothing can speed it up or slow it down.

Given enough time, investments that may otherwise seem unattractive may become highly desirable. The longer the time period over which investments are held, the closer actual returns in a portfolio will come to the expected average. This means short-term market fluctuations will smooth out.

The real challenge is to commit to a strategy and discipline of long-term investing and not be swayed by compelling investment distractions. With a long-term view, you can better choose investments that have the best chances for success. By adding the essential ingredient of time to your investment plan, you can *almost* be assured of success. Of course there's no guarantee that just adding time solves all your investment problems. There is still a little more to it.

Beware of approaches that measure rates of returns over one-year periods. While this is a conventional and widely used approach, a twelve-month time frame simply is not the best length of measure.

The news media has extremely short-term deadlines — often limited to that particular day! The media plays to the public's belief that gurus exist who can accurately predict when the market will turn up or down, and that a knowledgeable person can pick the *right* individual security or mutual fund. But every year, about half or more of the mutual funds don't outperform their benchmarks, and those in the upper half in one year have only about a fifty percent chance of repeating in any other year.

Uninformed investors believe that by regularly reading a financial publication such as the *Wall Street Journal* or a financial magazine, they become insiders to information that gives them some advantage.

When you look at long-term common stock investments, however, the ups and downs tend to straighten out. Wars and threats of wars merely become blips on the chart. Economic events are put in their proper long-term perspective.

The Global Equity portfolio shown in Figure 1.5 presents another way of looking at how time affects risk. Notice that one-year-at-a-time rates of return on common stocks over the years are inconclusive, showing both large gains and large losses. Shifting to five-year periods brings a considerable increase in consistency and regularity. The losses disappear, and the gains appear more consistently. Shifting to ten-year periods increases the consistency of returns significantly. Compounding over a decade overwhelms the single-year differences. *The gap between the lows and the highs narrows.*

Unless you're a day trader, you are probably not going to invest in a stock for only one day. Such a brief time period is clearly too short for investment in common stocks, because the expected variation in returns is too large in comparison to the average expected return. Such short-term holdings in common stocks are not investments; they are speculations.

Change measurement periods to longer time horizons, and expected rates of returns and variations in returns also change. If we measure an investment every three years, rather than every quarter, we can see satisfying progress that wouldn't be apparent on a quarterly measurement.

In most cases, the time horizon that investors use as the standard to measure results is far too short, causing dissatisfaction with investment performance. This is perpetuated because most stock brokerage firms reward their brokers on the basis of trades, not on how well their clients' portfolios perform.

Too often, people try to compress time. They have fantasies and dreams that can only be reached by getting rich quickly, but those attempts almost always end up on the losing side.

One investment strategy that puts time on your side, avoids the mistaken activities of market timing and stock selection, and eliminates a lot of needless worry by making investing automatic is *dollar cost averaging*. With this strategy, an investor buys by the dollar's worth rather than by the number of shares.

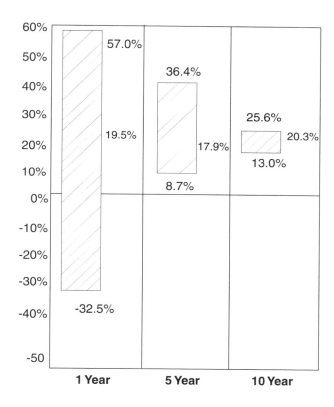

RISK OVER TIME
Global Equity Portfolio Returns:
January 1972- December 1997
Compound Annual Rates of Return

ROLLING PERIODS

Figure 1.5 Global equity portfolio returns showing risk over time. (Data from RWB Advisory Services, Inc.)

The Principle of Dollar Cost Averaging

This simply means investing equal dollar amounts at regular intervals: monthly, quarterly, semiannually, or annually. It's an effective method that can help you turn the characteristic fluctuations of common stock or mutual fund values into a benefit because you are investing over different time periods.

When prices are low, you're able to purchase more shares. When prices are high, you'll be purchasing fewer shares. In most cases, you will purchase a greater number of shares at a lower price level, making your average cost per share generally lower than the normal average. For this strategy to be effective, you should consider beforehand if you will indeed be able to invest equal amounts at regular intervals over time. If prices are low and you continue investing the same amount; you will be buying more shares at a lower price. In other words, with dollar cost averaging, the objective is to purchase shares at an average cost that is below the average price.

Figure 1.6 charts a $150 per month investment through a ten-month period. Share prices fluctuate during that time, but the investment amount holds constant. When prices are at their low, $2.00, an investor is able to purchase more shares (75). When prices are higher, $10.00, an investor purchases fewer shares (15), for the same purchase price. Over time, that investor will purchase a greater number of shares (342.5) at a lower price level, thereby making his or her average cost per share ($4.38) lower than the general average price ($6.00) at which shares are purchased. *In effect, the investor is buying in quantity at lower prices, and relatively little at exorbitantly high prices.* Just what an investor would want to do, right?

Investing becomes automatic with dollar cost averaging. It eliminates the worry of *should I or shouldn't I?* Mutual fund investors using dollar cost averaging also have less reason to fear market declines. Indeed, an occasional decline becomes a benefit, permitting the investor to buy a greater than normal number of shares at lower than average prices. The dollar cost averaging investor begins to almost wait in anticipation of the next mini-crash, instead of dreading it.

But beware. Even armed with this valuable knowledge, you may be vulnerable to another ever-present danger lurking about in investment "la la land." That danger is "dis-information" — the subject of the next chapter.

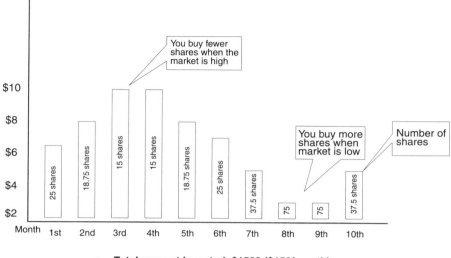

- **Total amount invested: $1500 ($150/month)**
- **Average price of these 10 purchases: $6.00**
- **Average cost per share: $4.38**
- **Total shares: 342.50**
- **Average cost per share: $150 month times 10 months = $1,500 divided by 342.50 (total shares) = $4.38 average cost**

Figure 1.6 The principle of dollar cost averaging.

2 Misleading Information

Misleading information is everywhere. Some financial professionals may sometimes disseminate misleading information because they are so anxious to compete or to look good that they don't take the time to do their homework. Also, the level of complexity in the industry has grown exponentially over the last decade, contributing to the problem. From brokers to advisors to online trading sites, the message is to *buy and sell* and you'll get rich. The explosion in the financial media has brought its own compounding effect into the confusion that influences investors of every type. There is an almost limitless number of television and radio shows, magazines and periodicals devoted to telling us how and where to invest, and there are numerous others in which investing is featured prominently. An entire industry has developed and grown around the necessity to engage in transactions and trading. Without this activity, the financial industry in its present form simply could not exist.

With all of this "space" in printed form and on the air which must be filled every single day, there is a need to find information to talk and write about. The result of all of these factors has been a proliferation of investment *dis-information*.

Dis-information presents a distorted view of reality and, generally, creates more problems than it solves. This dis-information consists mostly of reports on day-to-day activity, which is confusing and distracting. It may be misguided, sensational, and lack any theoretical foundation. False ideas can become so widespread that the public, for the most part, simply accepts them as fact.

What investors don't realize is that chasing the hot stock or attempting to time the market swings are strategies that are costly to implement, have an extremely low probability of success, and are ineffective in adding value. There are no gurus on Wall Street, and stock timing, or option trading, is a loser's game. What Wall Street calls an investment is many times pure speculation. Trading stock seldom translates into the highest returns. Although you may be up thirty percent one year, you may lose that much or more the next year.

Many investors get their information from the news media, magazines, or TV and have never heard of the academic theories of investing. Unfortunately, the dis-information (which may be intended to get you to trade) has been proven to be the exact opposite of what is necessary to be successful as a long-term investor.

It follows then that one of the most important issues affecting investors today is where we get the information we use to make decisions; in other words, whether our decisions are based on fact or fiction.

There is a better way! And that better way is to become an *informed investor.*

When you are able to take a step back, consider all the facts, and engage your newly acquired knowledge of how markets work, the logical errors of "accepted" investment strategies will become clear to you. You will become an informed investor. Informed investors understand how financial markets actually work. They focus on the overall investment strategy and portfolio, rather than viewing a specific investment in isolation, since academic studies tell us that each investment should be evaluated as to its contribution to a portfolio's total return. The best part about being an informed investor is that you will be able to properly evaluate the investment advice you receive, and you will never again fall prey to the misguided recommendations of uninformed advisors, investors, or journalists.

Why Not Just Buy a Plain Vanilla Mutual Fund?

What do you see in the chart shown in Figure 2.1? The top managers in any one year were at the bottom the next. It's not a conspiracy, but the people who work on Wall Street want you to believe that somebody is in control, that someone is driving the bus. But as you'll soon discover, nobody on Wall Street is keeping any secrets from you. Nobody knows if earnings are going to push a stock up, or what a stock will be worth in the future, because no one can accurately predict tomorrow.

TOP 20 MUTUAL FUNDS, 1995 TO 1996
ONE YEAR RANK VS. THE NEXT YEAR (1996)

1st Year	Next Year	1st year	Next Year
1	2898	11	7261
2	7268	12	7297
3	45	13	1705
4	7283	14	6
5	262	15	2497
6	6290	16	2719
7	7233	17	7050
8	3473	18	3256
9	7256	19	5383
10	7061	20	7351

Average run of top 20 in subsequent year = 4388
Average number of funds = 7857

Figure 2.1 Top twenty mutual funds.

No matter how many times a mutual fund has beaten the market in the past, it has only a fifty percent chance of beating the market in the future. These apparently random outcomes are consistent with market efficiency.

Edgar Barksdale and William Green examined the performance persistence of 144 institutional equity managers. They ranked the managers based on their results over a five-year period. They then tracked what percentage of these managers performed better than average over the subsequent five years. Their results show that, regardless of where a manager places in the first five years, he or she is as likely to rank above average as below average during the next five years. Again, it's a random pattern that is consistent with the laws of pure chance.

Ronald Kahn and Andrew Rudd studied the performance of equity mutual funds and fixed-income mutual funds. They found no evidence of consistency in performance for equity funds and insufficient consistency in fixed-income funds to validate their use (because the fixed income funds underperformed their benchmarks by a significant amount). Kahn and Rudd concluded, given only past performance information, that index funds are best for both equity and fixed-income investments. Studies of mutual fund performance now span more than forty years. The message is clear that, while an occasional mutual fund may beat the market, there is no indication to support the contention that performance may repeat or continue. There is actually more likelihood that it will *not*.

Your job is to become aware and avoid being misled by dis-information. When you listen to the nightly news, ask yourself, "*What does this really have to do with me?*" Worrying about the daily moves of the stock market is like watching another police car chase on the 6 o'clock news. It plays on viewers' emotions.

Basic Financial Blunders to Avoid

Aside from acting on misleading information, nothing can stop you from meeting your future financial objectives more than making the following seven investment errors. It is important for you to recognize these errors so you can avoid them.

1. Lack of follow-through on long-range goals. Concentrate on those instruments designed to fulfill your long-term financial plan instead of a hodgepodge of investments bought on tips, hearsay advice, or casual comments from friends. Customize your portfolio to reflect your objectives and your ability to assume risk. If you're a stock investor who likes to invest exclusively in one industry or sector, you may wish to consider abandoning this practice and instead diversify in several.
2. Riding the emotional roller coaster. To take the emotion out of purchasing stocks, you could use a mechanical means such as dollar cost averaging that demands a specified contribution on a regular basis, regardless of market conditions. This can help reduce vulnerability to certain cross-cutting variables, such as government policies or consumer preferences, and eliminate emotion-based actions.
3. Going against all the odds. Find out what is realistic and set your personal investment expectations to match reality. Start looking at stocks the way you look at life. Use guidelines to keep you from reacting to market fluctuations. The fact is, nobody knows what the market is going to do.
4. Confusing income with appreciation. Don't confuse saving with investing. Do not expect index funds to pay high dividends or income.

Understand your investments. Some stocks that have a high percent of earnings and dividends may be a poor investment in terms of growth. Many people believe that as stock dividends increase, so does the worth of their holdings.

5. Procrastinating. Becoming an investor is going to require some of your attention and time. How much time? Set time deadlines and take small easy investment steps, one at a time. But don't put off getting started.

6. Not having an emergency fund. Investments that lack liquidity either prevent you from getting your money quickly or force you to sell at discount prices. You should have six months' living expenses in liquid or cash equivalents. You never know when you may need an emergency fund. Make a game out of saving to cover living expenses and keep extending the time periods and your savings out further.

7. Not taking advantage of employer savings and/or tax advantaged investments. Tax-deferred stock option plans or 401(k) plans may have employer matching features. Talk to your benefits officer. Some investments can be made with "before-tax" dollars or can defer tax on interest/dividends that accrue on the investment. These advantages could grow your investment wealth more rapidly.

8. Failing to use professional advisors. Unless you have broad experience and plenty of spare time, you may save more in the long run by obtaining professional help than by trying to do it yourself. Advisers such as stockbrokers, financial planners, accountants, and tax attorneys can help you build and implement a comprehensive financial plan.

The real message is to control everything you can control. Take actions consistent with your financial goals, guided by sound advice. How do you know where to get sound advice? The answer depends on whether you are a do-it-yourselfer, verifier, or delegator — the subject of the next chapter.

3   Get a Financial Coach

I t is a lot easier to find a reputable investment advisor who understands investing and how the markets work than trying to do it yourself.

Get advice from a fee-based advisor or investment consultant. These are brokers who specialize in consulting on the process of investment management. This group also charges fees for services rather than commissions. In this way, they have no conflict of interest in the investments they recommend.

Fee-based advisors and consultants and almost all Wall Street stockbrokers now have access to more than just their own mutual fund families. There are now over 8,000 registered mutual funds, and 4,000 individual money managers. What these consultants do is direct you to the ones suited to your needs.

Brokers can provide you with free financial planning reports, which can cost hundreds, or thousands, of dollars elsewhere. For a fee, consultants in many large firms can help you establish your investment objectives, do the research and due diligence needed to find an appropriate money manager, and — most importantly — provide sophisticated monitoring and review of the money manager who is managing your account. (If you're a trustee of a pension plan, this service may help you comply with the Employment Income and Securities Act of 1974 — but we still recommend that you check with your legal counsel.)

One last note about brokers: you can't buy an individual issue of stocks, bonds, or municipal bonds without the services of either a full-service or discount brokerage firm. A full-service brokerage firm can help you research the issues and make recommendations. A discount house won't. That's the distinction.

Some mutual funds are offered directly to the public at net asset value without sales charges being added. A fund can do this because it does not maintain a sales staff. It simply advertises and markets its shares by mail or magazine.

How do you find a good consultant? Spend some time, and be sure to ask the following questions:

1. What is the advisor's education in investment consulting? Answer: Having a college degree doesn't qualify someone for investment consulting. A consultant should have a certification designation from either IMCA or IIMC.
2. What percentage of the advisor's practice is fee-based? Answer: Should be sixty to seventy percent or more.
3. What investment vehicles does the consultant offer? Mutual funds, individually managed accounts, annuities? Answer: You'd like for the consultant also to have access to asset class mutual funds. Since asset class funds and index funds are no-load, you pay no commission to buy the investment; you pay only an advisor or consultant fee as you would with an attorney or certified public accountant (CPA).
4. Ask for three references. Answer: Most fee-based advisors generally don't mind if you ask for references of current clients.
5. Ask about the advisor's investment history. The correct answer: The consultant is doing what he or she is advising you to do.
6. Has the consultant ever lost money? Answer: If so, did he or she learn something from the experience?

The exact role an advisor plays in your own investment arena is up to you. The more hands-on help you want, the more it will cost, but a solid foundation may be worth it. Include your family members in planning discussions, so their expectations will be in line with your strategies.

It's still up to you to do your own homework.

Problems

Many investors feel uncomfortable dealing with the financial services industry due to the transactional nature of the broker's or advisor's compensation. Many feel that the recommendations they receive are suspect, because of the inherent conflict of interest in a commission sale. Many investors are unsure how their portfolios are performing because their monthly brokerage statements are intimidating and difficult to understand. Tracking performance can be especially troublesome if there is more than one brokerage account involved. There is so much information to come to grips with that the potential investor often doesn't feel comfortable taking any action at all.

Most investors feel they need an effective filter, so they subscribe to such publications as *Money, Forbes, Fortune, Business Week,* or the *Wall Street Journal.* Frequently these periodicals contain conflicting recommendations, even though they draw from the same data. In today's information age, one huge challenge is dealing with information effectively and using it to advantage.

Working with a good, as opposed to merely average, financial advisor will make a significant difference in your success. Let's look at a 1995 study completed by Dalbar Financial Services, Inc., to see how big this difference can be.

The following study shows how individual investors fared working on their own compared to working with a financial advisor. For comparison, I've included the performances of three model portfolios for the same time period. You can see that there is a significant difference in returns realized by working with a qualified financial advisor.

The study measured the total returns over the past ten years earned by investors who purchased directly marketed investment products, vs. returns earned by investors who used the services of a financial advisor. While using a financial advisor did improve overall returns vs. do-it-yourself investing, it added value in only one dimension.

From January 1984 through September 1993, equity investors using a financial advisor realized total returns of 90.21 percent vs. a total return of 70.23 percent for the do-it-yourself investors. The study concluded that individuals who go it alone are more likely to try to time markets rather than to hold assets long-term. If you used the services of a financial advisor, you would have increased your returns twenty percent on average over time. That builds a pretty good case for working with an advisor.

Let's take it a step further. The language about investing is too complex and, therefore, creates confusion. Think of all the various professionals out there selling investments as being like different divisions of the armed services. There is the army, navy, marine corps, and air force. All have a similar objective and often even use the same type of equipment; they just carry out their missions differently. To the public, this can be confusing, and rivalries can result. Stock-brokers think they are at the top of the pecking order; bank representatives believe they sell on hallowed ground; and independent, fee-only financial advisors sense they are close to reaching nirvana. Yet they all may be selling the exact same investment product or offering the same service. The joint mission they all share, however, is to provide a service to the public. Unfortunately, not all advisors share this sense of mission. In fact, some have changed their titles to "financial planner" simply to gain a marketing advantage. Some of these individuals desire to sell you a product, not assist you.

Stockbrokers

Most investors have a good relationship with their traditional Wall Street brokers; in surveys these brokers score high marks. Many stockbrokers attempt to add value by following traditional investment strategies, such as trying to pick exceptional securities, stocks, or mutual funds. Some attempt to predict which way the market's going. All academic studies, however, conclude that market timing doesn't work.

Active strategies entail investigation and analysis expenses. These judgment calls may also involve the acceptance of a degree of diversifiable risk. The extra costs and risks can be substantial and must be justified by realistically evaluated return expectations.

Differences Between Wall Street Brokerage Firms and Discount Firms

The big Wall Street firms are known as "full-service," meaning they offer a wider variety of financial products than discount brokerages — while charging higher fees. Products they offer include stocks, bonds, options, annuities, and insurance. A full-service stockbroker solicits business and traditionally is paid mostly by commissions. These houses also offer investment advice, online services, and research.

Discount Brokers

Discount brokerages usually don't offer the full range of services provided by full-service brokers. Most do not offer advice — they simply transact trades. Because they manage fewer products than their full-service counterparts, discounters charge lower fees. Discounters also often offer online computer order entry services. Those that have live brokers generally pay them a set salary to execute trades. The brokers don't solicit and aren't paid commissions. Discount brokerages make money by doing business in volume, competing mostly on price and "reliability" of the service. If they have the lowest prices and the best service, they get the most trades.

Which broker should you choose? You need to determine what types of services you need. If you need lots of research backup and advice, you should go to a full-service broker. If you are happy doing your own homework and don't need the advice, a discount broker is preferable.

Investment Consultants

Investment consultants normally work for Wall Street firms and specialize in consulting with investors about their investments. They charge fees for services rather than charging commissions on transactions. They take a much broader approach and maintain a macro perspective of global, small cap, and large cap equities. They provide educational materials and attend training sessions. They help investors set financial goals and come up with comprehensive plans, rather than simply trying to sell particular investments.

Bank Investment Representatives

A broker-in-the-bank. For decades, consumers have listed banks as their most trusted source of financial products and advice. The primary reason is that bank savings and CDs are backed by the Federal Deposit Insurance Corporation (FDIC). Bankers, however, have traditionally known little about investments, financial planning, or diversification; having been trained simply in making loans, taking deposits, and issuing credit cards. Then a few years ago, though banks had been prohibited from offering investments, banks decided to cross over the line and offer investments through subsidiaries or affiliates. These bank affiliate advisors have the same securities licenses as other brokers and many have gone through traditional Wall Street training programs.

Independent Fee-Only Financial Advisors

There are many types of advisors, and many are very good. They are similar to the big Wall Street firms' investment management consultants. Like investment management consultants, these advisors have no incentive to sell a financial product for the commission they'll personally gain. They still have access to all the mutual fund vendors and meet with representatives of many mutual fund companies. The main difference is in how they are paid. The next step is to find one who understands and uses asset class investing.

Financial Planning

Figure 3.1 presents the results of a survey of 4,212 consumers who were asked which type(s) of financial advisors they considered reliable for investment advice. Consumers considered financial planners most reliable for this type of advice in nearly all demographic segments, while insurance agents were considered least reliable.

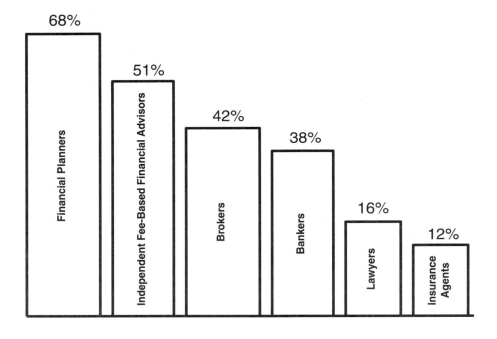

Figure 3.1 The most reliable sources of financial advice. (Data from Dalbar Study, January 1997.)

You should be aware that more than 200,000 women and men call themselves financial planners, including accountants, attorneys, stockbrokers, insurance agents, self-styled money managers, credit counselors, and the Internet junkie down the street. But only a small number are registered certified financial planners, a designation that guarantees a person has passed a rigorous set of tests in all parts of personal finance (investing, retirement and estate planning, taxes, insurance, and more), and has at least three years of experience in the field. However, this still doesn't mean they understand modern portfolio management.

Whatever the designation, many advisors get the bulk of their compensation through the commissions clients pay on investments they purchase as a result of the planner's advice – just as stockbrokers do. This sets up a potential conflict of interest for them and a proceed-with-caution sign for you: Since the advisor or planner will profit most from high-load and high-commission items, it's tempting to recommend those items, whether or not they best suit your pocketbook and goals. It's best to derail the profit motive and pay a set fee for a planner's advice. Following is a breakdown of types of financial advisors, including investment analysts and investment consultants.

- CFP (Certified Financial Planner): Designated by the Certified Financial Planner Board of Standards (based in Denver) to those who complete an approved course, pass an exam, and meet work-experience requirements.
- CPA/PFS (Certified Public Accountant/Personal Financial Specialist): Designated by the American Institute of Certified Public Accountants (based in New York) to CPAs who pass an exam and meet work-experience requirements.
- ChFC (Chartered Financial Consultant): Designated by the American College (Bryn Mawr, PA) to those who complete a ten-part course of study.
- CFA (Chartered Financial Analyst): Designated by the Association for Investment Management and Research (based in Charlottesville, VA) to those who pass a rigorous three-level exam (levels of exams must be taken one year apart), each administered by the association and covering investment principles, asset valuation, and portfolio management. Candidates must also have three years of investment-management experience.
- CIC (Chartered Investment Counselor): Designated by the Investment Counsel Association of America (based in Washington, D.C.) to those holding CFAs and currently working as investment counselors.
- CIMC (Certified Investment Management Consultant): Designated by the Institute for Investment Management Consultants (based in Washington, D.C. and Phoenix) to members who pass an exam and have at least three years' professional consulting financial experience.

- CIMS (Certified Investment Management Specialist): Designated by the Institute for Investment Management Consultants to associate members who pass an exam and meet financial service work-experience requirements.

These professional organizations will provide you with select lists of financial planners in your area.

- American Institute of CPAs — Lists CPA Personal Financial Specialists. Call 888-999-9256.
- The Institute of Certified Financial Planners — Lists financial planners with a CFP designation. Call 303-759-4900.
- LINC (Licensed Independent Network of CPA Financial Planners) — Lists members who are CPA/PFS fee-only planners in public accounting firms. Call 800-737-2727.

The exact role an advisor plays is up to you. The more hands-on help you want, the more you may end up paying in fees and commissions. You may opt for an advisor who analyzes your financial condition, strategizes with you on the best route forward and sends you on your way — in other words, who empowers you to take action on your own.

A critical factor often overlooked in successful investing is defining your own personal investment profile. This very individual profile includes your investment attitudes, objectives, and time frames.

We will now spend some time defining just what these are for you.

4   **Financial Personality Test**

Here's the problem: investors get saving and investing mixed up. People want to feel safe, so they're drawn to high yields on savings. But when they switch to investing, this higher yield attitude can become a trap. For instance, they may choose a mutual fund with the highest performance, without considering the amount of financial risk involved in achieving that return. Risk is an important consideration which can be measured.

What are the personality traits that make it difficult for you to save for important goals? Which characteristics will make you a successful investor, and which ones hinder you? The answers to these and other questions about your own financial style will help you understand your financial personality and determine what you can do to make the most of your money.

The quiz below, an abridged version of a financial personality test developed by the National Center for Women and Retirement Research (631-287-2888), is designed to identify aspects of your personality that may prevent you from making smart money decisions, and also identify those that can help you. Based on the landmark findings of the National Center's study on how personality influences investment choices, it will help you evaluate how you handle risk, cope with change, make decisions, and view the future. The score analysis that follows will explain how these aspects affect the way you control your finances and will tell you what steps you can take to become a wiser investor.

If you would like more in-depth information about your score and more thorough advice, the National Center for Women and Retirement Research and the editors of *Working Woman* have devised a detailed assessment that will be individually tailored to each respondent's quiz results. This service is *free*. Just send your quiz score sheet and a self-addressed, stamped envelope to:

Women Cents Money Quiz, National Center for Women and Retirement Research, Long Island University–Southampton College, Southampton, NY 11968.

THE QUIZ

For each statement, choose the response that most accurately reflects your feelings or behavior.

A. Exactly like me; B. Somewhat like me;
C. Generally not like me; D. Not at all like me.

Your attitude toward risk

___1. I like working with a safety net. For example, I will consider investments only when I'm guaranteed not to lose any money.
___2. Most people would describe me as adventurous.
___3. I think investing is just like gambling.

Your feelings about change

___4. I've sometimes stayed in a relationship or job longer than I should have because the idea of making a change was scary.
___5. I am open to considering new opportunities, whether they have to do with my career or my investments.
___6. I feel that change adds zest to life.

Your feelings about control

___7. I feel that I have control over the direction my life is taking.
___8. I rarely send back food in a restaurant, return something I've purchased or make a customer complaint, even when I'm very dissatisfied with the product or service.
___9. I'm so busy with work and taking care of my family that I rarely have time to tend to my own needs, financial or otherwise.

Your feelings about the future

___10. When I think of the future, I feel optimistic.
___11. I tend to be spontaneous and live for the present; planning ahead is not my style.
___12. I'm pretty good about saving money for things that I'll need soon, like a new car or a vacation. But I find it a lot more difficult to save for far-off goals like retirement.

Your attitude toward money

__13. I know I should save *something*, but in my heart of hearts, I don't believe financial planning really does that much good unless you have a lot of money.

__14. I tend to tune out when friends or colleagues talk about money.

__15. I believe that women are just as capable of investing and managing their money as men are.

Your money understanding

__16. Investment lingo and other financial terms intimidate me.

__17. I make most of the financial decisions in my household, either alone or with my spouse, and I feel pretty good about how we've done.

__18. I know very little about different types of investments and the basics of financial planning.

Your decision-making style

__19. I often put off financial decisions because I'm afraid of making a mistake.

__20. After making a big decision, whether about my job, money or a relationship, I often worry that I made the wrong move.

__21. When making most major decisions, I tend to listen to my heart.

What Your Answers Mean

21 to 36 Points: Danger Zone

If your score is in the Danger Zone, you may often feel that you're not in control of your life — a feeling that usually extends to financial matters. You probably don't know much about investing or the basics of financial planning, are intimidated by financial terminology and, in the end, may defer decisions about money matters to others. Your choices about where to put your money often reflect a strong preference for the familiar over the unknown, an aversion to risk, and difficulty in coping with change. For example, even as your income rises, you're likely to put your savings into money-market accounts, CDs, and other familiar vehicles that promise not to lose any money. Trouble is, they won't *make* very much money either — a fact that is likely to haunt you as you grow older and find yourself still struggling to achieve financial security.

What to Do

If your score is in the Danger Zone, don't despair — but don't delay in trying to get your financial act together. One of the biggest obstacles to your taking charge of your financial life is also the easiest to overcome: lack of knowledge. Learning more about how to manage your money will help you gain a sense of control over the direction your life is taking and increase your confidence in making money decisions.

Start by buying one of the many reference books now available that demystify money and investing, and read it a chapter at a time. An excellent choice is *Making the Most of Your Money*, by syndicated financial columnist Jane Bryant Quinn. You may also consider registering for a personal-finance course sponsored by a community organization or a local college. Invite a friend to join you to make it more fun.

You can help yourself further by working on some of the non-financial issues that keep you from taking an active role in managing your money. The sections of the quiz in which you scored lowest indicate the areas you need to focus on. For example, if you scored low in the control section, you might work on becoming more assertive by pushing yourself to send back restaurant food that is not to your liking or by demanding a refund for a faulty product. Similarly, if you're generally loath to try new experiences (and investing in stocks is a new experience for most Danger Zone women), practice — on a small scale. Try a new type of food or invite a colleague you don't know very well (but would like to know) to lunch. It's not how big but how new the experience is that counts.

37 to 52 Points: Caution Zone

The ups and downs of daily living preoccupy your thinking if you're in the Caution Zone. You believe you can't do much to shape the future, so you focus on the here and now rather than on long-term needs. When prioritizing financial matters, for example, you may be motivated to save for a new car but less so to put money aside for retirement and other faraway goals. You listen to your heart on most decisions, so when it comes to money and investing, you often make choices based more on feelings than on facts. You are likely to perceive financial planning as pointless unless you have a lot of money to work with, and to reject any investment that is not guaranteed to protect your principal as too risky. Like Danger Zone women, you prefer the familiar, which keeps you from exploring investments that offer higher returns over time than CDs and savings accounts.

What to Do

Your biggest challenge is letting go of preconceived notions about money and investing. Increasing your knowledge of the fundamentals of financial planning through the steps outlined in the Danger Zone section should help you change some of your attitudes toward money and get you to base your financial decisions on fact rather than feeling. To overcome your resistance to planning for the future, give some concerted thought to your wants and needs over the long term. Since the first step in achieving a goal is to visualize it, start by making a list of your financial priorities for the next year, five years, ten years and beyond. For example, you might shoot for a new car in one year, a bigger house in five years, a sizable college fund for your kids in ten years, and a comfortable retirement nest egg for yourself in twenty years or more. With these specific goals as incentives, set up separate savings accounts, specifically earmarked for each one, and add a little bit to each on a regular basis. To make the process easier, consider signing up for an automatic savings account at a bank or mutual fund company (described later in this book). Most important, be sure to put the money you allocate for long-term goals into growth investments that have historically outpaced inflation — that is, stocks and the mutual funds that invest in them.

53 to 68 Points: Comfort Zone

If you're in the Comfort Zone, you usually feel in control of your life. You're likely to be optimistic about the future and to realize the importance of taking responsibility for your finances. In addition, you feel capable of understanding money and investing and have learned at least the basics about investment types and financial-planning principles. The problem is that you are sometimes *too* comfortable. You may wish you were more active in managing your investments, but take solace in the progress you've made. Still, since you don't experience a sense of urgency and aren't alarmed by fears of failure, inadequacy or insolvency, it's easy to put off making financial decisions or investigating new investment options. In fact, you usually find conversations about money and investing boring.

What to Do

This is a wake-up call. Regardless of your current financial, career, marital, and health status, circumstances can and do change. To make sure complacency doesn't keep you from achieving financial security, make planning a top priority. Set aside at least an hour or two each month to review money matters — for example, researching a new mutual fund or checking to see whether you need to make any changes in your portfolio — and mark the time down in your calendar, as you would any important appointment. If you are considering a new investment or face another kind of financial decision, set a deadline by which you must make your choice. By doing so, you won't let yourself procrastinate indefinitely. To make the process more interesting and fun, consider joining an investment club. In fact, all-female groups are the fastest-growing type of investment club, as more women discover that these clubs are a great way to invest in the stock market and hone financial skills in a social setting. Call the National Association of Investors Corporation (810-583-6242) for more information.

69 to 84 Points: Action Zone

There's little to prevent you from becoming an accomplished investor. You are open to a wide range of investments and understand that you must put some money in riskier, growth investments like stocks to earn higher returns. You aren't easily intimidated by financial lingo, and you'll ask questions until you are sure that you understand. What's more, because you're generally assertive about your rights, you will challenge a financial professional who gives you poor service or questionable advice. Though you value your ability to enjoy the present, you want to be in control of your financial future, and you regard planning as essential to meeting that goal.

What to Do

Congratulations. You either are an active and accomplished investor or are set to become one. If you haven't fully taken the plunge, try to analyze why by examining your scores in the individual sections of the quiz. Are your totals similar in all seven sections, or are one or two substantially lower than the others? If so, these are the areas you need to work on to make smarter choices about your money. For example, if your scores indicate that you tend to procrastinate, set a deadline each time you are faced with a financial decision. If your totals are low in the financial-knowledge section, bone up on personal finance by reading books or magazines or by attending a financial-planning seminar. Whatever your weak spot, create a plan of action to overcome it. Then just do it.*

---

* We want to thank Christopher L. Hayes, director of the National Center for Women and Retirement Research at Southampton College of Long Island University, who developed this quiz in collaboration with *Working Woman* magazine.

Where to Learn More

The National Center for Women and Retirement Research, which spear-headed the survey project, is a nonprofit organization at Long Island University's Southampton College. This organization conducts research and provides seminars and educational materials on preretirement financial planning for women. Prudential Securities provided a grant to underwrite this project.

The National Center for Women and Retirement Research also offers its own financial-planning seminars, "Money Matters for Women," throughout the country. For additional information on the center and its programs, call 631-287-2888.

5 | How to Determine Your Needs and Goals

You now know more about your own investment attitudes. It's time to determine your financial needs and goals. This is an absolute must before investing. Four questions and answers are of primary importance:

1. What do you want your investments to do for you?
2. What is your current financial situation?
3. What is the level of risk you will tolerate to achieve your goals?
4. What is the time frame for achieving your investment goals?

Investment choices are driven by your needs. These needs must be more specific than "to get a higher return." Knowing why higher returns are needed helps determine the correct course of action. And action cannot be taken until a possible investment choice is evaluated in concert with your other accounts, investments, and assets, and until you have an idea of your risk tolerance.

A retired couple in their mid-60s had $50,000 to invest. They wanted a higher rate of interest than a savings account could provide, and they wanted to withdraw the interest to supplement their income. This is all the information they initially disclosed.

Filling their needs seemed fairly straightforward: They needed a higher return and current income. There are several good investments that could immediately provide what the couple was requesting. However, when they were led to answer questions about their life situation, their level of investment experience, their other needs and assets, and time horizons, the picture changed. Facts are discovered through inquiry that often alter the initial impression and eliminate several possible investments that first come to mind. The husband was seriously ill, so the couple would be ill-advised to commit that money for the long-term or tolerate risk to the principal, since the $50,000 should be readily available for medical expenses. They are better off leaving the money in a savings account.

With further discussion, they revealed that ten years prior they purchased a bond mutual fund and were continuing to reinvest all of its income. They were advised to simply start taking systematic income payments from their existing bond mutual fund to get the added income they needed.

In the beginning, the couple didn't feel it was necessary to disclose much about their life situation and other assets. They just wanted a simple answer to their immediate problem of what to do with $50,000 to get more income. Acting on what they felt was adequate to disclose at the outset would have resulted in a poor investment choice in meeting their real underlying needs.

The following worksheet may help you get a better understanding of your own investment needs and goals. This *Financial Needs Discovery Worksheet* will help you determine important facts now and will prepare you to communicate these facts to your advisor or consultant. It also contains a section for listing your current assets, accounts, and investments. The worksheet is designed for self-discovery.

FINANCIAL NEEDS DISCOVERY WORKSHEET

Step 1: Define Your Financial Goals
Identify whether or not your needs are for immediate income, and/or if you want to set aside some assets for future growth. Do you need monthly income? Are you saving for a house? When do you plan to retire? Are you saving for your children's or grandchildren's college education? Please take a moment and list your three most important financial goals. (Perhaps make a long list of everything that comes to mind, then hone in on three major goals.)

1. _____
2. _____
3. _____

Your choice of investments should always be driven by what you want your money to do for you. You may want your investments to fill very specific needs — provide cash to buy a house or car, pay college costs, or help support your retirement. Or, your goals may be more general, simply to build wealth, as an example.

Step 2: Set Your Time Horizons

Next, assign a time horizon to each goal. If you are saving for a special event, like funding college, estimate when you will need the cash to meet your goal. If your objective doesn't have a definite deadline, estimate how long it will continue to be important to you; for instance, if your primary concern is earning income, for how long will you want to continue an income based program?

Setting time horizons for your goals is critical. Why? Because you should follow a very different strategy when you invest for the short term than when you invest for longer periods.

Step 3: Consider Your Personal Risk Profile

To find how much risk you are willing to tolerate, answer the following questions. Be honest to avoid coming to an incorrect assessment of your risk tolerance. Total your score and compare it to the key that follows the quiz.

Personal Risk Profile Questionnaire

1. How would you describe yourself when it comes to investing?

   - Risk avoidance   1
   - Conservative   2
   - Risk taker   4
   - Aggressive risk taker   5
     Score _____

2. What would you do if your investments suddenly declined in value 10 percent?

   - Sell them   0
   - Hold them   2
   - Buy more   5
     Score _____

3. How important is it to you that the value of your investments stays consistent from quarter to quarter?

- ■ Critical   0
- ■ Very important   2
- ■ Important   3
- ■ Not important   5

  Score _____

4. Do you need to make regular withdrawals from your investment account?

- ■ No   5
- ■ Yes   0

  Score _____

5. Do you foresee a major expenditure in the next five years?

- ■ No   5
- ■ Yes   0

  Score _____

6. What length of time do you feel is appropriate to wait before assessing the performance of your investments?

- ■ Less than 1 year   0
- ■ 1 year   1
- ■ 2 years   2
- ■ 3 years   3
- ■ 5 years   4
- ■ Over 5 years   5

  Score _____

7. How much do you expect to make on your investments?

- ■ 0-4%   0
- ■ 5-7%   2
- ■ 7-10%   3
- ■ 10-12%   4
- ■ Above 10%   5

  Score _____

  Total score _____

Once you have completed the risk profile questionnaire, take a moment to total your score. Your total score, between 0 and 35, will reveal your attitude toward risk. The closer to zero you are, the more risk averse you tend to be as an investor. The higher the score, the more risk you can tolerate.

Plot your range on the scale below and, at the same time, note the corresponding category and percentage of return associated with the level of risk in each category. For example, if you have a score near zero, you probably have regular cash-flow needs, and will most likely fall into the defensive column.

Risk/Return Scale

0   5–10   15–20   25–30   35

Risk Reward Categories

Defensive   Conservative   Balanced   Moderate   Aggressive

Step 4: Find the Investment that Matches Your Risk Profile

You can find investments that may be right for you in every time horizon: short-term, mid-term, and long-term.

The investment pyramid concept can provide a visual framework for you to review your financial choices. The first two lower levels of the pyramid make up the foundation and contain safe investments that will provide your financial security. As you move up the pyramid, you'll find investments that offer higher opportunities for growth. Less of your money should be invested, the higher up you go.

For example, stocks are liquid and historically have more potential for growth than fixed-income securities, but also have a higher level of risk associated with them. That is why they rest higher on the investment pyramid.

Step 5: Reaching Your Goals

Most people underestimate the amount of money they need, because it's impossible to know what the future will bring. All you can do is make an educated guess. Obviously, the shorter the time horizon, the easier it will be to make an accurate estimate.

Step 6: Rethink Your Investments Periodically

This investing business is a lifelong process. Since your assets, needs, and goals are always changing as you go through life, you should update your goals by taking out this chart and reworking it once a year. Meeting annually with your advisor to review your goals and investment performance will complete your yearly check-up.

All the principles described here boil down to four simple rules:

1. Set clear financial goals.
2. Choose investments that provide the combination of risk, reward, and enough time to achieve your goals.
3. Minimize your risk by diversifying as broadly as your resources permit.
4. Use the services of a professional financial advisor you trust.

UNDERSTANDING HOW MUTUAL FUNDS WORK

Contents

6 All About Mutual Funds

T hink of a mutual fund as a financial intermediary that makes invest-ments on your behalf. The mutual fund pools all its investors' funds together and buys stocks, bonds, or other assets on behalf of the group as a whole. Each investor receives a certificate of ownership and a regular statement of his or her account indicating the value of the shares of the total investment pool. A mutual fund, in other words, is an investment company that makes investments on behalf of its participants, who share common financial goals.

Mutual funds continually issue new shares of the fund for sale to the public. The number of shares and the price are directly related to the value of the securities the mutual fund holds. A fund's share price can change from day to day, depending on the daily value of its underlying securities.

The manager of the mutual fund uses the pool of capital to buy a variety of stocks, bonds, or money market instruments based on the advertised finan-cial objectives of the fund. These objectives cover a wide range. Some funds follow aggressive policies, involving greater risk in search of higher returns. Others seek current income and no risk. Since each mutual fund has a specific investment objective, the investor has the ability to select a variety of funds to meet asset allocation and diversification needs.

Net asset value is the value of the fund's total investment, minus any debt, divided by the number of outstanding shares. For example, if the fund's investment value is $26,000, with no debt and 1000 shares outstanding, the net asset value (NAV) would be $26 per share. The NAV is not a fixed figure because it must reflect the daily change in the price of the securities within the fund's portfolio.

In a regular mutual fund, which includes thousands and often millions of shares, the NAV is calculated on a daily basis without commissions, in full and fractional units, with values moving up or down along with the stock and bond markets.

The biggest mistake that most investors make when buying mutual funds is looking first (and sometimes only) at the prior performance of the fund or paying too much attention to the current bond fund yield. Fund costs are an equally important factor in the return that you earn from a mutual fund. Fees are deducted from your investment. All other things being equal, high fees and other charges depress your returns.

Because of the large amounts of assets under management, investment companies are able to offer "economies of scale," or competitive fee schedules, to their customers. The management fees charged depend on the complexity of the asset management demands. Foreign equity management requires substantially more research, specialized implementation, and transaction costs than the management of a U.S. government bond fund. Asset management fees reflect those differences. Equity mutual fund fees are higher than bond mutual fund fees.

Fee comparisons are particularly important. Remember to compare the proverbial apples to apples — in this case, similar equities to equity mutual funds; and similar bonds to bond mutual funds.

Mutual fund	Annual Performance	Management Fees	Net Performance
Foreign Equities	12.50%	1.25%	11.25%
US Large Cap	12.50%	1.00%	11.50%
US Small Cap	13.00%	1.20%	11.8%
Investment-Grade Bonds	7.80%	0.65%	7.15%
High-Yield Bonds	9.25%	0.75%	8.50%
Foreign Bonds	9.25%	0.90%	8.35%

Figure 6.1 A comparison of mutual fund fees.

Keeping a Careful Eye on Costs

You can put more money to work for you in your investment by keeping a careful eye on costs. It's simply common sense — lower expenses translate into higher overall returns. Your goal should be to keep acquisition costs as low as possible. There are two basic kinds of costs, described below.

Sales Charges

In the past, all commissions were simply charged up front, but that has changed. There are now several ways that mutual fund companies charge fees (Figure 6.2).

The sales charge is called a "load" and is subtracted from the initial mutual fund investment. A no-load fund does not have this charge, although other fees or service charges may be buried in its cost structure. Don't be misled: nearly all mutual funds have a sales charge. Some are hidden, some are not. Let's talk about the ones that you can see.

Figure 6.3 shows that about half of the 2.6 trillion dollars invested in mutual funds are split evenly between load and no-load. A "front-end" load mutual fund charges a fee when an investor buys it. Loaded mutual funds can also be "back-end" load — having a deferred sales charge — and are sometimes known as B-shares. This option has higher internal costs. If you decide to redeem your shares early, usually within the first five years, you pay a surrender charge, as illustrated in Figure 6.2.

A customer who redeems shares in the first year of ownership would typically pay a five percent sales charge. The amount would drop by an equal amount each year. After six years, the shares could be redeemed without further charge. There are brokers who will tell you it is better to invest in B-shares, since you will not pay an up-front fee. If you invest a large amount, you will get a breakpoint inside an A-share mutual fund and your annual costs will be lower.

- ∎ With A-shares you pay the commission all at once.
- ∎ B-shares have a contingent deferred sales charge. They are more popular with brokers because you don't pay an up-front load, but every year an amount equal to one percent is deducted to pay the broker.
- ∎ C-shares typically have even higher internal expenses, and pay the selling broker up to one percent per year based on the amount of the assets. This fee comes directly from your investment performance. C-shares may have no up-front fee, but a possible one percent deferred sales

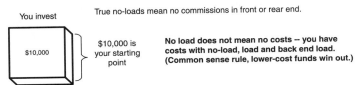

(NO-LOAD) MUTUAL FUNDS

Sales loads are commissions paid to brokers and financial advisors who sell mutual funds. They typically range from 4 percent to as high as 8.5 percent of the amount you invest.

FRONT-END (LOAD) MUTUAL FUNDS

BACK-END (LOAD) MUTUAL FUNDS

Some no-load mutual funds have redemption fees that scale down the longer you hold them. The broker/advisor is paid his commission by the mutual fund company. If you leave the fund earlier than the schedule, that percentage will be subtracted from your proceeds.

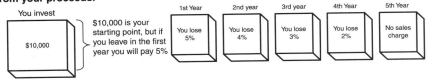

Figure 6.2 Types of mutual fund sales charge (loads).

charge in year one (sometimes longer), and higher annual expenses (up to one percent extra per year). I would avoid them.

You will notice in Figure 6.4 that the offering price is different from the net amount invested column. The offering price, known as the *ask* price, is greater than the fund's NAV (net asset value). The NAV is identified as the amount per share you would receive if you sold your shares.

No-load mutual funds do *not* mean *no cost*. Some no-load funds charge a redemption fee of one to two percent of the net asset value of the shares to cover expenses mainly incurred by advertising. Buying a no-load mutual fund is like doing your own plumbing work. You can save money if you know what you're doing; but if you don't have the required time and expertise, you can make a serious mistake. We highly recommend working with

100% = 11,317 mutual funds

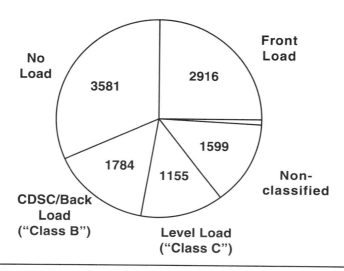

The load/no-load distinction is becoming more blurred because many mutual funds now charge other fees: 12b-1 fees, short term redemption fees, transaction fees, and maintenance fees. Furthermore, many load funds are now being sold at NAV (without the load) and many no-load funds are being sold as part of wrap and advisory programs.

Figure 6.3 Growth of mutual funds; load and no-load. (Data from *SIMFUND*, December 1997.)

	Sales Commission as a percentage of:	
Purchase Amount (A Shares)	Public Offering	Net Amount invested
Less than $50,000	5.00%	5.26%
$50,000 but less than $100,000	4.00%	4.17%
$250,000 but less than $500,000	3.00%	3.09%
$500,000 but less than $1,000,000	1.00%	1.01%
$1,000,000 or more	0.00%	0.00%

Figure 6.4 The commission schedule of a typical mutual fund.

an investment advisor who can offer the same no-load funds. Another important fact to remember is that when you call the toll-free number of the mutual fund company with a question, you are serviced by an employee of the mutual fund company, and the advice you receive may be biased.

Investors who are truly devoted to learning about financial matters, and who follow financial news, reading enough to keep themselves well informed, may be able to do this for themselves — but most investors are not in this category and are well advised to seek professional guidance for their investments.

Operating Expenses

Fees pay for the operational costs of running a fund — employees' salaries, marketing, servicing the toll-free phone line, printing and mailing published materials, computers for tracking investments and account balances, accounting fees, and so on. A fund's operating expenses are quoted as a percentage of your investment; the percentage represents an annual fee or charge. You can find this number in a fund's prospectus in the fund expenses section, entitled something like "Total Fund Operating Expenses." A mutual fund's operating expenses are normally invisible to investors because they're deducted before any return is paid and are charged automatically on a daily basis.

Other Things You Should Know

Dividends

Dividends and capital gains (the profits from a sale of stock) are paid in proportion to the number of mutual fund shares you own. So even if you invest a few hundred dollars, you get the same investment return per dollar as those who invest millions. The problem is you will have to pay taxes on this amount even if it is reinvested. You can use a variable annuity to defer those taxes until you plan to spend the money.

Prospectus and Annual Reports

Mutual fund companies produce information that can help you make decisions about mutual fund investments. All funds are required to issue a prospectus, and you can now get many of these off the Internet. You can take a look at the past performance of the funds and see what asset classes they really fall into.

Statements

Any mutual fund in which you participate will send you a year-end statement itemizing the income you've received. You should save this sheet along with other records of dividends, tax-exempt interest, and capital gains distributions, as well as records of the amounts received from the sale of shares, for tax purposes.

Full-time Professionals

When you invest in a mutual fund, you are hiring a team of professional investment managers to make complex investment judgments and handle complicated trading, record keeping, and safekeeping responsibilities for you. People whose full-time profession is money management will sift through the thousands of available investments in order to choose those that, in their judgment, are best suited to achieving the investment goals of a fund as spelled out in the fund's prospectus.

Full-time professionals select the portfolio's securities and then constantly monitor investments to determine if they continue to meet the fund's objectives. As economic conditions change, professionals may adjust the mix of the fund's investments to adopt a more aggressive or defensive posture. Having access to research analysis and computerized support, professional management can help identify opportunities in the markets that the average investor may not have the expertise or access to identify.

Diversification

Diversification is one important characteristic that attracts many investors to mutual funds. By owning a diverse portfolio of many stocks and/or bonds, investors can reduce the risk associated with owning any individual security.

To go it alone, you would need to invest money in at least eight to twelve different securities in different industries so that your portfolio could withstand a downturn in one or more of the investments. A mutual fund is typically invested in twenty-five to a hundred or more securities. Proper diversification enables the fund to receive the highest possible return at the lowest possible risk given the objectives of the fund.

Mutual funds do not escape share price declines during major market downturns. For example, mutual funds that invested in stocks certainly declined during the October 27, 1997 market crash, when the Dow Jones plunged 554.26 points. However, the most unlucky investors that month were individuals who had all of their money riding in Asian mutual funds. Some fund shares plunged in price by as much as thirty to forty percent that month. Widely diversified mutual funds were least hit.

Low Initial Investment

Each mutual fund establishes the minimum amount required to make an initial investment, and then how much additional is required when investors want to add more. A majority of mutual funds have low initial minimums, some less than $1,000.

Liquidity

One of the key advantages of mutual funds stems from the liquidity provided by this investment. You can sell your shares at any time, and mutual funds have a "ready market" for their shares. Additionally, shareholders directly receive any dividend or interest payments earned by the fund. Payments are usually made on a quarterly basis. When the fund manager sells some of the investments at a profit, the net gain is also distributed, but net losses are retained by the fund. Inside the mutual fund, when the dividends or capital gains are disbursed, the NAV is reduced by the disbursement.

Audited Performance

All mutual funds are required to disclose historical data about the fund through their prospectus — returns earned by the fund, operating expenses and other fees, and the fund's rate of trading turnover. Having the Securities and Exchange Commission (SEC) on your side is like having a vigilant guard dog focused on the guy who's responsible for your money. Remember, all mutual funds are registered investments.

Automatic Reinvestment

One of the major benefits of mutual funds is that dividends can be reinvested automatically and converted into more shares.

Switching

Switching from one mutual fund to another accommodates changes in investment goals, as well as changes in the market and the economy. Again, this switching between mutual funds creates tax implications. For instance, say you redeem a Franklin Growth and Income Fund and buy a Franklin NY Municipal Bond Fund, you have to pay taxes on the gains you earned.

Low Transaction Costs

When an individual investor places an order to buy 300 shares of a $30 stock ($9,000 investment), he or she is likely to get a commission bill for about $204, or 2.3 percent of the value of the investment. Even at a discount broker, commissions are likely to cost between $82 (0.9 percent) and $107 (1.2 percent). A mutual fund, on the other hand, is more likely to be buying 30,000 to 300,000 shares at a time! Their commission costs often run in the vicinity of one tenth of the commission you would pay at a discount broker. Where your commission might be $0.35 a share, the mutual fund would only pay $0.05 a share or even less. The commission savings can (and should) mean higher returns for you as a mutual fund shareholder.

Flexibility in Risk Level

An investor can select from among a variety of different mutual funds, finding a risk level he or she is comfortable with, and goals that match his or her own.

1. Stock funds. If you want your money to grow over a long period of time, funds that invest more heavily in stocks may be most appropriate.
2. Bond funds. If you need current income and don't want investments that fluctuate in value as widely as stocks, more conservative bond funds may be the best choice.
3. Money market funds. To protect your invested principal from dropping in value, because you may need your money in the short-term, a money market fund or a guaranteed fixed interest investment may best fit your needs.

No Risk of Bankruptcy

A situation in which the demand for money back (liabilities) exceeds the value of a fund's investments (assets) does not occur with a mutual fund.

The value can fluctuate, but this variation doesn't lead to the failure or bankruptcy of a mutual fund company. In fact, since the Investment Company Act of 1940 was passed to regulate the mutual fund industry, no fund has ever gone under.

In contrast, hundreds of banks and dozens of insurance companies have failed in the past two decades alone. Banks and insurers can fail because their liabilities can exceed their assets. When a bank makes too many loans that go sour at the same time and depositors want their money back, the bank fails. Likewise, if an insurance company makes several poor investments or underestimates the number of claims that will be made by insurance policy holders, it, too, can fail. But mutual funds are held in separate accounts and are not part of an insurance company's assets.

Custodian Bank

A custodian — a separate organization — holds the specific securities in which a mutual fund is invested independent of the mutual fund company. The employment of a custodian ensures that the fund management company can't embezzle your funds or use assets from a better-performing fund to subsidize a poor performer.

How Do these Various Parties Work Together?
How a Mutual Fund Works

After you have written your check to the mutual fund, the mutual fund company sends that check on your behalf to an organization functioning as a "transfer agent." Here your investment is recorded and processed and the real safeguards come into play. The agent transfers the money, not to the mutual fund's portfolio manager (the individual or firm that makes the investment decisions, technically known as the "investment advisor"), but to a "custodian bank."

Once that custodian bank receives the money, it notifies the mutual fund that new money is available for investment. The fund manager checks a daily account balance sheet and "new monies" are invested according to the mutual fund's investment policy.

The requirement of the Investment Company Act of 1940 that there should be independent custody for each mutual fund's assets has turned out to be the key provision that has sheltered the industry from potential trouble

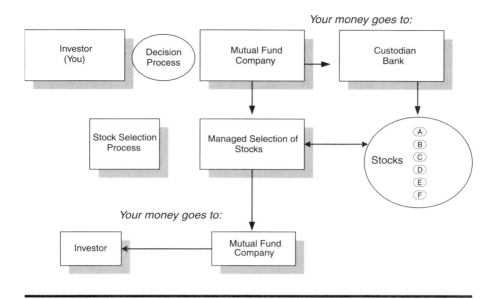

Figure 6.5 The relationship of various parties of a mutual fund.

for half a century. Separate custody means a mutual fund's parent company can go belly-up with no loss to the fund's shareholders, because their assets are held apart from other funds and apart from the parent fund.

Contrast this business structure with the far less restrictive set-up between, say, individual investors and a real estate promoter; or investors and a stockbroker who may have direct access to clients' accounts. In any number of notorious incidents, individuals in such a position have taken the money and run.

The limited partnership of the 1970s and 1980s was an excellent example of a poor business structure. During those years, many unregulated and unregistered limited partnerships were formed and investors sent their money directly to the limited partnership company. An unscrupulous promoter could simply write himself or herself a check. Financial scandals were numerous.

A money manager of a mutual fund has no direct access to investors' cash. The fund manager only decides how to invest shareholders' money. The custodian who controls the underlying securities allows them to be traded or exchanged with other institutional investors only after getting proper documentation from the manager. The upshot of independent custody is that it's very difficult for a fund manager to use the money for his or her own purposes.

The Investment Company Act adds other layers of investor protection as well. Independent accountants must regularly audit every fund. A fund's board of directors, who serve as modern-day trustees, negotiate prudent contract terms with the fund's service providers and generally oversee the operation. The SEC has the power to inspect funds and bring enforcement action against those that break the rules.

In addition, mutual fund firms have legions of compliance lawyers — essentially in-house cops — paid to make sure that portfolio managers, traders, and others follow the rules.

A Code of Conduct

Under SEC rules, fund managers are required to abide by strict codes of conduct. The codes require advance reporting of personal securities transactions so that there can be no conflict of interest between a manager's personal trades and what he or she does with the fund's securities. A manager otherwise could "front-run" the fund, personally buying or selling securities before the fund trades in them, to his or her gain and possibly the fund's loss. To avoid such potential for self-dealing — that is, favoring one fund at the expense of another — the SEC has set down strict guidelines for when funds in the same company trade a security between one another rather than on the open market.

Major Types of Mutual Funds

The number of mutual funds has nearly tripled since 1980. In the current universe of approximately 8,000 funds, there are portfolios that suit most investment risk objectives. Likewise, the number of options has skyrocketed. There are funds that invest in high quality growth stocks, or smaller aggressive growth stocks, or stocks that pay high dividends. Mutual funds that invest in corporate and government bonds are also available.

Many fund management companies offer a number of different types of funds under one roof, often referred to as a "family of funds." A fund may include a growth stock fund, an aggressive growth stock fund, a fund that invests in stocks and bonds, a tax-exempt bond fund, a money market fund, and perhaps many others. Most mutual funds permit its customers to exchange from one fund to another within the group for a small fee, if their personal investment objectives change.

Following is a description of how, roughly, the $2 trillion currently invested in mutual funds breaks down. Despite endless variations, there are basically three broad categories of mutual funds: those aimed at providing immediate income; those oriented toward long-term growth or appreciation; and those that stress tax-free returns. The fund's objectives will be stated at the opening of the prospectus, indicating whether the fund emphasizes high or low risk, stability or speculation. Funds generally fall into one of the following major types: growth, growth and income bond, money market funds, tax-free, metals, foreign, and specialized.

Stock Funds

Following are the various types of stock funds.

Growth Funds

These stock funds emphasize growth. Dividend payouts will typically be low. These funds stress capital appreciation rather than immediate income. A typical growth fund would be the Vanguard S&P 500 index fund. This is a fund that consists of U.S. large cap stocks and has the primary objective to equal the return of the 500 largest U.S. stock companies.

According to Morningstar.com, as of June 30, 1996 the average growth mutual fund had returned 12.0 percent over the last ten years, but only 9.4 percent after tax (assuming maximum brackets). This reduction in return is due to dividend and capital gain distributions made by the funds, which are taxable to investors.

Aggressive Growth Funds

Aggressive growth funds invest in smaller, lesser-known companies, giving these companies time and room for enough upward movement to perform spectacularly during a bull market. As the name implies, these funds are invested for maximum capital gains, capital appreciation, and performance. This type of portfolio can be highly volatile and speculative in nature. The old adage, "high risk, high return," would fit. Historically, the more aggressive funds, or small cap funds, have outperformed the larger "blue chip" growth funds. You should be aware though that these returns also come with higher volatility, meaning the roller coaster ride has much bigger dips.

Balanced Funds

These portfolios stress three main goals: income, capital appreciation, and preservation of capital. This type of fund balances holdings such as bonds, convertible securities, and preferred stock, as well as common stock. The mix varies depending on the manager's view of the economy and market conditions. We generally do not believe in these funds unless they have a static ratio of stocks to bonds. We normally look for the manager to keep sixty percent in stocks and forty percent in bonds.

Growth and Income Funds

Combining stocks and bonds, this type of fund makes a serious effort at capturing both modest income and a long-term rise in the stock market. The manager is typically looking for blue chip companies that pay high dividends. Another strategy is to place a large percentage of the portfolio in equities and a portion in fixed income to generate the dividends. The concept of these funds is that they will have lower volatility and a more predictable and consistent return.

Income Funds

Their advertised investment objectives are safety and income, rather than capital appreciation. Income funds invest in corporate bonds or government-insured mortgages; if they own any stocks at all, these are usually preferred shares. The danger is chasing higher yields and not looking at the risks.

Utility Funds

Utility funds invest in stocks in utility companies around the country. Like bonds, utility stocks generate high income. Utilities are defensive investments in services that are needed, no matter how bad things get. The concept here is that everyone needs electricity, gas, water, etc. The problem is that we may need them, but sometimes the amount of regulation on these companies and the cost of distributing energy can negate the benefit

of constant demand. Utility funds need to be treated as risk-based investments like any stock mutual fund.

Specialty Funds

Specialty funds are also known as sector funds because they tend to invest
in stocks in specific industries. Sector funds should be avoided for large
percentages of a portfolio. Investing in stocks of a single industry defeats a
major purpose of investing in mutual funds — you're giving up the benefits
of diversification. A sector fund would be something like the India Fund or
a gold fund. They can be used to build a portfolio, but only in small amounts.
I would caution anyone from placing a large percentage of a portfolio in
these types of funds.

Specialty funds tend to carry much higher expenses than other mutual
funds. The only types of specialty funds that may make sense for a small
portion (ten percent or less) of your investment portfolio are funds that invest
in real estate or precious metals.

Gold Funds

A gold fund is a cost-effective way to participate in the possible increase in
the price of gold. Some funds invest only in South African stocks owning
shares of mining firms. The down side is that gold can be highly volatile.
These types of funds can help diversify your portfolio because they can do
better during times of higher inflation — not today.

Global Equity Funds

U.S. international and global funds focus their investments outside of the
U.S. The term *international* typically means that a fund can invest anywhere
in the world except the U.S. The term *global* generally implies that a fund
can invest anywhere in the world, including the U.S.

Hybrid Funds

Hybrid funds invest in a mixture of different types of securities. Most commonly, they invest in bonds and stocks. These funds are usually less risky
and volatile than funds investing exclusively in stocks. Hybrid mutual funds
are typically known as balanced or asset allocation funds. Balanced funds

generally try to maintain a fairly constant percentage of investment in stocks and bonds.

Asset Allocation Funds

Asset allocation funds tend to adjust the mix of different investments according to the portfolio manager's expectations. The only problem is, no one can accurately predict the actions of the market.

Bond Funds

Bonds are essentially IOUs. When you buy a bond, you are lending your money to a corporation or government agency. A bond mutual fund is nothing more than a large group (pack) of bonds. Most bond funds invest in bonds of similar maturity (the number of years to elapse before the borrower must pay back the money you lend). The names of most bond funds include a word or two to provide clues about the average length of maturity of their bonds.

For example, a short-term bond fund concentrates its investments in bonds maturing in the next few years. An intermediate-term fund generally holds bonds that come due within seven to ten years. The bonds in a long-term fund usually mature in twenty years or so. In contrast to an individual bond that you buy and hold until it matures, a bond fund is always replacing bonds in its portfolio to maintain its average maturity objective.

Bond funds are useful when you want to live off dividend income or when you don't want to put all your money in riskier investments such as stocks and real estate (perhaps because you plan to use the money soon).

Global Bond Funds

Global bond funds invest in foreign as well as U.S. bonds. Historically, global bond funds have outperformed domestic bond funds, but you do assume additional risk.

Money Market Funds

Money market funds are the safest type of mutual funds if you are worried about the risk of losing your principal. Money market funds are like bank savings accounts in that the value of your investment should not fluctuate. This type of fund could be used as your core saving strategy.

Index Funds

Think of these funds as whole baskets of stocks, representing the various stock market indexes. The S&P 500 index fund is by far the most common index fund for both institutional and individual investors. It tracks the performance of the Standard & Poor's 500 Index, a capitalization-weighted index of 500 large U.S. stocks. It is estimated that over ninety-five percent of all retail indexed monies are invested in S&P 500 index funds.

Following is a list of the indexes:

- The Wilshire 5000 includes all 5,000 stocks on the New York Stock Exchange Annex, as well as stocks traded over-the-counter (OTC). The Wilshire essentially takes the entire market as an index.
- The NASDAQ 100 — the National Association of Securities Dealers Index of stocks traded over-the-counter via its automatic quoting system "NASDAQ". The NASDAQ one hundred measures price changes in 100 of the largest OTC industrial stocks.
- The S&P 500, also known as Standard & Poor's Composite Index of 500 stocks consisting of the New York Stock Exchange-listed companies plus a few of the American Exchange and OTC stocks. Also, seven percent are non-U.S. companies and investment companies that can be affected by currency translations. One of the downsides of the S&P 500 is that the companies are chosen by committee, rather than by market efficiency.
- The Schwab 1000 Index, possibly a better index, makes it possible for you to invest in one thousand American companies with just one investment. It includes common stocks of the one hundred largest publicly traded U.S. companies measured by market capitalization. This represents eighty-two percent of the U.S. stock market value. It's a broader index, a broader diversification; not selected by a committee or Charles Schwab, but according to a formula of market capitalization. The fund invests in large and mid-size growth companies and is designed to track the broad U.S. stock price in dividend performance in order to keep pace with the market.
- Morgan Stanley EAFE (Europe Australia and Far East Index) is actually two subindexes of a thousand stocks traded in Europe and the

Pacific Basin; it is the most commonly used index for mutual funds that invest in foreign stocks.

Other Types of Index Funds

Be cautious with these index hybrids. Some brokers are now using these strategies to combat index investing and advising clients they can trade the hybrids as they would a stock (which you now know doesn't work in the long run).

Anyway, this new strategy is called SPDRS, "spiders," or Standard & Poor's Depository Receipts, available on the American Stock Exchange. SPDRS combine the advantage of index funds with the superior trading and flexibility of common stocks.

SPDRS buy and sell shares only to adjust the changes in the composite of the S&P index, without the need to meet investor redemptions the way an index fund does. When individual investors want to take money out, they simply sell shares on the American Stock Exchange.

If you want an index other than the S&P 500, there's Standard & Poor's Mid-cap, 400 Depository receipts; and globally, there are SPDRS called "World Equity Benchmark Shares," or WEBS, at select major international equity markets. The ticker symbols are SPDRs (SPY), Midcap (MDY), and Diamonds (DIA).

For information on SPDRs, call 800-The-Amex or click www.amex.com. On WEBS, call 800-810-WEBS or click://websontheweb.com.$.

Companies that provide financial services include

- Vanguard Group, 1-800-962-5160, www.vanguard.com
- Merrill Lynch, 1-800-MERRILL ext. 2896, www.plan.ml.com/zine/tax You can order the book, *You and Your Money, A Financial Handbook for Women Investors.*
- Charles Schwab and Co., 800-806-8481, www.schwab.com
- Fidelity Investments, www.fidelity.com. You can ask for a rollover IRA kit, kit for retirees, mutual fund kit, brokerage kit, and retirement planning for small business.
- Microsoft Money '98 Financial Office, www.pcmall.com/money98
- National Discount Brokers, 1-800-888-3999, www.ndb.com

Asset Class Mutual Funds

For a moment, think of mutual funds as being like a huge auto mart that offers everything from everyday economy cars to sports cars. You have to be wary of the seductive luxury cars with lot of extras that drive up the price. There are lemons among them.

Asset class mutual funds are composed of financial instruments with similar characteristics. Unlike managers of index funds, asset fund managers actively manage costs when buying and selling for funds. The most important attributes of asset class mutual funds are low operating expenses, low turnover, and low trading costs.

Low operating expenses: an important study of retail equity mutual funds by Elton et al.* finds the more expensive a fund is, the worse it performs on average. Low expenses is one of the main reasons to use asset class mutual funds.

Low turnover: active mutual fund managers do a lot of trading — this is how they think they are adding value. As a result, the average retail mutual fund has an annual turnover rate of eighty-six percent. This represents $86,000 of traded securities for every $100,000 invested.

High turnover is costly to shareholders because each time a trade is made there are transaction costs involved. These costs include commissions, spreads, and market impact costs. These hidden costs may amount to more than a fund's total operating expenses.

Retail mutual funds have high turnover because they're under tremendous pressure to perform. Good short-term performance leads to a bonus for the manager and a flood of new money for the fund. If they are performing poorly, they often try to make up ground by changing the composition of their holdings.

If a mutual fund sells a security for a gain, they must make a capital gain distribution to shareholders. This is because mutual funds are required to distribute ninety-eight percent of their taxable income each year, including realized capital gains, to stay tax-exempt at the corporate level. No mutual fund manager wants to have his or her performance reduced by paying corporate income taxes.

Low trading costs compared to high turnover products which include commissions, bid/ask spreads, and market impact costs.

The four major equity asset classes are

---

* Elton, Edwin J., Martin J. Gruber; Sanjiv Das; and Matthew Hlavka, "Efficiency with Costly Information: A Reinterpretation of Evidence from Managed Portfolios," The Society for Financial Studies (1993).

1. U.S. large company stocks
2. U.S. small company stocks
3. International large company stocks
4. International small company stocks

These four equity asset classes represent more than 5,000 different stock positions in fourteen different countries. U.S. large stocks mean domestic companies with capitalizations of over $50 million; small means under $50 million. Research shows that large and small company stocks have low correlation with each other.

When the equity markets decline, fixed income securities will dampen the fall. The two major equity asset classes are (1) fixed income and (2) international fixed income

U.S. Equity Asset Class Mutual Funds

U.S. equity asset class funds and pure index funds have portfolios that are market-capitalization weighted. In other words, the fund manager allocates money to U.S. companies based on the size of their markets, measured by market capitalization.

International Equity Asset Classes

Global investing is a hot topic on Wall Street and among money managers, many of whom, for various reasons, would rather have U.S. investors park their funds at home. They, therefore, discourage international investing for their clients. These managers and advisors have even come up with ways that investors can seemingly play markets abroad using domestic assets. This theory holds that the way to make a global play — without taking on true global securities exposure — is to buy the stocks of U.S. multinational firms doing a great deal of business abroad.

This idea seems clever on first glance, but there are difficulties. What most undermines this concept is that stocks of multinational firms tend to follow the movements of their local markets rather than the international market. This is true regardless of the degree to which their operations are globally diversified. For example, Colgate gets about eighty percent of its revenues from foreign operations, yet its stock price still closely follows the U.S. market. Because stocks of U.S. multinational firms are so highly correlated with the U.S. market, they lose their diversification power.

It has become conventional wisdom that you should put some of your money in international equities. The two reasons most often given for this recommendation are (1) foreign stocks have historically outperformed U.S. stocks, and (2) foreign stocks provide good diversification due to their low correlation with U.S. markets. While it is true that international stocks measured by Morgan Stanley Capital International's EAFE Index have outperformed the S&P 500 since 1970, this occurs only because foreign currencies have outperformed the U.S. dollar. In local currency terms, the returns of foreign and domestic stocks are about equal.

The international and U.S. equity markets have a low correlation; they do not tend to move together. The data indicates that U.S. and foreign stocks have equal expected returns; therefore, true global diversification is desirable.

Most international asset class funds and pure index funds have portfolios that are market-capitalization weighted. In other words, the fund manager allocates money to countries based on the size of their markets, measured by market capitalization. Currently, Japan is the largest of any market outside the U.S. Therefore, a market-capitalization-weighted international fund will allocate more money to Japan than any other country. This approach probably puts too much money in Japanese stocks. The overweighting occurs because, in Japan, it is common for companies to invest in the stocks of other companies.

These cross holdings are counted twice, which overstates the market capitalization of Japan relative to the rest of the world.

Fixed Income Asset Class Mutual Funds

Fixed income securities are an important part of a comprehensive portfolio because they provide stability to counterbalance the high volatility of equities. While they have lower expected returns than stocks, they add value to the portfolio by reducing overall volatility. Bonds are the primary tools for pinpointing your portfolio to your target risk level. A higher allocation to bonds reduces portfolio risk and a lower allocation to bonds increases portfolio risk.

A bond represents a loan to an issuer, such as the U.S. government or a major corporation, usually in return for periodic fixed interest payments. These payments continue until the bond is redeemed at maturity (or earlier if called by the issuer). At the time of maturity, the investor receives the face value of the bond.

Many investors buy long-term bonds because they normally have higher current yields than shorter-term bonds. Investors consider them safe, but in reality long-term bonds have many different kinds of risk. These risks include reinvestment risk, call risk, purchasing power risk, liquidity risk, and interest rate risk.

The major risk you face with long-term bonds is interest rate risk. Because prices of bonds move in the opposite direction of interest rates, when rates rise, prices of bonds fall, and vice versa. For example, consider a newly issued twenty-year Treasury bond with a six percent coupon. If over the next twelve months, interest rates increase by two percent, new twenty-year Treasury bonds will be offered with eight percent coupons. Therefore, the old six percent bonds will be worth less than the new bonds since the new bonds have higher coupons. This illustrates how falling interest rates force bond prices up. Alternatively, interest rates may rise and force bond prices down. This inverse relationship between interest rates and bond values is an important risk of fixed income investments. It can create significant volatility, especially for long-term bonds.

To give you an idea of the volatility of long-term bonds, consider the historical rates of total return of twenty-year Treasury bonds over the last six decades. During the 1980s, long-term bond investors enjoyed one of the best decades ever, with gains averaging 12.7 percent per year. Bond prices soared during this decade due to declining interest rates. Because of these high returns, long-term bonds became very popular in the late 1980s and early 1990s, since investors frequently place too much importance on their most recent experiences. Psychologists call this *cognitive bias*. We call it *rear view mirror* investing. It is like trying to drive a car while only looking where you have been through the rear view mirror. It is crucial to analyze all statistical evidence available when making financial decisions.

In contrast, consider the decade of the 1950s. This was the worst decade for long-term bond investors because they experienced an average annual return of negative 0.1 percent including reinvested interest. Most investors don't realize that the volatility of long-term bonds is close to the volatility of common stocks.

The higher risk of long-term bonds would be acceptable if investors were sufficiently rewarded with higher rates of return. Eugene Fama of the University of Chicago has studied the rates of return of long-term bonds from 1964 to 1996 and found that the term premium for longer-term bonds is not reliable. His research shows that long-term bonds have wide variances in their rates of return and, most important, that bonds with maturities beyond five years don't offer sufficient reward for their higher risk.

The predominant investors in the long-term bond markets are institutions, such as corporate pension plans and life insurance companies. These investors are interested in funding long-term obligations, including fixed annuity payments or other fixed corporate responsibilities. In general, they are not concerned with volatility of principal or with the effects of inflation, since their obligations are fixed in maturity date and amount. You, on the other hand, should be concerned with inflation, as well as volatility. This is because you are an individual living in a variable rate world. You have a limit to the amount of volatility with which you feel comfortable.

Given the data, you should own fixed income investments to provide stability to your portfolio, but not to generate high returns. High returns should come from equities. Fixed income securities can help offset the risk of your equity holdings and, therefore, lower the risk of your overall portfolio. You can best do this by using short-term fixed income securities rather than long-term bonds. Short-term bonds have less volatility and a lower correlation with stocks and are a better choice for your portfolio. They will allow you to invest a larger percentage of your money in stocks while maintaining low portfolio risk.

International Fixed-Income Asset Classes

This asset class includes foreign government bond markets — including the markets of Japan, the United Kingdom, Switzerland, the Netherlands, Germany, and France.

The Emerging Market Asset Classes

Many institutional investors now recognize emerging markets as a separate and distinct asset class. The term "emerging markets" refers to the stock markets of the world's developing countries whose economies are growing fast enough to deserve the term "emerging."

It is also important to keep in mind that while these markets may be defined as emerging, the companies whose stocks are being purchased are well-established companies in these countries. The countries must have well-organized markets that provide ample liquidity and also have a developed legal system that protects property rights and upholds contractual obligations. Typical holdings are national banks, land developers, and phone companies of various countries.

These emerging countries are experiencing rapid growth and improvements in their political, social, and economic conditions. You might conclude that the higher rates of economic growth in these countries should lead to

Rate Of Return & Risk Objectives

Asset Class	Expected Return	Standard Deviation
Money Market	4.90%	3.30%
Fixed Income	6.70%	3.90%
US Large	13.60%	20.30%
US Small	19.40%	38.50%
International Large	13.60%	20.30%
International Small	19.40%	38.50%
Emerging Markets	16.00%	29.00%

Figure 6.6 Asset classes, expected returns, and standard deviations. We have identified the specific return/risk profiles of each optimized model portfolio. You can use these ranges of returns of each risk level as the framework to determine your return expectation for your portfolio, as well as its component asset classes.

higher stock returns. This is a common message communicated by the financial press and investment professionals. While it is true that emerging market countries have higher economic growth rates than the developed world, this alone does not mean their stock returns will be higher.

What is not so widely understood is that emerging market returns are *not* due to faster economic growth. Higher returns are a reward for accepting higher risk.

Emerging market investing involves substantial risks, including political instability, extreme market volatility, lack of liquidity, dramatic currency devaluation, high transaction costs, and regulatory risk. And because of a lack of reliable information, low accounting standards, and very poor financial disclosure, investors should avoid these funds unless they are a small part of an overall asset class portfolio.

Even though investing in emerging markets seems risky, you may be surprised to see the volatility of the emerging markets asset class is actually less than that of U.S. small company stocks. You may also be surprised to see that international small company stocks and U.S. small cap have approximately the same standard deviation or risk level. In the next section you will learn how to combine these asset classes to lower risk while enhancing returns.

The Rating Game

The mutual fund rating game works much the same way as the old dating game on television. Investors use ratings of mutual funds that are listed in newspapers and magazines as a guide to help them pick funds that are the right ones for the portfolio.

Choosing an A-rated fund is a quick and easy way to choose a fund, but are these ratings actually useful? Let's consider mutual fund ratings in the *Wall Street Journal* as compiled by Lipper Analytical Services. Lipper awards

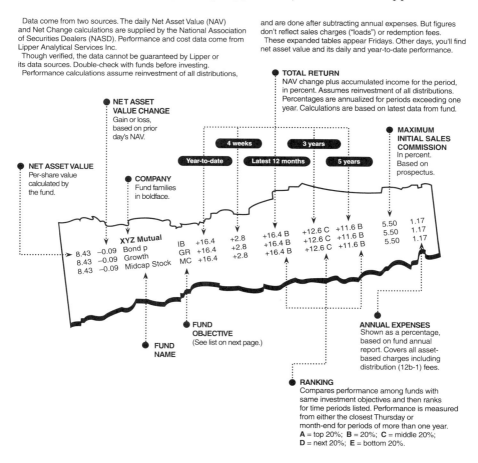

Data come from two sources. The daily Net Asset Value (NAV) and Net Change calculations are supplied by the National Association of Securities Dealers (NASD). Performance and cost data come from Lipper Analytical Services Inc.
Though verified, the data cannot be guaranteed by Lipper or its data sources. Double-check with funds before investing.
Performance calculations assume reinvestment of all distributions,

and are done after subtracting annual expenses. But figures don't reflect sales charges ("loads") or redemption fees.
These expanded tables appear Fridays. Other days, you'll find net asset value and its daily and year-to-date performance.

● **TOTAL RETURN**
NAV change plus accumulated income for the period, in percent. Assumes reinvestment of all distributions. Percentages are annualized for periods exceeding one year. Calculations are based on latest data from fund.

● **NET ASSET VALUE CHANGE**
Gain or loss, based on prior day's NAV.

● **MAXIMUM INITIAL SALES COMMISSION**
In percent. Based on prospectus.

4 weeks   3 years

Year-to-date   Latest 12 months   5 years

● **NET ASSET VALUE**
Per-share value calculated by the fund.

● **COMPANY**
Fund families in boldface.

XYZ Mutual

8.43	−0.09	Bond p	IB	+16.4	+2.8	+16.4 B	+12.6 C	+11.6 B	5.50	1.17
8.43	−0.09	Growth	GR	+16.4	+2.8	+16.4 B	+12.6 C	+11.6 B	5.50	1.17
8.43	−0.09	Midcap Stock	MC	+16.4	+2.8	+16.4 B	+12.6 C	+11.6 B	5.50	1.17

● **FUND OBJECTIVE**
(See list on next page.)

● **FUND NAME**

● **ANNUAL EXPENSES**
Shown as a percentage, based on fund annual report. Covers all asset-based charges including distribution (12b-1) fees.

● **RANKING**
Compares performance among funds with same investment objectives and then ranks for time periods listed. Performance is measured from either the closest Thursday or month-end for periods of more than one year. **A** = top 20%; **B** = 20%; **C** = middle 20%; **D** = next 20%; **E** = bottom 20%.

Figure 6.7 How to read newspaper mutual fund tables. Remember, don't use the publications as your main source of financial information. (From Chambers, L., *The First Time Investor*. New York: McGraw-Hill, 1998. With permission.)

an A to funds whose returns are in the top twenty percent of their category. The next twenty percent get Bs and so on, through C, D, and E. For the period ending December 31, 1997, the Vanguard Index 500 is awarded an A, the highest rating possible, while the Vanguard Index Small Company Fund is worth only a C.

This means that the Vanguard Index 500 Fund is ranked in the top twenty percent of all similar funds, and the Vanguard Index Small Company Fund only ranks in the middle of its peer group. Likewise, for the last three years, the Vanguard Index European Fund managed the highest rating of A, while the Vanguard Index Pacific Fund gets only a D for the previous twelve months. Something seems amiss with these ratings.

Because index funds should be easiest of all funds to rank, they simply mirror broad market segments and disclose exactly what's in their portfolios. Active managed funds are much harder to classify than index funds because they have changing styles, moving asset allocation, and other complications. Good ratings bring money into mutual funds, bonuses to managers, and so on. Naturally, managers will do whatever they need to do to improve their ratings.

For example, a recent study by Kelly, Brown, Van Harlow, and Starks* found that mutual fund managers increased the risk level of their portfolios right in the middle of the year if they were not ranked among peer group performance leaders. If they were successful and their funds' rank improved, the managers would give bonuses and the fund would get increased assets from investors. If the gamble failed, the fund performed worse than it would have if it had not made any changes. The mutual fund rating game is a loser's game.

A Barometer of Ups and Downs

When the stock market is said to be up ten points, what is usually meant is that the venerable Dow Jones Industrial Average (DJIA) went up ten points. The DJIA is based on the average prices paid for thirty blue chip stocks. The up-and-down fluctuations of the New York Stock Exchange has been recorded since 1896, and general upward and downward movements of stock prices are symbolized on Wall Street by bulls and bears.

* Kelly, Brown, Van Harlow and Laurel Starks, "On Tournaments and Temptations, An Analysis of Managerial Incentives in the Mutual Fund Industry," *Journal of Finance*, March 1996, pp. 85–110.

What is the Dow Jones Industrial Average?

In the widely watched Dow average, only one stock, General Electric Co., remains from the original twelve chosen in 1896. The Dow reflects the U.S. economy. When the average ended its first day at 40.94, twelve years before Henry Ford made his first Model T, the average included such stalwarts as U.S. Leather and Tennessee Coal & Iron. If it hadn't changed, the average wouldn't be an accurate barometer of the economy. It's true that there are only thirty companies, but they are thirty of the best-known and largest companies.

Narrow as it is, the DJIA is easily the most popular gauge of the U.S. stock market. The public follows the Dow more than academics or even the Wall Street crowd. All three television networks acknowledge the popularity of the Dow as a yardstick by citing it on their nightly news reports.

The Dow industrials are a big brand name, and in that way have become synonymous with the fortunes of U.S. stocks generally. Investors who want to know if stocks are up or down ask about the Dow the same way customers ask for a soft drink or facial tissue. We ask for a Coke, or we ask for a Kleenex.

Rival stock-market averages and indexes don't have the Dow's cachet. That was even more the case in the 1930s. They watched the stocks, but the Dow in most people's minds was an indicator of what the market was doing.

Dow Jones, publisher of the *Wall Street Journal*, helps ensure that the Dow industrials stay prominent. The biggest newspaper in the country, with a daily circulation of 1.8 million readers, the *Journal* usually features its average first when writing about the stock market.

They promoted the Dow average, and once a generation or two was trained on it, it just became the easy thing to follow.

Of late, the Dow industrials have beaten the broader Standard & Poor's 500 Index, the seventy-year-old benchmark that gauges 500 stocks. Since the current bull market began in October 1990, the Dow has surged 144 percent, topping the S&P 500's 129 percent gain.

To understand the importance of the Dow Jones Industrial Average, investors must return to the closing years of the nineteenth century.

Charles Dow was ahead of his time. When he decided in 1896 to create the industrial average, he sensed where the country was going. At the time, the NYSE did very little trading of industrial shares. They were too low-brow, and were considered speculative — like we would consider junk bonds today. The only stocks regarded as investment-grade were railroads and utilities. By giving investors a measuring instrument, Dow helped popularize stocks in general.

Big business was relatively unknown before 1880, when most companies were family-owned. The next twenty-five years saw the creation of national businesses, companies such as GE and U.S. Steel. Charles Dow recognized the growing importance of manufacturing and the opportunities available to investors.

The Dow average's popularity grew because investors needed a way to compare their gains with the overall stock market.

Professional money managers think of the Dow as a crude average because no allowance is made for the size of a company. The price of all thirty stocks is added up; but instead of being divided by thirty, the total is multiplied by a divisor that is adjusted to maintain historical continuity.

That method doesn't take into account that a ten percent rise in International Business Machines Corp., whose shares sell for $109, has a far greater impact on the broad market than a ten percent move in Bethlehem Steel Corp's $12.75-a-share stock. By contrast, the S&P 500 Index is weighted by a company's size and is the benchmark by which mutual fund managers usually measure their performance.

The Dow seldom changes its average unless forced to by a merger or acquisition or spin-off. No change has been made in the Dow industrials in the five years since Walt Disney Co., Caterpillar Inc., and J.P. Morgan & Co. were added to the average, replacing Navistar International Corp., Primerica Corp., and USX Corp.

Some analysts think the Dow industrial average will continue to evolve, perhaps by adopting leading NASDAQ Stock Market companies, such as Microsoft Corp. or Intel Corp., which are regarded as proxies for the computer industry.

It's also possible that Dow Jones editors will broaden the average by enlarging it beyond thirty names. After all, they expanded the original list of twelve companies to twenty in 1920 and enlarged the average to the current thirty in late 1928. It's not been a static index. They've added companies and taken companies out. Generally, when they update the index, they add a company that's a little more responsive to what's going on in the economy.

The Standard & Poor's 500 Index, the Value Line Composite Index, and the New York Stock Exchange Composite Index are ostensibly more accurate indices and are also more widely followed. These are broader-based, which should make them somewhat more accurate in a large market. Since the DJIA consists of only thirty large companies, it may not truly reflect market performance.

What If You've Bought a Bad Fund?

What if you're in a mutual fund that isn't performing according to its or your stated goals? Despite our advice on the subject of market timing, this is an exception — sometimes you just buy a bad fund. Let's look at the telltale signs of a bad mutual fund:

- Above average expenses — those higher costs take a bigger bite out of the return earned by the stocks, meaning lower return to you. If your fund investment loses three percent, for example, and has a two percent annual expense ratio, you've actually sustained a five percent loss for the year. (You can find the expense ratio in your fund's prospectus.) Lipper Analytic says the average stock mutual fund has an annual expense ratio of 1.54 percent. The average fixed income fund is around 0.96 percent.
- Poor communications — troubled funds often fall behind on providing information in a timely fashion. If information isn't arriving on time, and you don't get a satisfactory explanation, it's appropriate to get nervous.
- Lack of discipline — the best investments all take a consistent approach. The worst type of funds pursue whatever is hot. If your fund has changed its focus, or if the manager has changed his or her style, the fund could be chasing a hot sector, trying to enhance returns.
- Managers change — if the managers keep leaving, there's something going on. The fund owes you an adequate explanation. They need to tell you what the new guy can do to help turn it around.
- The biggest indicator: shrinking assets. Funds get bigger when they're making more money and they shrink when they lose. When investors lose confidence, the shrinking can be dramatic.

Mutual Fund Names

Titles can mislead investors. There are some strict rules being proposed. When you hear *Fidelity Magellan*, or *Putnam Voyager*, what does it really tell you? Are they going on a voyage? No. You don't have a clue as to what they're investing in. That fact would make them exempt from a proposed federal regulation that would require mutual funds to have at least eighty percent of their assets in securities that match the name of the fund, instead of the sixty-five percent now required. So, for instance, ABC Japan fund would

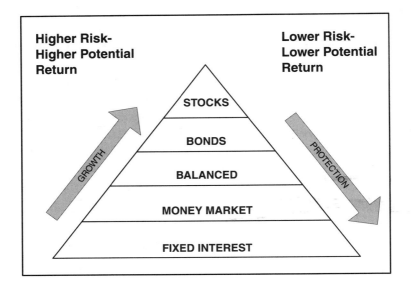

Figure 6.8 Relationship between risk and return.

have eighty percent of its assets invested in Japan, instead of the sixty-five percent required now. The point is to prevent investors from being misled by fund names.

Now we will look at the underlying investments that make up these different mutual fund categories. Think of a pyramid. At the top of that pyramid would be stocks. If you combined stocks and bonds for less risk, they would make up the middle. Fixed interest investments would be at the bottom of the investment pyramid, because of their low risk.

7 Understanding Stocks

Equity mutual funds are made up of many individual stocks. A stock is a security issued by a corporation or by a government as a means of raising long-term capital. The ownership is divided into a certain number of shares; the corporation issues stock certificates which show how many shares are owned.

The capital a company raises through the sale of these shares entitles the holder to dividends and to other rights of ownership, such as voting rights.

Prices of stocks change according to general business conditions and the earnings and future prospects of the companies that have issued the stock. If the business is doing well, stockholders may be able to sell their stock for a profit. If it is not, they may have to take a loss when they sell.

Large corporations may have many thousands of stockholders. Their stock is bought and sold in marketplaces called stock exchanges. A stock exchange occupies an important position in our country's financial system by providing a mechanism for converting *savings* into physical and portfolio *investment*. It also performs two major functions; it provides a primary or new-issues market, in which new capital can be raised by issuing financial securities, and a secondary market for trading existing securities that facilitates transferability of securities from seller to buyers.

The shares of stock represent the value of the corporation. When the corporation has made a profit, the directors may divide the profit among stockholders as dividends, or they may decide to use it to expand the business. Dividends are paid to the stockholders out of the corporation's profits. When profits are used to expand the business, the directors and stockholders may issue more stock to show that there is more money invested in the business. This new stock will be divided among the old stockholders as stock dividends.

Stocks are issued in two forms: common and preferred.

Common Stock

Common stock represents true ownership shares in a company. Stockholders share directly in growing company profits through increasing dividends and an appreciation in the value of the stock itself. As the holder of common stock, you are a part-owner in the company issuing the stock. The purchaser of common stock not only receives a share of any dividends paid by the corporation, but also gets the right to vote for corporate directors who, in turn, choose the corporate officers and set the corporation's policies. When a broker uses the term "stock," he or she is normally referring to *common* stock.

Preferred Stock

Preferred stock, like common stock, represents ownership or equity, and not debt. Preferred stockholders have a claim on profits which precedes — or is preferred to — the claim of the common stockholder. The preferred stockholder has a right to receive *specified* dividends (for example, ten percent of the face value of the preferred share) before the common stockholder can be paid any dividend at all.

On the other hand, the preferred stockholder does not have the possibility of large gains open to the common stockholder.

If the preferred stockholders share with the common-stock holders in dividends beyond the specified percentage, the stock is called participating preferred.

Preferred stock may also be cumulative. That is, if there are no dividends given in a year, the preferred stockholders must be given double their dividend the next year. This is paid before anything is paid to the common stockholders. This principle continues for as many years as dividends are not paid.

More Terms

Price/Earnings Ratio

This is how you measure the value of a company. The price/earnings ratio measures the stock's price divided by the company's earnings per share (or EPS) over the past twelve months. If a company is earning $1 a share and the public is buying the stock at $10, the market price is divided by the earnings. In this case, ten is divided by one; this tells us that the stock is selling at ten times earnings (10P/E or 10x). If you invest in this company and paid $10, theoretically you are paying ten years' worth of earnings to own it. When the market is low you will see 10x. Today the average is 25 to 30 times earnings.

Dividend Payout Ratio

This is the ratio of a company's indicated annual cash dividend per share to its earnings-per-share (EPS), and can range from zero to one hundred percent. A utility that pays out $4 in dividends for each $5 of earnings would have a payout of eighty percent. The payout is above fifty percent for the average large industrial company and even higher for the typical utility. The higher the dividend payout, however, the less room there is for dividend increases, since less profit is available to reinvest for future growth.

Dividend Yield

This measures the annual dividend divided by the stock price. For example, if a utility's dividend is $4 and its stock sells for $50 a share, the yield would be eight percent. When the EPS (in general) is high, yields will be low.

Blue Chip Stocks

These high-quality companies are typically large, old, and well established, such as those represented in the Dow Jones Industrial Average. Blue chips are often considered income stocks by virtue of their fairly high dividend payouts. Many of the companies included in the S&P 500 would also qualify as blue chips.

Stocks can be lumped into any of several broad categories. These are general classifications, and a stock may simultaneously fit into two or more categories. For example, a "blue chip" may also be classified as "growth and income" and "defensive." A "growth" company may be categorized as "speculative."

Where Is the Stock Traded?

A stock exchange provides a marketplace for stocks and bonds in the same way a commodity exchange does for commodities.

To most investors, "the stock market" means the New York Stock Exchange. The New York Stock Exchange has been in existence for more than 200 years. Needless to say, it has come a long way since twenty-four merchants and auctioneers met at the site of the present exchange to negotiate an agreement to buy and sell stocks and bonds issued by the new United States government, along with those of a few banks and insurance companies. It wasn't until 1817 that the exchange adopted an approved constitution, whereby it named itself the New York Stock and Exchange Board. The exchange did not cross the million-share daily threshold until 1886. Its dullest day ever was March 16, 1830, when only 31 shares changed hands. In 1997, the exchange witnessed the first day when 1 billion shares were traded.

There are also many other North American exchanges trading stock, from the American Stock Exchange (called AMEX) on down to the Spokane Stock Exchange. In addition, thousands of equities are not traded on any exchange but are, rather, sold over-the-counter (OTC). Prices for OTC stocks are readily available through the NASDAQ, an acronym for the National Association of Securities Dealers Automated Quotations system, the hottest market today. Many unlisted industrial securities are more speculative than listed ones.

There is a distinct difference between OTC stocks and exchange-listed equities, revolving primarily around eligibility requirements. Each stock exchange has listing requirements that must be met before a company may take its place on the exchange floor. For example, before a stock can be listed on the NYSE, the company must have at least one million shares outstanding (available to the public). Those shares must be held by at least 2,000 different stockholders, each of whom owns at least 100 shares. The company must also have earned a pre-tax profit of at least $2.5 million the year preceding the listing, and the pre-tax profits in the two prior years must have been at least $2 million each year. The AMEX and the regional exchanges have similar (though less stringent) listing requirements, but no such limitations exist for OTC listings.

How Does a Stock Exchange Operate?

Federal and state laws regulate the issuance, listing, and trading of most securities. The Securities and Exchange Commission (SEC) administers the federal laws.

Stocks handled by one or more stock exchanges are called *listed stocks*. A company that wants to have its stock listed for trading on an exchange must first prove to the exchange that it has enough paid-up capital, is a lawful enterprise, and is in good financial condition.

How Do Stocks Trade on the Exchange?

Probably one of the most confusing aspects of investing is understanding how stocks actually trade. Words like "bid," "ask," "volume," and "spread" can be quite confusing if you do not understand what they mean. Depending on which exchange a stock trades, there are two different systems.

The New York Stock Exchange and the American Stock Exchange (composed of the Boston, Philadelphia, Chicago, and San Francisco Exchanges) are both listed exchanges, meaning brokerage firms contribute individuals known as "specialists" who are responsible for all of the trading in a specific stock. This is known as "an open auction market." Volume, or the number of shares that trade on a given day, is counted by the specialists.

These individuals control stock prices by matching buy and sell orders delivered by the floor brokers shouting out their orders. The specialists change the prices to match the supply-and-demand fundamentals. The specialist system was created to guarantee that every seller finds a buyer, and vice versa. This process may sound chaotic, but specialists do succeed in their function of maintaining an orderly market and matching sellers to buyers. In return for this service, the specialist charges the buyer an extra fee of 6.25 or 12.5 cents per share, depending on the price of the stock.

The Over-the-Counter Market

The NASDAQ stock market, the NASDAQ SmallCap, and the OTC Bulletin Board are the three main over-the-counter markets. In an over-the-counter market, brokerages (also known as broker-dealers) act as market makers for various stocks. The brokerages interact over a centralized computer system managed by the NASDAQ, providing liquidity for the market to function. One firm represents the seller and offers an ask price (also called the "offer"), or the price the seller is asking to sell the security. Another firm represents the buyer and gives a bid, or a price at which the buyer will buy the security.

For example, a particular stock might be trading at a bid of $10 and an ask of $10.50. If an investor wanted to sell shares, he would get the bid price of $10 per share; if he wanted to buy shares, he would pay the ask price of $10.50 per share. The difference is called the spread, which is paid by the buyer. This difference is split between the two firms involved in the transaction.

Placing an Order

A person who wishes to buy stock places an order with his representative. The representative gets a quotation (price) and relays the order to the floor of the exchange. The entire transaction may take only a few minutes.

How do you do it? What types of orders can you place? Let's look at the major types of orders.

- Buy order: the order you place when, obviously enough, you want to buy shares. Simply tell the broker how many shares you want to purchase.
- Buy at market: you instruct the broker to buy a specified number of shares at the prevailing market price.
- Buy at a limit: you instruct the broker to buy a specified number of shares, but only at a specified price or lower. For example, you might say: "Buy 100 shares of IBM at a limit of $50." In this case, you are only willing to purchase shares of IBM if you can do so at $50 or less.
- Sell order: an order you place when you want to sell shares.
- Sell at market: an order to sell your shares at the prevailing market price.
- Sell at a limit: an order to sell your shares only at the price that you specify or higher.
- Sell at a stop limit: you instruct your broker to sell your stock if it falls to a certain price. For example, you buy IBM at $50 and you instruct your advisor/broker to sell if it falls to $45. This would be a Sell Stop at $45.

Shorting Stocks

Shorting a stock is the reverse of buying a stock. In effect if you sell a stock by borrowing it from a broker hoping that its share price will go down, you are "short" the stock. The idea is to buy the stock back later at a lower price and then return the shares to the broker and keep the difference. Although shorting is not the place you should be, you still understand how it works.

The basics of the shorting transaction are straightforward. You first contact your brokerage in order to determine whether or not they can borrow shares of the stock you want to short. When you receive the borrowed shares, you immediately sell them and keep the cash, promising to return the shares at some future time. The plan is to eventually repurchase the shares at a lower price and return them, keeping the difference yourself. But if the stock's price rises, you might have to buy back the shares at the higher price and thus lose money.

Summary: Just think of a mutual fund as the house and individual stocks and bonds as the people who live inside.

8 Understanding Bonds

What is a "bond"? Don't be ashamed if you don't know. A recent survey indicates that more than ninety percent of the general public is in the dark in this area. In fact, the majority of people who have actually invested in stocks and bonds don't really understand what makes a bond different from all other types of investments. A bond is the legal evidence of a debt, usually the result of a loan of money.

When you buy a bond, you are in effect lending your money to the issuer of the bond. The issuer agrees to make periodic interest payments to you, the investor holding the bond, and also agrees to repay the original sum (the principal) in full to you on a certain date — known as the bond's maturity date. Interest rates can soar and you, the customer, will still be repaid the entire principal at maturity. Even a mutual fund with a stable NAV will be affected to some extent by changes in interest rates.

More important is "what backs" the bond. In the case of many corporate securities, nothing more is behind them than the full faith and credit of the companies that issue them. These bonds, usually called debentures, are probably the most common type of debt issued by industrial corporations today.

Public utilities generally issue bonds with specific assets as collateral against the loan. These are called "mortgage" bonds or "collateral trust" bonds. Some utilities, however, issue debentures and some industrial corporations issue collateralized bonds.

Kinds of Individual Bonds

There are three main categories of bonds, issued by (1) the U.S. government or one of its agencies; (2) corporations; and (3) municipalities. While these three types have some different characteristics, they share a basic structure.

U.S. Government Notes and Bonds

The U.S. government issues both Treasury notes (maturities of two to ten years) and bonds (maturities over ten years). U.S. Government securities are considered to have no credit risk. The government auctions U.S. Government securities on a regular quarterly schedule.

In a normal yield-curve environment, U.S. Government notes typically have yields 50 to 250 basis points higher than those on Treasury (T)-bills, and the same spread lower than a U.S. Government bond. (100 basis points equals one percent.) Notes are the most likely investment for an individual investor because of the maturity range. Institutional investors and traders actively trade the thirty-year bond.

Corporate Bonds

Corporations of every size and credit quality issue corporate bonds, from the very best blue chip companies to small companies with low ratings. Corporate bonds are not easy to evaluate, especially those with longer maturities when call provisions may apply and the credit outlook is less certain. Many investors simply choose to stay in shorter maturities, or with extremely sound companies such as utilities. Corporate bonds may be backed by collateral and are fully taxable at the federal, state, and local levels.

Yields are higher on corporate bonds than on a CD or government-issued or -insured debt. The coupon is fixed and return of principal is guaranteed by the issuer if the investor holds it until maturity. If the investor sells the bond prior to maturity, the bond will be subject to market fluctuation. Investors who want to be able to check the prices of their bonds in the newspaper should buy listed bonds, preferably those listed on the New York Stock Exchange.

The fully taxable nature of corporate bonds (as opposed to municipals or Treasuries) has an effect on yield. When buying a AAA-rated corporate bond, you are buying a security that has more risk than a U.S. Government bond. For the risk you are taking, you should receive an additional 25 to 50 basis points in yield.

Municipal Bonds

What are municipal bonds? Very simply, they are investment instruments used to finance municipal governmental activities. They are not always guaranteed by the municipality.

Investors whose goal is simply to conserve capital and generate returns that keep up with inflation often look to municipal bonds with the idea that these bonds are fairly safe. Investors may believe this because "munis" issuances often have language stating they are "backed by the full faith and credit" of the issuing authority. In addition to the safety that conservative investors think they are gaining in municipal bonds, investors may also believe that the tax-free status of these bonds offers additional rewards. The combination of safety and tax-advantaged reward seems irresistible to many who are not especially sophisticated about the securities markets and who are seeking simply to avoid making an investment mistake.

Munis attract many wealthy investors for the above reasons. They're not looking for growth, they've already made it. The largest part of Ross Perot's holdings are in muni bonds.

However, if rates fall and prices rise, you're not necessarily going to be able to take advantage of your good fortune because the municipalities may hurry to call the bonds away from you. And tax-free certainly does not mean risk free: remember the Orange County debacle of the early 1990s or the New York City municipal difficulties of the 1970s.

Municipal bonds have high trading costs due to large bid/ask spreads and significant market impact costs. Because of their high trading costs, municipal bonds are only suitable for buy-and-hold investors who want to hold longer-maturity bonds or high-yield municipals.

Municipal Bond Funds

Municipal bond funds are nothing more than a large grouping of various municipal bonds. They may be appropriate when you are in high federal (twenty-eight percent and up) and state (five percent or higher) tax brackets. Most municipal bond funds invest in municipal bonds of similar maturity (the number of years before the borrower, in this case the municipality, must pay back the money to you, the lender).

The key advantage of a bond fund is management. Fund managers can switch bonds from time to time within a fund. A bond fund is always replacing bonds in its portfolio to maintain its average maturity objective.

What Are the Risks?

The main form of market risk for a bond is the risk of interest rates changing after a customer buys the bond — called "interest-rate risk." If market interest rates go up, the bond loses principal value; if market rates go down, the bond gains principal value. The longer the term of the bond, the more the price will be affected by changes in interest rates. Whether the U.S. Government, a corporation, or a municipality issues the bond, the risk is similar.

Bonds are also subject to "call risk," the risk that the bond issuer will choose to redeem (call) the bond before the maturity date.

A Look at Interest Rates

A bond's current value is directly affected by changes in the interest rates. The effect of higher interest rates on bonds is to lower their prices. Conversely, lower rates raise bond prices. The fluctuation is due to the fact that the price of the bond must offer a prospective purchaser current market rates.

When Should an Individual Buy a Bond, Rather than a Bond Fund?

There is a lot to understand before buying an individual bond. It is a somewhat different process from buying stocks or mutual funds. Large companies have millions of shares of stock outstanding, and all shares of common stock are the same. To buy a bond, on the other hand, the customer can't simply consult the *Wall Street Journal*, pick a particular bond, and place an order. Buying a bond means finding the owner (such as an institutional trading desk) of a bond that meets your needs.

The owner of individual bonds has much greater control of both cash flow and tax consequences. The investor controls when to take profits and losses based on what is in his or her best interest. If it matters to an investor whether a tax gain is taken in December or January, a bond allows that choice.

Any institutional investor buys bonds more cheaply than a single individual, and the bonds in a mutual fund have been purchased at the institutional price. The institutional investor also pays a minuscule portion of total price in transaction costs, whereas transaction costs can be significant for an individual — and it gets worse if the individual must pay for safekeeping the securities. A bond fund does, however, pay a management fee that might equal in yield the transaction cost an individual would pay.

The mutual fund pays dividends monthly since it owns bonds with so many different payment dates, whereas individual bonds pay out only semiannually. Following is information an investor should consider before making a bond purchase:

- Security description: type of bond, purpose of the bond, and the issuer.
- Rating: for example, AA is better than A.
- Trade date: date the bond is purchased in the market.
- Settlement date: the date the purchaser pays for the bond and interest starts accruing.
- Maturity date: the date the purchaser will be repaid the principal and last interest payment.
- Interest payment dates: dates interest payments are made, usually semiannually.
- Coupon: fixed annual interest rate (interest income) stated on the bond.
- Price: dollar price paid for the bond. (An offer price is the price at which the individual investor buys the bond; the bid price is the price at which the individual can sell the bond.)
- Current yield: the coupon divided by price, giving a rough approximation of cash flow.
- Yield to maturity: measure of total return on the bond at maturity.
- Par amount: face amount of the bond when it was issued, normally $1000.
- Accrued interest: the amount of interest income (coupon income) earned from the date of the last coupon payment to settlement date.
- Whether the bond uses a 360-day or 365-day basis to calculate interest payments.

Bond Rating Services

There are two major independent rating services: Moody's and Standard & Poor's. Investment-grade ratings range from AAA to BBB– (Standard & Poor's), or Aaa to Baa3 (Moody's). Lower-rated bonds are considered speculative. Ratings are intended to help you evaluate risk and set your own standards for investment.

The price of any bond fluctuates in harmony with the rise and fall of interest rates in general and the stability of the underlying corporation or agency issuing the bond.

Grades AAA through BBB are considered investment grade, although many advisors will confine their attention to bonds rated A or above. Ratings

Bond Ratings	Moody's	S&P	Fitch Prime
Credit Risk	Aaa	AAA	AAA
Excellent	Aa	AA	AA
Upper Medium	A-1, A	A+, A	A
Lower Medium	Baa-1, baa, a	BBB+, BBB	BBB
Speculative	Ba	BB	BB
Very Speculative	B, Caa	B, CCC, CC	B, CCC, C
Default	Ca, C	DDD, DD, D	DDD, DD, D

Figure 8.1 Bond ratings.

attempt to assess the probability that the issuing company will make timely payments of interest and principal. Each rating service has slightly different evaluation methods.

Summary

Almost all muni bonds have had a tough last few years, in part because the stock market continues to steal their thunder. According to a white paper published by the Investment Company Institute, for the first five months of 1997, the amount of investor dollars put in muni bond funds shrunk from $3.1 billion to $2.53 billion. The outflow followed a similar decline in 1996.

Today, munis offer rare tax breaks for small to medium sized investors, particularly attractive in high-income-tax states such as New York and California.

Tip

To determine if a muni bond fund makes sense for you, compare your after-tax return to another type of bond fund. For example, if a muni fund pays five percent versus six percent on a corporate bond fund, which fund works better for someone in the twenty-eight percent tax bracket? Divide five percent by 0.72 (100 minus the twenty-eight percent tax bracket). The answer, 6.94, is your after-tax return. So the corporate fund needs to yield 6.94 percent to measure up.

Good job. You are now ready to pull it all together, build your core investing strategy, and put some advanced strategies to work. In this next section, you will learn how to use effective diversification to build your own portfolio — one asset class at a time.

HOW INVESTMENTS WORK TOGETHER

Contents

9 How Investments Work Together

C hoosing a time horizon is as important as the investments you choose. This is because over long periods of time, very high returns and very low returns tend to average out. This enables you to recoup any losses you may have incurred. Over long periods of time, you can also fully realize the benefits of compounding.

Time is your greatest ally. Because the effects of short run volatility are reduced over time, a longer time horizon affords you greater flexibility in constructing your investment portfolio.

Now it's time to apply what you have learned to your current stage in life. Speak with your advisor before making important investment decisions. The following ratios are merely suggestions. Emergency money and day-to-day cash are not included.

Life Stages

Early Years (20 to 40): Your Investment Strategy

Build wealth by investing more of your assets in growth-oriented investments. When you are just starting out, your investment time horizon is long and your primary investment goal should be accumulation of capital. You do not need to use your investments to enhance your current income. Under these circumstances, stock investments should be a large part of your portfolio. Your diversified portfolio might include fifty percent in common stock mutual funds with potential for long-term growth, and twenty percent in balanced mutual funds invested in both stocks and bonds. If you need cash reserve, keep five percent in a money market or short-term (three to six) treasures.

Middle Years (40 to 50): Your Investment Strategy

In mid-career, even though your salary is increasing, so too are your expenses. You may want to include a conservative fixed-income component to preserve capital and provide regular current income if needed. Your investment mix for the middle years might include twenty-five percent in stock mutual funds, twenty-five percent in balanced stock and bond mutual funds, twenty-five percent in high-grade corporate bonds or bond mutual funds, and twenty-five percent in bank accounts. To minimize tax problems, variable annuities and tax-free municipal bond funds can be substituted for part of the stocks and mutual funds.

Pre-retirement Years (50 to 60): Your Investment Strategy

During these peak earning years, with your children's education complete, you should have a larger pool of assets and you may find income taxes increasingly burdensome. At the same time, you should start directing your efforts towards securing your retirement. Your investment mix for these years might include twenty percent in stock mutual funds, thirty percent in balanced stock and bond mutual funds, twenty-five percent in high-grade tax-free municipal bonds or bond mutual funds, and twenty-five percent in guaranteed accounts.

Retirement Years (60 to 70): Your Investment Strategy

As your investing time horizon shortens, you may want to shift more of your stock investments into fixed-income investments. A diversified portfolio might include ten percent in stock mutual funds, thirty percent in balanced stock and bond mutual funds, and thirty percent in bonds and bond mutual funds if you need income — or thirty percent in fixed and variable annuities if you don't. You may want to have some of your bond funds in tax-free municipals if you are in the higher tax brackets.

You'll probably retire during this stage of your life. When you do, your financial goals will center on protecting the assets you have accumulated over the years. In addition, you should focus on generating income to supplement Social Security and pension income.

The Late Years (70 plus): Your Investment Strategy

You've been retired for a few years and your main goal now is to receive income and preserve your capital so you don't outlive your money. A secondary consideration is to leave the most money possible to your heirs and loved ones. Your diversified portfolio might include twenty-five percent in balanced stock and bond mutual funds that can be accessed for income if necessary, thirty-five percent in bonds and bond mutual funds or fixed annuities, and the remaining forty percent might be in bank accounts and short-term government bonds.

10 The Seven Deadly Mistakes

T he other day, Cindy told us that her friend Bob, a local stockbroker, had said that if a man and a woman invested the same amount over the same time period, at the end of five years the average man would have five times the amount of money the average woman would have because of better investment decisions. She said that fact really discouraged her and made her think that a man should make investment choices for her.

Women and men have been programmed to think that men make the best investment decisions, and this is one more example of that kind of conditioned, baseless thinking. Bob may think that men will do better because they are more aggressive, but there is no factual study proving his assessment.

There is an old story, a true story, about a woman who beat Wall Street. Her husband had died and left a large portfolio of ordinary common stocks. She decided that she would hold onto those stocks and never sell them. So, for the next thirty years, she just collected the dividends, never buying or selling or having any concern for the prices of her holdings.

But as time went on, she wondered if she was doing the right thing. She contacted a Wall Street investment advisor and asked him if he could do better than she had done over all those years. He promised a review of her holdings and an accurate estimate of how much his firm could have made for her over the same period.

A few weeks went by and he never called back. Finally, she called him. He sounded embarrassed on the phone. He told her that her account had out-performed his firm in every one of the last thirty years and, in fact, her portfolio had outperformed all the other major money managers on Wall Street. He asked, "How did you do it?" "I don't know," she answered. "I just held onto my investments."

Cindy smiled as if she had a budding confidence that women can make money in the stock market. I warned her not to take this story too much to heart. A prudent person would review holdings at least annually. I advised her to learn how to review value line sheets on companies and to educate herself with the help of a trustworthy financial expert.

That expert can be a stockbroker or investment management consultant, either of whom is involved closely with the day-to-day stock and bond markets. Financial planners and CPAs, though well-versed, do not usually have a computer on their desk with timely information, stock quotes and news, or a squawk box with a variety of professionals delivering updates all day long. There are exceptions, but brokers and/or consultants employed by large national and regional firms usually have instantaneous information and high tech computer systems available to them that other financial folks do not have. Since stock brokers are highly regulated, they are continually educating themselves. Use them. They have good information.

Deadly mistake one — Following advice from the misinformed, or dumb and dumber. Cindy's friend, Bob, while meaning well, was projecting his own aggressive nature and mistaking it for truth. You don't have to be aggressive to win, you just have to invest. Aggression may be good in selling, but not necessarily in making money on Wall Street.

Bob's belief that being aggressive leads to high profits is mistaken. The stock market is highly efficient. Due to the abundance of very bright and capable investment analysts and the instantaneous flow of computerized information, securities data is analyzed and responded to continuously. Each stock represents the appropriate price based on all information available at that time. Numerous studies have shown that, on average, a person (as in the case of our passive widow) can perform as well as a professional analyst just by holding stocks. Studies have also shown that stock selection strategies may actually reduce rates of return and increase portfolio risk, especially in cases where little attention is given to effective diversification by the broker. One study in particular, by Brinson, Hood and Beebower, discovered that because of high commissions and trading costs, investment professionals have not been able to consistently outperform the random selection of stocks. Sorry Bob! Being passive wins over aggressive or active trading. But this is not to ignore that stocks and bonds must be monitored, reviewed, and occasionally sold due to negative fundamental changes within a company. This is wisely managing the risk side of a portfolio.

Mistake two — Failure to plan. Many investors end up owning a hodge-podge of investments bought on tips, hearsay advice, or casual comments from friends. A better strategy is to create an investment plan first, then concentrate on those instruments designed to fulfill your financial plan, and stick to it. Your plan should be based, first of all, upon solid asset allocation — and secondly, on adequate investment style diversification. Make sure you understand these two terms: asset allocation and diversification (see Chapter 19). They will be responsible for at least ninety percent of your long-term success!

Mistake three — Idealizing the future. Believing that when this or that happens, the future will suddenly be different and so much better for investing than the present is a common mistake. Examples can be overheard every day: "When I get that job or promotion," "When I win the lotto," "When Uncle John passes on." The reasons for delaying beginning an investment program are endless. The problem is that the future often doesn't measure up to your imagination. As soon as the future becomes the present, new fantasies emerge to replace the old ones that didn't happen as expected. That perfect time to invest gets pushed again further into the future.

Mistake four — Fear! Being too cautious. If you are going to make money investing, you are going to have to take risks. If you take the time to understand the nature of what we call investment risk and learn how to live with it, you will become a better investor.

Mistake five — Lack of detailed records. Many investors just don't keep accurate financial records because they simply don't bother. Make the effort. It can help you monitor your investment performance as well as aid your heirs after you're gone. Keep a list of all your assets in a safe deposit box so your survivors have ready access to them.

Mistake six — Not understanding risk. Many investors buy mutual funds blindly out of the back of magazines. Remember, these are simply clever ads. Market timing and individual stock selection have proven to be unreliable techniques. Diversification offers the most academically sound approach to investing. Not understanding the level of risk taken in a particular fund versus its stated return is the major mistake most people make.

Mistake seven — Not giving your investments enough time. The stock market goes down one year out of every four years, and no one has ever been able to predict accurately which year it will go down. For that reason, use a five-year or even ten-year horizon — and design your portfolio so that when there's a down year, the storm can be weathered.

11 | Planning Your Route

S ue sought advice at the age of 33, a year after her father had died; her mother had died ten years earlier. Sue was an only child, making her the sole beneficiary of her family's multimillion dollar estate. Fortunately, her father had left his finances in good order.

Sue's father had hired a personal attorney, a CPA, and a banker, and they had placed her inheritance in certificates of deposit. These powerful men had controlled her assets for the year since her father's death, and now she wanted to take the reins. This was a big step for her. These family advisors told Sue that she should keep her money securely at the bank. But her CDs were paying less than three percent and she saw advertisements in magazines of mutual funds that had made twelve and fifteen percent returns. She didn't like the fact that her father's advisors, who were much older than she, were treating her like an innocent child who needed to be protected. She wanted to make her own considered decisions. She was told that if she ventured out on her own, she would surely lose everything her father had worked so hard for. She felt she was being controlled, yet she felt guilty for even looking into alternative investments.

After we spent some time getting to know one another, Sue revealed that she felt completely overwhelmed and did not understand investments or what her choices were. I explained that investments could be divided into three simple categories: stability, growth, and income — or a combination of all three.

> Stability: Protecting your principal from risk of loss, also known as preservation of capital.

Growth: Increasing the value of your principal through capital gains reflected in price appreciation. The best investment for growth is stocks.

Income: This simply means you need current income and have enough saved that you are not concerned with growth; your main concern is avoiding risk. Fixed investments such as bonds, annuities, or saving accounts provide income.

Or a combination of all three: This category is where most of us want to be. We want some income, safety, and a component of growth which translates into larger income down the road.

It's important to recognize the basic categories of investments and where you best fit in. At first, Sue was taken aback by the suggestion that she fit into a typical category, but at the same time it helped her to clarify in her own mind what she wanted most out of her investments. She could see more clearly that by having everything invested in CDs and bank savings, she had stability but no growth.

The faster your money grows and compounds, the less you need to save each year to reach your goals. Earning just a few extra percentage points per year on your investments can dramatically decrease the amount you need to save. The younger you are, the more dramatic the effect.

12 Achieve Balance

The first step to achieving balance is to accept the world as it is. As children, we gradually learn how to control certain aspects of ourselves — how we dress, how we act, how to win friends — but then, as young adults, we start to develop rigidity about who we are. Many adults tend to see all investments as being risky and to be avoided. But investments do not always act the same way consistently and cannot be judged once and for all.

Here is the common response from investors when asked to define their investment objectives: "I want the highest possible return with the lowest possible risk in the fastest period of time." Well, sorry, but this is totally unrealistic. That attitude will ensure failure. A more reachable objective would be to balance risk to achieve the highest financial gain.

Answer the following questions: First, how would you feel about taking risk if you had evidence that you would come out ahead over time? Second, how would you redefine your investment objectives if you knew you couldn't lose?

If you knew you couldn't lose, investing starts to take on a whole new appearance. The most important element needed to make this come true is more time. Smart advisors tell their clients that they can't get high investment returns without high risks, and that by adding the element of time, they can significantly lower risk.

Study Figures 12.1 and 12.2, which show the correlation of risk during time, and the effects on a portfolio. Do you see a pattern developing? The secret to successful investing is the addition of time to your investment strategy. Once you understand that lengthening your time horizons is the key to success, you are ready to step off the emotional roller coaster that most investors ride.

Lengthening time horizons requires patience. Uncertainty often causes investors to run out of patience with their investments at the worst possible times — say, at the top of a bull market, or the bottom of a bear market. In bull markets, for example, the emotional element often causes investors to increase their holdings in stocks by selling the "underperforming" fixed income portion of their portfolio, only to become overexposed in expensive stocks at market highs.

These same investors often do just the opposite in bear markets. They liquidate stocks that have declined in value precipitously and buy fixed income securities at market lows. Then, when the stock market recovers, they are no longer positioned to take advantage of it.

The ability to maintain patience during difficult times requires more than just an understanding of the stock markets. It also requires an understanding of your own reactions to uncertainty. Only then can you arrive at a working balance between the desire to achieve the highest return and the need to preserve your capital.

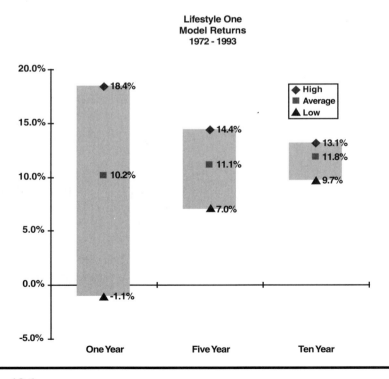

Figure 12.1

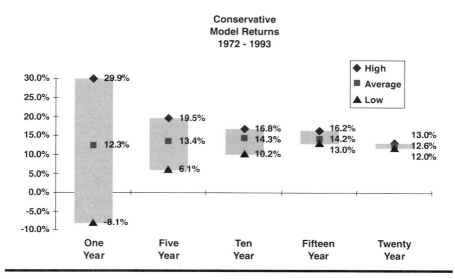

Figure 12.2

13 Lowering Investment Risk

Remember the two principles for investing that have withstood the test of time, and that will both reduce risk and likely increase what you earn. One is diversification; the other is asset allocation. These simple, yet powerful concepts are the keys to investing safely and wisely. The central premise of both of these principles is to select several different types of investment products, providers, and asset categories — with different risk and return potentials.

First, let's focus specifically on what diversification is and how it works. Diversification is simply investing in a broad variety of investments so all your eggs are not in one basket, so to speak. The idea behind this is that your overall performance should be less volatile than if all your money was in a single investment or type of investment. The graphs in Figure 13.1 illustrate the importance of diversification.

The graph illustrates a single investment of $10,000 that averages an eight percent return during twenty-five years. It also illustrates diversifying the same $10,000 into five $2,000 amounts representing five investments averaging various rates of return. While three of the five investments showed a lower return (including one that lost money) than the single investment, the total for the diversified side was substantially higher.

One type of diversification is to spread your investments in different types of securities, such as bonds, stocks, bank accounts, and other short-term investments. Each of these investments has different risks and will fluctuate in value during time. Selecting different types of investments will help reduce the risks present with owning only one type of security.

You should also choose different kinds of those investments as well. For example, when it comes to bank accounts, don't just use CDs, use money

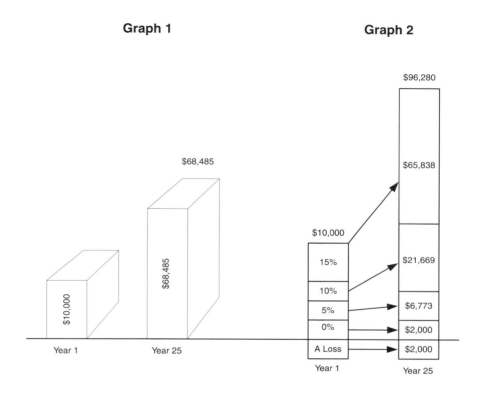

Figure 13.1 Diversification.

market accounts and savings accounts. The same applies to mutual funds. Choose stock mutual funds, bond funds, and balanced funds when appropriate. It's a good idea to use several different providers as well. In other words, don't put all your money in one type of investment (mutual funds, for example), or in the same kind of mutual funds (stocks, for example) or all with the same mutual fund company. The more you diversify, the more you're protected.

Now consider the difference between diversification and asset allocation, the other time-tested principle for decreasing risk and increasing return. Asset allocation is subtle, often misunderstood, yet significant. Asset allocation is spreading your money out to asset categories you purposely choose because their values generally move in opposite ways to each other.

Diversification is spreading your money among different investments and investment providers that fall within the same asset categories. For example, if you are a car buff and you bought a restored 1933 Chevy Coupe and a 1932 Ford three-window coupe, you would be diversifying. Your total investment would be protected; if Chevys went down in value, Fords might go up. But if the entire classic car market went down, your total investment would be in trouble. One way to guard against this occurrence is to also buy some collectors stamps. Why stamps? Because their value moves independently of what happens in the classic car markets. The optimal mix would be to buy an asset that always moves in a direction exactly opposite that of the classic car market, if there was one you could identify. The search for an investment value moves opposite of another investment to hedge against declines has led to the popularization of foreign stocks, for example, in recent years. Their values often move opposite to American stocks. This is the wisdom of asset allocation.

Research has shown that asset allocation — how you split your investments up among various asset categories such as stocks, bonds, and cash — has by far the greatest impact on your overall investment performance. More than 90 percent of your total return is due to the asset allocation of your portfolio. In contrast, market timing and investment selection account for less than seven percent.

Although often used interchangeably, don't confuse asset allocation with diversification. They are not the same thing. Asset allocation is a means of reducing the overall risk in a portfolio by matching different asset classes. During any given time period, some asset classes will be up and some will be down. The result is that you mathematically reduce risk to a greater degree than by simply diversifying.

The strategy to help you make a successful transition into the world of investing is simple. Build a conservative foundation first; own common stocks for growth; invest in bonds and stocks for enhanced income; diversify to spread out investment risk; and allocate your money between different asset classes to optimize your over-all return. Following this strategy, you will build your investment portfolio based on reasonable expectations, not guesswork.

14 How to Choose a Money Manager

When an investor chooses a money manager she will be faced with two of her main investment concerns: keeping her principal, while letting her investments grow. She will also need to define her specific objectives and work with an advisor. Once she understands her objectives the search can begin for an appropriate money manager.

The next step concerns the all important issue of qualifying the manager, which is the subject of this chapter. This qualifying process, better known as "due diligence" by the investment industry, simply means that care must be taken to substantiate the suitability of a manager. However carefully done, hiring a money manager is subjective in nature and difficult to qualify.

All investors have individual investment requirements. Some investors have tax considerations, others do not. Some need income, while others want growth of capital. Most importantly, investors seek out the knowledge of experts because they believe professional managers can do a better job than they can do themselves. These separate investment needs often cause managers to handle portfolios in different ways. The way managers choose to report on those portfolios also leads to hard-to-discern performance results. Consequently, performance numbers often tell less about a manager than the investor assumes.

Choosing a money manager was once a simple process. The world of investment management was the private domain of large pension managers and bank trust departments. Selecting a manager for a pension depended more on the manager's client list than his investment track record. For individual accounts, most investors felt bank trust departments were a safe and conservative place to keep their money. From the Great Depression to the late '60s, inflation remained low and the stock market had one of its biggest run-ups in history. During this period, most people had few complaints about the growth of their money because the underlying buying power of their investment continued to increase.

Starting in the '70s and early '80s, the number of investment managers began to grow rapidly, due to several factors. From the administrative side, new government regulations made administrating pensions of all sizes cumbersome. Under the new regulations, fiduciaries found themselves personally liable for lapses in their pension's administration. At this time, individuals and pension administrators also discovered that inflation was rising while the stock market was not. Passive investing no longer resulted in the rising purchasing power of savings. Investors began to look beyond the big pension managers and bank trust departments for outside talent to invest their money.

The demand for managers with new ideas spawned the rapid growth of what is now the independent investment manager. Both the large number of new managers and the rapid increase in assets under their management reflect this rapid growth. But with the influx of new capital looking for managers, a large number of newly established managers have arisen. Many of these start-ups manage assets in the hundreds of millions of dollars. Today it is not uncommon to find management firms, not even in existence just a decade ago, controlling over half a billion dollars in assets.

How can you gather knowledge about these managers? *Request a copy of the manager's ADV form.*

No matter how impressive the manager's general marketing information, investors should keep in mind that marketing information serves the purposes of the manager and not the investor. Disclosures usually reflect what the manager wants the investor to know. Knowledgeable investors do have other alternatives for gathering information about managers. Because the Securities and Exchange Commission (SEC) regulates investment managers, additional information on disclosure statements is on file with the government.

Most important of these disclosure documents is the ADV. By law, the manager must provide Part II of the form (or equivalent disclosure) to prospective clients. While Part II is the only form legally required to be furnished to the public, it never hurts to request both parts. The ADV provides basic background information on the manager's state registrations, disciplinary or legal problems, ownership, potential conflicts of interest with fees or commissions, financial condition, and the background of the firm's principals. Investors should keep in mind that the SEC never passes on the merits or accuracy of the information provided in the ADV. Its purpose is to place basic information about the manager on public record. By having an ADV, the investor has an opportunity to do some basic background checking. Obvious areas of interest are prior employment of the firm's principals and their educational backgrounds. When legal actions against the firm are discovered, investors should try to obtain copies of the court-filed complaints. By checking with the SEC's enforcement division, the investor may uncover actions taken by the SEC against the manager for regulatory violations.

The Form 13F Filing

If the manager manages $100 million dollars or more in equities, then SEC regulations require that a quarterly Form 13F filing be made. The filing states the equity positions and the number of shares held by the manager. Some managers may argue that, because portfolio adjustments often occur between filings, the 13F is an inaccurate performance measure. Most managers have portfolio turnovers of about twenty-five percent a year or higher. Even at forty percent turnover a year rate, the average quarter has only a ten percent change in portfolio positions — a relatively small amount. This gives the investor using the Form 13F filing another way of comparing the manager's publicly reported performance with his SEC Form 13F filings.

Managers with Public Funds

While it's more the exception than the rule, investors should always check to see whether the manager also manages a mutual fund in addition to his individual accounts. If so, then compare the performance of the manager's individual composites with his mutual fund. The two should be similar in performance since it is unlikely that different investment styles are being applied to them.

The Brokerage Network

Most full service brokerage houses have the in-house capability of tracking the performance of managers. Upon opening a managed account, the brokerage firm begins to monitor the account's performance. Quarterly reports compare the manager's performance with other managers. The broker assigned to the account often receives these reports. By tracking a large number of portfolios from a particular manager, it becomes possible to measure the performance and consistency among the manager's different accounts.

In addition to tracking performance, many full-service brokerage houses make on-site inspections of the managers they monitor. By combining information from house accounts and visiting managers, these brokerage firms are often the best repository of information on managers. Investors should always try to find out whether a brokerage has excluded a manager from doing business with any brokerage firms. Similarly, it helps if a manager's name is on the brokerage's approved list of managers.

The Manager

It is unlikely that most managers will talk voluntarily about possible reasons for not doing business with them. A manager's disclosure is, by nature, a one-sided viewpoint. There are numerous questions we could list here that would be prudent to ask the manager. For the sake of brevity, we will limit ourselves to two questions. First, it is important to understand the history of the management team. If managers have come and gone, then it is important to know who they were and why they left. As with any organization, a management team must work well together if it is going to succeed. If there is dissension among those making decisions, then portfolio consistency may suffer.

The second question, if truthfully answered, is one of the most telling pieces of information about any manager. Ask the manager to state the total asset value of his accounts, and the number of new accounts acquired and lost during the past five years. A good manager has little to fear from this question. On the basis of this one piece of evidence alone, most investors could save themselves much trouble.

Other information investors might want to know includes the size of the firm, how long the firm has been in business, the clientele list, and who the firm lists as referrals. Common sense dictates that these basic questions be explored. Investors should be careful of firms growing so fast that service and performance could suffer. The faster growing manager must place additional time and attention on the administration of his business. This is, sometimes, to the detriment of securities research and portfolio performance.

15 Understanding Manager Styles

Many investors often chase an investment manager's performance history in searching for the pot of gold. Rainbow chasing comes into play when an investor finds an investment manager who did exceptionally well and hires him, only to find out later that it was the manager's style that did exceptionally well, not necessarily the manager himself.

When you hire a money manager, it is important for you to understand the style of manager with whom you are working. It is also important to understand when a particular style works well and when a style doesn't work at all. An understanding of which segment of the manager's performance cycle you are looking at is also important. As an investor, you are also buying the opportunity that these managers will pick companies that will grow in adverse or stormy environments.

How do you quantify what good performance is without falling into the trap of rainbow chasing as a method of trying to "beat the market"?

You want to look at the level of risk that a manager is taking and volatility. This is something many investors tend to overlook. However, this is what a professional investment management consultant can bring to the surface. A consultant should highlight the advantages of lower volatility, high relative returns, and why a particular manager's performance is leading or lagging the market. This is a key element in identifying a trend and getting in front of it. This goes way beyond just identifying the managers who have had exceptionally good performance near term.

Therefore, when making a manager selection, or when contemplating the termination of a manager, one must look at how long the manager's performance was lagging behind market averages. Keep in mind that the market average is a compilation of all the different stocks that fall into every one of the management disciplines. The certain segments that will be leading will actually be the ones that are influencing the averages in certain areas. For example, over the last few years, when the larger capitalization stocks did exceptionally well, the top one hundred stocks in the S&P 500 represented over sixty percent of the market capitalization. Therefore, they influenced the S&P index considerably, whereas the bottom one hundred stocks in the S&P 500 represented only about two to three percent of the market capitalization.

When the smaller cap stocks start to move, they really won't have much influence on the S&P 500 averages and, consequently, you will see a large percentage of small and medium-cap managers actually outperforming the market averages. As a result, some investors may be compelled to hire one of these managers well into the first leg of the cycle for small and medium-cap managers. They may be too late, however, to take advantage of the trend.

An investor may be correct in identifying a trend. However, he may be identifying it after the first leg, only to ride down the correction phase before the second leg up for this particular style. If an investor is going to identify a manager solely on performance, then he'd better understand what portion of the cycle that manager is in. That is the fallacy of looking at a manager who has had great performance over five- and ten-year periods.

Therefore, when making a manager selection, or when contemplating the termination of a manager, it is important to understand his or her investment style. Let's look at individual managers' styles and how they relate to the investment process.

Value Managers

The primary motivation of the value manager is to select securities based on known information. This information may take the form of price/earnings screens, or screens for other financial characteristics. When using a P/E screen for example, the "P" in the ratio is today's price and "E" is the trailing twelve months' earnings. The value manager's style has a strong emphasis or discipline based on the price/earnings — or other prescribed — selection methods. The value manager tries to find stocks where the price is thirty to fifty percent less than break-up or replacement of company assets.

Value managers would come into play predominantly after a long market decline or at the bottom of a market cycle. Also, they do well in periods where market prices are cheaper, pessimism is very high, and economic problems are widespread. A value manager is not necessarily going to focus on the economy, as much as on the pricing of individual securities relative to their book value or replacement costs, etc.

Growth and Emerging Growth Managers

Some people confuse growth managers with emerging growth managers. Emerging means the investment is in a smaller company that is emerging in size, hence the smaller capitalization, whereas growth stocks are companies that have earnings that are generally above average for the market.

Growth Managers

Growth managers are more attractive in periods when the market is doing well. A growth manager buys companies that are doing well within the market, and showing very strong earnings growth. A high degree of volatility comes into play with growth managers because they manage higher multiple stock. The P/E multiples are higher, consequently the volatility of the stocks is greater.

Now, we can break growth into large-cap growth and small-cap growth. There will be periods when growth stocks in the large-cap sectors do exceptionally well because there is a high level of safety, meaning higher quality and better capitalized companies. Unfortunately, growth stocks with smaller capitalization will be overlooked to a wide extent, because small or medium-cap stocks might happen to be out of vogue with the market at that time.

One type of growth management company, such as Frontier Capital Management in Boston, Massachusetts, tracks growth of earnings using a thematic approach. They identify companies, both domestically and internationally, that will be able to take advantage of trends that are unfolding. Recent examples would be companies in communications, health, and international telecommunications. Companies in these areas are enjoying good growth that is not tied to normal business cycles. Such companies have done exceptionally well throughout the entire recession because their stocks have had uninterrupted earnings growth.

When applying an earnings growth approach, you have to be definitive about whether you are talking about large-caps or small-caps. If you want to employ a value approach, and large-caps have already made their big move but small-caps haven't, and you are willing to accept a higher level of volatility, then perhaps smaller capitalized companies will be more attractive.

The year 1991 was a perfect example. In the middle of 1990 to 1991, smaller capitalization stocks were down significantly. Between January 1989 and October 1990 was devastating for the smaller-cap stocks. When the market declined in May of 1990 through October of 1990, the S&P was down 14.5 percent while the Nasdaq was down 27.8 percent. However, from October of 1990 through December 1991, the S&P was up 42.6 and the Nasdaq over-the-counter was up 81 percent. So, we look at the year of 1991 as a market year: the S&P was up 30 percent, but the Nasdaq was up 59 percent.

During the 1989 to 1990 period, the value of some small-cap stocks remained exceptionally high, even in the face of the recession and the war in the Middle East, and the earnings momentum for many of these stocks was strong. But the market in general didn't participate in this. Now, the market is starting to participate and identify those small-cap stocks. As a result, the performance over the last two-year period is very much in line with managers who had a very good 1990.

Relative Value Managers

A relative value manager looks at different sectors — for instance, financial, energy, and consumer staples — and tries to determine the best value in each sector. Such a manager may buy stock in one sector that has a much higher P/E ratio than a stock in another sector.

Relative value managers do a bottom-up analysis within a sector. This may sound like a sector rotator manager, looking for values in each sector to determine which sector is going to do the best. A relative value manager, however, does not want to be limited to any one sector in case that sector goes out of favor. He does not let absolute value force him to be overly concentrated. Therefore, this type of manager looks at the relative value of stocks in each sector, and buys the best values within many sectors.

Emerging Growth

Emerging growth managers tend to buy stocks that have a high degree of price volatility. This is a bottom-up style of management in that the primary motivation for buying a particular stock is inherently in the stock itself. These are the "stock pickers." Some buy based on price momentum or earnings momentum that is not based on a passing change in the way a company is perceived by the public.

Quality Growth (Hybrid Index)

The primary purpose is to replicate the performance of the market. An example would be to own a majority, if not all, of the stocks in the upper half of the S&P 500. Many quality growth managers perform as well as the market with lower relative market risk; some perform better than the market with equivalent market risk.

Balanced Growth

These managers typically do not buy overly aggressive stocks, but they do rely heavily on earnings forecasts. This is a style that is usually devoid of extremes, not too much income and not too much risk. If you were going to place all of your assets with one manager, this style would most likely be the best choice.

A trend that is unfolding, which appears to be transparent to many investors, is the growth of the convertible bond market. Owning high yield securities that can be converted into equities has been very attractive. Inherent in convertible securities is the fact that more middle-capitalization sized companies issue convertible debt; this reduces the yield on the bond that is issued.

Income Growth

The primary purpose in security selection is to achieve a current yield significantly higher than the S&P 500. The stability and rate of growth of the dividend are also of concern to the income buyer. These portfolios may own more utilities, less high-tech, and may also own convertible preferreds and convertible bonds.

Income growth is primarily to fund higher income needs. Growth is achieved through exposure to equities, the intent being to increase cash flow and increase the value of the portfolio, perhaps to maintain or stay ahead of inflation.

Industry Rotators

The primary emphasis is on finding industries that will outperform the market as a whole. These managers begin with a top-down approach after making projections and forecasts on general economic conditions. This "macro" approach then leads them to overweight or underweight certain industries that are consistent with their economic scenario.

Lastly, various industry categories are filled with individual stocks believed to be the strongest in these industries.

An industry rotator is a manager who identifies specific industries that have moved. These industries are either undervalued or have moved into a trend that the market is supporting highly. For example, in the early 1980s, oil stocks were doing exceptionally well as an industry; a rotator at that time would most likely be heavily involved in owning those stocks. As we moved further into the 1980s, rotator managers moved into aerospace stocks, and away from oil and gas stocks.

These managers can do a very effective job, provided they have analytical expertise in industries in which their clients are interested. For example, during the mid-1980s, many high-tech oriented managers who found themselves in small-cap stocks, but who were more experienced in the area of high-tech stocks, performed poorly. This was due to the style of management to which they were adhering.

Fixed Income

This style strictly uses cash flow generating instruments: bonds, notes, CDs, preferred stocks, etc. These advisors will primarily try to maximize highest yields while attempting to protect principal by adjusting maturities to take advantage of rising and falling interest rates.

Cash Management

Using short-term fixed instruments insures a portfolio's liquidity. Maximizing principal protection becomes the primary objective of a cash management portfolio. Even though these accounts have short-term (one-day) liquidity, they typically pay more like 90- to 180-day CDs versus passbook or one-week CDs.

Fixed income and cash management are usually driven by immediate need for money. A short time horizon for liquidity is usually the major factor in the decision to use a fixed income or cash manager.

Indexing

The index number is driven more predominantly by certain components within the index, not the entire index. Because that is the case, the components that led the index over the past year or two may not necessarily be the components that are going to lead the index in the future. Therefore, it is important for an investor to subscribe to the style of manager most appropriate for his own quality requirement, considering limitation of risk and volatility.

The fact of the matter is that every manager ideally wants to beat the market. The questions an investor should ask a manager in this regard are: What market is the manager comparing himself to? What time period is the manager using for comparison? If the manager's criterion is to beat the market, does he mean the S&P 500, the value line index, or the convertible bond index? More importantly: What is the manager's tolerance for risk and volatility? What is his longer-term return requirement and expectation? Is the manager's style at a good point in the market cycle, or is it at the tail end of a cycle?

The problem is that every investor has expectations of having immediate positive performance and those expectations may not be compatible with a particular manager's style at certain points in time. A good approach is to lengthen the time horizon beyond a three- or five-year period and then look at a manager's style, concentrating on the quality of securities and level of volatility and risk control, to determine what type of investor will be comfortable with this manager's style over a long period of time.

If an investor has enough resources to hire more than one investment manager, that can increase his chance of being in the right place more than once during a complete market cycle. This strategy can also lower overall volatility.

16 Investment Performance Confusion

Anyone who has heard sales pitches about investment programs from different stock brokerage firms will probably agree that there is a lot of confusion around investment performance. It would appear that each brokerage house represents the number one manager in the country. How can this be? Everybody can't be number one, or can they?

There will be some period of time when a manager will show top quartile performance of all money managers in the country; even a broken clock is right twice a day. The brokerage or money management firm will pick the best time period to represent its performance.

Mutual funds, banks, brokers, insurance companies, and money managers use various methods to calculate investment returns. While the different approaches are usually perfectly legitimate, they can make comparisons difficult.

One thing to keep in mind, performance figures you see in brochures are there for one reason — marketing.

But as an investor, you aren't helpless. You can either solicit help from an investment management consultant, or take the time to get a better understanding of how performance is reported and how risk-and-return statistics work. In these ways, you can reduce the chance of falling victim to inflated sales pitches.

If a manager shows that three years of returns on an investment portfolio totals 27 percent, did the investment earn 9 percent a year or 6.96 percent a year? Both answers, and numerous others, could be correct. How can this be?

The difference arises from the use of two types of return calculations. The simplest is the "average," where the returns for any number of past periods are added up and divided by the number of periods.

The second calculation, more widely used by investment firms, is the "compound," or annualized, rate of return. This figure is the rate at which $1 would have to grow in each of several periods to reach an ending amount.

Unlike the average, the compound return takes into account the sequence of earnings or losses. That's because a gain or loss in any one year directly affects the amount of money left to build up in subsequent years. Thus, a big gain in an earlier year generates a higher compound return than if the same gain had occurred more recently.

In addition, the bigger the swings in returns from one period to the next, the lower the returns compared with average calculations.

Both return calculations can be useful in checking an investment's track record. The average return is going to give you some information about what is most likely to happen, but used together with the compound return, you also get the idea of the risk involved, so it's nice to look at both.

Time versus Dollar Weighting

While average and compound calculations produce different returns over several periods, the choice between so-called time-weighted and dollar-weighted calculations produces different return figures for the same period.

The dollar-weighted, or internal, calculation shows the change in value of a portfolio for the average funds invested in the period, including cash added or withdrawn by the investor. That sounds like it covers all the bases, but those cash flows can be a problem in calculating the true performance of the investment manager. Because the manager can't control the size and timing of money flowing in and out of an account, a time-weighted calculation can be made to figure the value of $1 invested for the entire period, eliminating distortions from cash flows.

For the question of how your investment manager is doing, you want a time-weighted return. For the question of how your money is doing, you might want to calculate the dollar-weighted rate of return.

The difference between the two types of return calculations is illustrated by the following two investors, each of whom opens a $100 account with the same money manager. The manager buys two shares of the same $50 stock for each client. A year later, each share has risen to $100. Client A adds $100, which the manager uses to buy another share of the same stock. Finally, after another year, the stock is back to $50.

On a time-weighted basis, the return on both accounts is zero because $1 invested at the start of the period was still $1 at the end. But on a dollar-weighted basis, Client A's account shows a negative 18.1 percent return, as the $150 invested fell to $100. Client B, with $100 both at the start and end of the period, had a zero dollar-weighted return.

Over short periods of, say, a month — or when there isn't any cash flow — the difference between time-weighted and dollar-weighted calculations usually isn't significant. But the difference grows in importance as time and cash flow increase.

Per-share values of mutual funds are calculated on a time-weighted basis. Returns for savings accounts paying a constant rate are the same whether calculated on a time-weighted or dollar-weighted basis.

Volatility

It might appear that a ten percent investment gain in one period, followed by a ten percent loss the next period, would leave you no worse off than when you started — but the math doesn't work out that way. What first grew to $110, in this example, would shrink to $99 in the next period.

The distortion is greater with bigger numbers. A fifty percent loss on $100, followed by a fifty percent gain, leaves you with $75, still a long way from the original $100. In fact, after a fifty percent loss, a one hundred percent gain is required to get back to the original $100 investment.

Such big swings reflect high volatility that can eat deeply into portfolio results over time. Cautious investment professionals continuously warn that risk and returns are usually linked, as evidenced most recently by the performance of the high-risk, high-yield junk bond market. A loss in just one year will put a dent in investment results for years to come, so it's well worth reviewing volatility as closely as returns.

By looking at only raw rates of return, you often have a very incomplete picture of why a manager earned what he did. The important thing to determine is the kinds of risk a manager took to get that rate of return. The AIMR Performance Presentation Standards can give you some insights into how the managers reported their results. These are a set of guiding ethical principles intended to promote full disclosure and fair representation in the reporting of investment results.

The objective of these standards is to ensure uniformity in reporting so that results are directly comparable among investment managers. To this end, some aspects of the standards are mandatory. These are listed below. However, not every situation can be anticipated in a set of guidelines. Therefore, meeting the full disclosure and fair representation intent means making a conscientious good faith interpretation of the standards consistent with the underlying ethical principles.

Mandatory Requirements

- Presentation of total return using accrual as opposed to cash basis accounting. (Accrual accounting is not required for dividends, nor is it required for retroactive compliance.)
- Time-weighted rate of return using a minimum of quarterly valuation (monthly preferred) and geometric linking of period returns.
- Size-weighted composites using beginning of period values to weight the portfolio returns. (Equal-weighted composites are recommended as additional information, but are not mandatory.)
- Inclusion of all actual, fee-paying, discretionary portfolios in one or more composites within the firm's management (no selectivity in portfolios, no simulation or portability of results within composites).
- Presentation of annual returns at a minimum for all years (no selectivity in time periods).
- Inclusion of cash and cash equivalents in composite returns.

Mandatory Disclosures

Prospective clients must be advised that a list of all of a firm's composites is available.

- For each composite, disclosure of the number of portfolios, the amount of assets, and the percentage of a manager's total assets which are represented by the composite. For composites containing five or fewer portfolios, disclosure of composite assets and percentage of firm assets, plus a statement indicating that the composite includes five or fewer portfolios.
- Historical compliance is at the discretion of the manager. When the firm's historical performance record is presented, a disclosure must

be made that identifies the in-compliance periods from the periods that are not in compliance.

■ The firm must also disclose that the full historical performance record is not in compliance. If semiannual or annual valuation periods are used to calculate returns and weight composites for retroactive compliance, this must also be disclosed.

■ Disclosure of whether balanced portfolio segments are included in single-asset composites and, if so, how the cash has been allocated between asset segments.

■ Disclosure of whether performance results are calculated gross or net of fees and inclusion of the manager's fee schedule in either case.

■ Disclosure of whether leverage has been used in portfolios included in the composite and the extent of its usage.

■ Disclosure of settlement date valuation if used in place of trade date.

■ Disclosure of any non-fee paying portfolios included in composites. What about when a manager uses the total return of a balanced composite to market a balanced account strategy? When a manager uses the total return of a balanced composite to market a balanced account strategy, but wishes to present the portion of the balanced composite as supplemental information in presenting the balanced strategy, the segment returns can be shown without making a cash allocation as long as the returns for each of the composite's segments (including the cash portion or segment) are shown along with the composite's total return.

■ In fixed-income strategies, or other single-asset strategies, a cash allocation to each of the segments must be made at the beginning of the reporting period.

For example, if a manager is using the equity-only returns of the equity portion of the balanced composite as an indication of expertise in managing equity-plus-cash portfolios, the manager must assign a cash allocation to the equity part at the beginning of each reporting period. That segment can then be included on the firm's list of composites.

For retroactive compliance, a manager must make a reasonable and consistent cash allocation to each of the composite segments and must disclose the methodology used for assigning cash.

When the results of the balanced segments are added to single-asset composites, a cash allocation needs to be made to each of the segments. This prevents a manager from mixing asset-without-cash returns to asset-plus-cash returns.

17 | Making that Final Choice

Most money management firms do an excellent job of quantifying the return objectives and risk tolerance of the investor, but the investor must still make the final choice of managers from those the firm recommends. The information in the manager profiles will help you here, but you still need a structured approach to making that final choice. There are three key areas you should examine as you narrow down the field.

How can you tell if a manager earned enough extra return to justify the risk taken? Fortunately, there is a way to compare apples to apples here. It's called the reward-to-risk ratio.

This analogy may be useful. Consider automobiles for a moment. The mileage range of a car on a single tank of gas can be compared to the returns of a manager. The "market line" for this analogy would plot the mileage range on the vertical axis and the gallons, or cost, on the horizontal axis. The miles-per-gallon figure puts two cars on a comparable basis and allows you to determine which car is a better value. The reward-to-risk ratio is nothing more than miles-per-gallon in the car analogy.

Most consultants can provide an investor with manager profiles and all the information needed to calculate reward-to-risk ratios. The returns are listed in the table; the risk can be read from the Market Line chart. There's one refinement that should be made, however. The so-called "Risk-Free Rate of Return" (i.e., Treasury Bills) should be subtracted from the manager's return. Why? Well, think back to the car analogy. If the first fifty miles of the trip were downhill, you could coast without using any gas (risk) at all, and your miles-per-gallon would be infinite! Obviously, what's important is how your car does after the coasting. Since any car can coast at no cost, you should subtract those fifty miles from the total range. Similarly with the manager's returns.

Second, and more important, is analysis of the philosophy and strategy. There are important aspects of the manager's investment philosophy to consider.

The first question should be: is his strategy sound and logical? Said another way: does the manager's approach to investing make sense? Don't be fooled into believing that a successful investment philosophy must be incomprehensible to mere mortals. We're not speaking of the details of investing; those may indeed be complex. We're speaking of the underlying principles the manager goes by. And, as one investment consultant said a few years ago, "If the manager can't explain how he invests, he probably doesn't understand it himself!" That's not the kind of manager you want to be comfortable with!

Third, and most important, is analysis of the investment process. If the investment decision process is systematic, disciplined, and understandable, then you can have confidence that the experience you have had in the past with a manager will be continued into the future.

To analyze the investment process, look for five key elements:

> The first is *security selection criteria*. Ask, for example, how criteria are determined, and what causes them to change (if anything). In my opinion, explicit, well-defined criteria for security selection is a fundamental cornerstone.

> The second element is the *security selection process*. Sensible criteria are of little value if not applied. And that application should be to a sufficiently large "universe" of choices to make sure that no opportunities are missed.

> The third is *portfolio implementation*. If the manager picks great securities, a client should feel confident that he will own those securities in his portfolio. Otherwise, great security selections are meaningless. We utilize a centralized investment decision making system to make sure that each portfolio has the right securities in the right proportions.

> The fourth is *portfolio monitoring*. Once securities are in the portfolio, there should be an effective method for making certain that each portfolio stays invested according to a firm's policy and strategy (in the context of client guidelines). One firm employs a weekly

system of accountability for all portfolio managers, using the computer to compare each account with an appropriate model account.

The fifth element, and maybe the most important, is *security sell disciplines* — for after all, the bottom line is income and realized gains. Taking profits and minimizing losses is the goal of any investment system.

Ask questions like: who keeps the system running? Find out if the process depends on one or two key individuals. If these individuals own the firm, that may be OK — but if not, what happens if they leave the firm? Once again, your goal in analyzing a manager's investment process is to gain confidence that the results of the past are reasonably likely to continue into the future.

The Final Breakthrough

By now, you should have strong reasons to invest and, to a lesser degree, an understanding of the external signals of the economy. You may even have discovered where your fears come from, and have gained an understanding of the particular personal emotional obstacle course you must face when dealing with money and investments. Hopefully, you have done your card work, planned your investment route, and are now headed in a more balanced direction. You've put in many hours of study. Now it's time for the payoff. In this section, you're going to learn to trust your inner signals, break through your fears, and take the needed steps for financial security. You'll also learn how to teach your children about money and investing.

Perhaps you feel a bit uneasy about taking this next step, but you shouldn't. If you've done all of the preliminary work outlined in the previous chapters, you are ready. Any hesitancy or uncertainty you may feel at this time is just the normal worry that any new investor faces. You are ready to get going. It's time for action! It's time to make that final breakthrough. The first requirement of the breakthrough is trusting your internal guidance system.

18 Trusting Internal Signals

W hen one of our clients was in an attorney's office in Hawaii to write a check for a large initial investment in real estate, all his internal signals came to full alert. His stomach hurt so badly that he had to leave the room. He didn't act on any of his internal signals; he went against his instincts, and wrote the check. Financing couldn't be obtained and the project collapsed two months later. Looking back, he should have boarded the first plane for home. So there really is something to that feeling that you get in the pit of your stomach. If it doesn't feel right, if what somebody is saying doesn't add up and you get that churning feeling, stop. Take a few days to think about it, or just simply don't invest.

Investments like bonds and CDs are conservative types of investment. Stocks and mutual funds are more risky and this is where feelings of insecurity will pop up.

Notice if the areas you are most knowledgeable about, or have experience in, are where you feel most secure. If you're worried, there's usually still some insecurity in your mind.

The more secure you feel, the more confidence you will have in taking new "risks" in forging your financial destiny. The question to ask yourself in any situation is not "Am I secure or insecure now?" but rather "What can I do to make myself more secure?"

You might feel, "I'm insecure because I've never dealt with mutual funds before." "I'm insecure because I'm intimidated by people who work in brokerages and investment firms who can talk knowledgeably about investments." So what can you feel secure about when thinking about investing? You may think, "I'm at least secure in understanding what mutual funds are. I can make myself internally secure by learning as much as I can about mutual funds before I talk to an investment advisor." In other words, insecurities can be reduced or eliminated by actions.

Another one of our clients, a college professor, once felt very insecure every time she taught a course. She would learn as much about the subject as she could, and think about how her students would relate to the subject and to her. After a while her anxiety was replaced by a sense of humor and her fear was replaced by a sense of cooperation. The class became play. She had gone from being very insecure to secure. The key to making this change is to recognize that the difference between feeling secure and insecure is often a matter of how much you know about the subject.

This exercise creates a holistic attitude towards investing. The beauty of this is that the more you learn about investing, and the more you can transform your insecurities into securities, the further your investment plan will unfold, naturally. The side benefit is that you won't worry.

Within you are numerous sources of internal signals competing with external forces for control of your life. Internal signals operate as thoughts, feelings or intuitions, or the voice within you.

Some researchers have used the term "locus of control" to differentiate external from internal types of people. When your life is predominantly controlled by signals coming from outside yourself, you are said to have an external locus of control. Psychologists estimate that seventy-five percent of the people in our western culture are externally controlled. These outside signals maneuver us and manipulate us to make decisions based on someone or something outside ourselves. When it comes to investing, most people believe that somebody else has superior knowledge and can pick investments better than we can. There is a sense that experts can actually predict the future. The truth is that there are no studies that have shown stock pickers or stock market timers have been able to outperform any stock market indexes ever! In fact, they underperform them.

Here is the problem. When external controls dictate decisions for you, this can result in conflicts with your inner signals. That makes your mind repress your inner feelings. If somebody else began to dictate how to raise your children, or what you must do to earn a living, that this was better for you than that, you might start to feel a lot of anxiety or fear. On the other hand, becoming attuned to your internal signals can give you a real sense of security, peace of mind, and power. The more you trust your internal signals and rely less on external cues, the more you will experience the locus of control in your own hands, where it belongs.

Advertisements in back of investment magazines are a strong source of external cues. Sit quietly and ask yourself where these ads generate from. "Do

I feel trust, or is this ad a manipulation to get me to feel at ease so I will not do my homework, and just send in my check?"

The point is to keep external signals from blocking out your internal impulses in situations such as investing in which you are more apt to react to the external controls of others. Okay, it's impossible to eliminate external centers of control over our lives. We all live in this world together and constantly interrelate. No man or woman is an island. I just want you to be able to recognize the difference between internal and external signals. It will make you a better investor.

One more hurdle to jump on your way to becoming more internally directed is to overcome external signals that tell you that you are selfish if you take too much control of your own life. Women are most conditioned to feel that way.

We've heard this faulty statement a hundred times: "All of the wealth in the world is controlled by women." This is simply not true. Stockbrokers like to say that a majority of assets are owned by women and controlled by women. The fact is that a large number of women in the world live below the poverty level.

Write down any areas in your life where the locus of control is external. In other words, somebody's telling you what to do, or you perceive that you have no choice in the matter. Then write down areas in your life where the locus of control is internal. You determine what happens. Now imagine what would happen if the two areas were reversed. What if your investments were controlled by someone besides you? Or, what if you had total control of your financial life?

What if you countered your fears around money and investing with love? Love creates unity and causes us to react in ways that integrate. Consider investing as the ultimate act of love. Setting up an investment program will nurture your family and yourself in the future. Wouldn't this orientation change your attitude about investing? You might wake up happier that you are creating a better financial future, and this leads to peace of mind.

19 Monitoring and Controlling Risks

D iana is what I call a free spirit. She is not who you think of when you imagine the typical investor. She is in her late fifties, wears sweats and a fanny pack, and drives her own mobile home around the country. She has accumulated $750,000 and has four different money managers managing her portfolios and real estate. Her concern is with how to control her risk and not lose what she has accumulated.

We met and discussed a technique that is the cornerstone of modern portfolio theory, that is to assemble a portfolio of dissimilar investments — investments that don't have historic correlations with each other. This means that they will tend to move in very different cycles. By investing this way, an investor can increase diversification, decrease risk, and increase profit.

With dissimilar investments, one may move up, a second down, while a third may have no movement at all. The movement of the different investments therefore tend to cancel each other out. The overall portfolio has a much lower volatility and higher compound rate of return than the individual asset classes that make up the portfolio.

The prudent investor will strive to combine a series of investments within a portfolio that have the lowest possible correlation coefficient. This technique enables the financial planner to take advantage of relatively high-risk, high-return stocks within a conservative portfolio. These stocks can be included within a portfolio if they have a low correlation coefficient with, say, your real estate portfolio.

Many investment portfolios that are diversified in more than one stock are ineffectively diversified in only one type of investment vehicle, such as large company stocks. That way all the investments in a portfolio move together. The overall risk in a portfolio is *not* the average risk of each of the investments; it is actually less if your investments do not move together. By including investments in your portfolio that don't move in concert, you can eliminate the specific risk of individual investments for which the market does not reward you.

Since 1973, major institutions have been using the money management concept known as modern portfolio theory. This theory was developed at the University of Chicago in 1952 by Harry Markowitz and Merton Miller, and later expanded by Stanford's Professor William Sharpe. Markowitz, Miller and Sharpe won the Nobel prize in Economics in 1990 for this investment methodology. The five-step process of developing a strategic portfolio using modern portfolio theory is mathematical in nature and can, at times, appear daunting. It is important to note that math is nothing more than an expression of logic and, as you examine the process, you can readily see the common sense approach that these researchers have taken — which is counterintuitive to what Wall Street's "soothsayers" have shared with the media.

For every level of risk, there is some optimum combination of investments that will yield the highest rate of return. Combinations in a portfolio exhibiting this optimal risk/reward trade-off form the efficient frontier line. The efficient frontier is determined by calculating the expected rate of return, and standard deviation, and utilizing this information to optimize the portfolio to get the highest expected return for any given level of risk.

By plotting each portfolio representing a given level of risk and expected return, we are able to create a line connecting all efficient portfolios. This line forms the efficient frontier.

Most investor portfolios fall significantly below the efficient frontier. Portfolios such as the S&P 500 fall below the line, in that investors could have had comparable rates of return with much less risk or higher rates of return for the same level of risk.

By combining investments in your portfolio that don't move in concert and have low volatility, and by globally diversifying, owning institutional asset class funds, and designing your portfolio to be efficient, you may achieve the magic of increased overall returns with lower overall risk.

20 The Twelfth Step — Teaching Your Kids

As with any good twelve-step program, the last step is to go out and teach it. How to manage money is one of the most important lessons you can teach your children. Children who are excluded from open discussions of family financial affairs or sheltered from the financial realities of life can sometimes develop distorted ideas about money. They may make extravagant demands, often creating unnecessary conflict about money, simply because they are uninformed about the family's financial resources. When these children grow up, they can be ill-equipped to manage their own finances or unable to exercise good judgment in financial matters.

The key is to teach your children to think about money and financial management from a positive point of view. Of course, introducing your children to money management is a very personal matter, and you as the parent must decide what is best for your child. Here are some tips you may find helpful:

■ Be open with your children about money matters. Many families hold regular conferences, children included, to review finances. Every family member should be encouraged to speak out freely about his or her own priorities or goals. This way you can illustrate that priorities need to be set and that trade-offs are sometimes necessary for effective use of money. Even a fairly young child, for instance, should be able to understand that paying for shelter and groceries takes a higher priority over a new bike or a trip to an amusement park. Attending these sessions can give your children a sense of involvement and a greater willingness to work toward meeting family financial goals.

■ Give your children regular allowances. You can begin when they reach school age, and be sure to include at least some money they are free to spend as they like without accounting to anyone. That way your children gain experience in deciding how to spend their own money. A recommended way to start is by giving a young child a small amount of money every day or two for little toys or treats. As the child gets older, you can spread out the payment periods and increase the size of the allowances and the purpose for which it is used. The child can have a greater voice as the years go by in determining what the allowance should be. A teenager, for example, might receive a monthly allowance that covers school lunches and supplies, hobbies and entertainment, and clothing. This can teach the child to plan and to save for necessities and special purchases, and to shop carefully for good buys. Giving an occasional advance against an upcoming allowance may be appropriate, but if your child overspends constantly, work with him or her to bring spending in line with available income.

■ Teach your children the value of working for extra money. Children should learn at an early age that money must be earned. You do not want to pay your child for every routine household task, of course, but you might consider paying for special household chores, above and beyond the allowance.

■ Encourage your children to save for special goals. You might begin with a piggy bank and advance to a passbook savings account so that each child can see firsthand how money deposited regularly can earn money through interest and grow faster. A child can open a savings account at any age, but remember, banks generally require a social security number for all depositors. Once a child has a passbook account, he or she should have the freedom, within reason, to withdraw funds at will when necessary.

■ Introduce your children to checking accounts once they are old enough. Opening checking accounts for your children when they are in their mid-teens is one way for them to learn about simple transactions — how to make deposits, write checks, and balance checkbooks.

■ Expose your children to the basics of investing. Since money management is sometimes more than balancing your checkbook or opening a passbook savings account, you should also try to involve your child in an investment. By actually owning a stock, a child can watch the stock market fluctuate, learn how investments help the growth of the American economy, and gain an understanding of basic investment principles. And, as a stockholder, your child will periodically receive information on his or her investment, including an annual report, that may be interesting as well as educational.

■ Teach your children about credit once they are mature enough. Credit has become such a substantial part of the American way of life that teaching your children to use it properly is an important element of their financial education. Many stores permit teenagers to use family credit accounts with their parents' consent. You should supervise their use of credit closely, of course, to make sure they keep credit purchases modest and pay bills promptly.

■ Set a good example. This is the best way to teach your children the principles of sound money management. No matter how much training you give them, many of their attitudes toward money will be influenced by the way you spend and save it.

TAX-DEFERRED INVESTING FOR RETIREMENT IV

Contents

21 Investing for a Longer Retirement

W hen it comes to retirement planning, most people have overly ambitious goals, inadequate funding, and either no investment strategy or the wrong kind of strategy, as we have seen. In the unlikely event that you stay with the same employer all your working years (although statistics say that you won't), the best you can hope for is to retire on half your average annual earnings. You can't expect Social Security to fill in the gaps, since most employers' retirement formulas count half of the monthly Social Security benefit as part of your pension income.

To reach your financial goal, you will have to develop a dependable income stream, control costs, and beat the inflation robber. Investors need only make the decision to invest and then decide how much risk they can tolerate in a given time span.

Table 21.1 shows how much you would need to save every month, starting now, to have a million dollars at age sixty-five. It also shows that the earlier you start, the richer, by far, you'll be.

With tax deferral, your money will grow faster than the same return rate would grow without the tax deferral. Even after withdrawing all of your money and paying current taxes, you will most likely still have more dollars than by paying taxes as you go. The reason is that you are able to earn interest on dollars that would have normally gone to pay taxes.

Table 21.2 shows the tax equivalent yield and helps you calculate what you will need to earn on a taxable investment to achieve the same annual growth.

For instance, let's say you are in the 28 percent bracket and have a tax-deferred or tax-free investment earning 5 percent. Find the 28 percent tax rate

Table 21.1 How to Have a Million Dollars

Starting Age	Amount You Have To Invest per Month		
	8% Return ($)	10% Return ($)	15% Return ($)
25	310	180	45
30	470	300	90
35	710	490	180
40	1,100	810	370
45	1,760	1,390	760
50	2,960	2,500	1,640
55	5,550	5,000	3,850
60	13,700	13,050	11,600

Table 21.2 Tax Deferral Calculator

Interest rate	Tax Rate				
	15%	28%	31%	36%	39.6%
	What a Taxable Investment Must Earn during Accumulation				
2.5	2.94	3.47	3.62	3.91	4.14
3.0	3.53	4.17	4.35	4.69	4.97
3.5	4.12	4.86	5.07	5.47	5.79
4.0	4.70	5.56	5.80	6.25	6.62
4.5	5.29	6.25	6.52	7.03	7.45
5.0	5.88	6.94	7.25	7.81	8.28
5.5	6.47	7.64	7.97	8.59	9.11
6.0	7.06	8.33	8.70	9.38	9.93
6.5	7.65	9.03	9.42	10.16	10.76
7.0	8.24	9.72	10.14	10.94	11.59
7.5	8.82	10.42	10.87	11.72	12.42
8.0	9.41	11.11	11.59	12.50	13.25
8.5	10.00	11.81	12.21	13.28	14.07

Equivalent yield formula: Tax-deferred rate divided by (1 – tax rate). For example, 6.0 (tax-deferred) divided by (1 – 28%) = 6.0 ÷ 0.72 = 8.33%.

and the 5 percent interest rate and you see they meet at 6.94 percent. This means you would need to find a taxable investment paying 6.94 percent to achieve the same growth rate, after paying taxes, as the tax-deferred or tax-free investment.

Retirement Plans

There are a number of special plans designed to create retirement savings, and many of these plans allow you to deposit money directly from your paycheck before taxes are taken out. Employers occasionally will match the amount (or a percentage of that amount) you have withheld from your paycheck up to a certain percentage. Some of these plans permit you to withdraw money early without a penalty in order to buy a home or to pay for education. For those that do not allow early withdrawals without a pen-alty, sometimes you can borrow money from the account or take out low-interest secured loans with your retirement savings as collateral. Rates of return vary on these vehicles depending on what you invest in, since you can invest in stocks, bonds, mutual funds, CDs, or any combination.

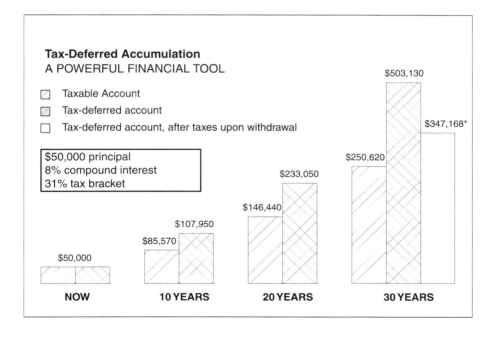

Figure 21.1 Tax deferral.

Why start now? The age at which you begin does make a dramatic difference. If you start putting $150 a month at age twenty-five into a retirement account that's tax-deferred, by the time you're sixty-five you'll have approximately $840,000. If you wait until you're thirty-five, you'll have around $300,000.

You can do it yourself or use a broker or investment advisor. They screen investment managers across the country and across investment disciplines to ensure compatibility with your financial goals. They not only monitor the money managers on an ongoing basis, but they also help you monitor and evaluate your personal portfolio with a quarterly performance report. Next, let's take a look at the different types of retirement plan and which one best fits your needs.

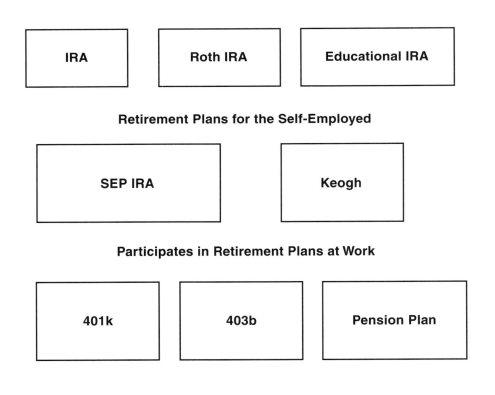

Figure 21.2 Retirement plans.

Individual Retirement Account (IRA)

Individual retirement account (IRA) contributions are no longer deductible if either you or your spouse is covered by another retirement plan, such as corporate pension; SEP IRA accounts; Keogh plans or 401(k) company-sponsored plans.

If your adjusted gross income is under $35,000 (single) or $50,000 (joint), you are allowed $1.00 in IRA deductions for each $5.00 below those limits. In other words, you can still get a tax credit for the full $2,000 IRA contribution, if your adjusted gross income is no higher than $25,000 (single) or $40,000 (joint) and you or your spouse is covered by a pension plan or a Keogh.

IRA Checklist

Consider putting money in an IRA if:

■ You are among those whose contributions are fully deductible — couples filing jointly with gross income of less than $40,000, singles who make less than $25,000, or anyone who is not covered by a pension, profit-sharing, or other tax-advantaged retirement plan.
■ You qualify for a partial deduction and are sure that you will not need the money in your IRA before age 59.

Contributing to an IRA is probably not worthwhile if:

■ You are ineligible for a deduction, especially if you think that your tax rate when you retire will be higher than now.
■ You can use other tax-favored retirement savings plans such as a 401(k).

The basic rules of contributing to any type of IRA (with the exception of educational IRAs, which are really not retirement accounts) are based on taxable compensation. This includes wages, salaries, tips, professional fees, commissions, and self-employed income. Your annual contribution to all IRA accounts cannot exceed the lesser of your compensation, or $2000 plus up to an additional $2000 for a non-working or low earning spouse. The IRA is simply a tax shelter. For example, say you accumulate $50,000 in a deductible IRA by the time you reach age forty. If your account averages a ten percent annual return for the next twenty-five years, you'll generate

$492,000 of earnings. And if you withdraw that as a lump sum and pay a thirty percent average tax rate, you'll net around $344,000. On the other hand, if you have that $50,000 in a taxable account, your earnings are subject to an average tax rate of thirty percent and you net only seven percent per annum instead of ten percent. At that rate, your $50,000 earns about $221,000 over the next twenty-five years. So that's the benefit of compounding. You get an extra three percent provided by the IRA tax shelter.

Even though your stocks are riskier in the short run and there may be volatility over the long run, IRAs participate in the growth of the economy.

Educational IRAs

Educational IRAs limit contributions to $500 a year; and while the earnings compound tax-free, they have to be used for tuition or other allowable college costs. The IRS would penalize you if your child decides to buy a car with it instead. If the funds are used for any purpose other than education, income tax and a 10 percent penalty are slapped on the earnings. Also, when you cash in an educational IRA, you become ineligible for new tuition tax credits during that calendar year. And finally, if you're ready or not, you must withdraw any remaining funds by your youngest child's thirteenth birthday. I know that sounds silly.

Another idea for your children's education may be to set aside your spare change, unused dimes, and quarters every day. Once a month, write a check equivalent to the total to a mutual fund company. They'll accept a small contribution of $50 a month. If you earn eight percent a year, in ten years, your child could net $9,064.

The Roth IRA

The new Roth IRA, available since 1998, is a valuable new kind of IRA. It differs in that contributions are not deductible. However, distributions of funds held in the IRA for more than five years from the date you set up the Roth IRA will be totally *tax free* if used for up to $10,000 of first-time home-buyer expenses or after the occurrence of death or disability, or you reach age fifty-nine.

The Roth IRA will be most valuable when it holds investments that compound at a high rate — such as growth stocks — for a long period of time. That's because the ultimate value of the compound investment returns will be distributed *tax free*, instead of being taxed at normal rates, as are distributions from regular IRAs and other retirement accounts.

Children's IRA Opportunity

A Roth IRA is an excellent investment account to open for children as soon as they have earned income. The extra years of compounding available to a child can produce a tax-free payoff that will give the child a big head start on lifetime financial security.

Roth IRA for Yourself

You can make a full $2,000 contribution to a Roth IRA if your adjusted gross income (AGI) is less than $150,000 for a joint return or $95,000 for a single return. The contribution gets phased out from $150,000 to $160,000 (joint) and $95,000 to $110,000 (single). If your AGI doesn't exceed $100,000, you'll be able to convert existing IRAs into Roth IRAs. To do this, you'll have to first withdraw your IRA assets and pay the taxes on the gains. If you convert after 1998, you must pick up all of the income in the year of conversion.

Whether it will pay to convert a regular IRA to a Roth IRA will depend on several factors, such as:

■ Your current and expected future tax rates.
■ The length of time you expect to keep your funds in the IRA.
■ The rate of return that you expect to earn.
■ Whether you can pay the tax due on the conversion from non-IRA funds.

A Roth IRA offers advantages in addition to the tax-free distributions — you can withdraw the amount of your regular contributions to a Roth IRA any time.

A good comprehensive booklet on IRA answers is available from Schwab (1-800-806-8481), *Schwab IRA Answers, New Laws, More Choices.*

Retirement Plans for the Self-Employed

Keogh

This is a special type of IRA that doubles as a pension plan for a self-employed person. The self-employed person can put aside up to $30,000 a year, significantly more than the normal $2,000 cap on an individual IRA. You can do this asset class investment program inside a self-directed Keogh.

If you are self-employed, sock away twenty percent of your income — up to a maximum of $30,000 — in a Keogh plan. You can establish a Keogh plan with any bank, brokerage firm, or mutual fund. You may also want to explore the advantages of a SEP plan.

Simplified Employee Pension (SEP) Plan

A simplified employee pension plan (SEP) is like a giant IRA. SEPs were created so that small businesses could set up retirement plans that were a little easier to administer than normal pension plans. Both employees and the employer can contribute to a SEP.

A SEP lets you contribute thirteen percent of your net earnings from self-employment up to $24,000 — without the paperwork of a Keogh.

You can actually save more in a SEP account than you can in a 401(k). A SEP allows you to put away as much as 13.034 percent of pretax self-employed earnings or $24,000 a year, whichever is less. The nice thing about a SEP account is that you can wait until the last minute to invest in it.

Participate in Retirement Plans at Work

The 401(k)

Things have changed dramatically in the last few years. If you participate in a 401(k) retirement plan at work, you need to know that any investment mistakes you make come out of your retirement nest-egg. In other words, investment results are your responsibility and not those of the sponsor of the plan. This makes it even more important for you to understand your investment choices and make smart decisions.

Some employers will match your contribution. That's like found money. So your contribution and your employer's contribution could be compounding tax-deferred until you retire.

403(b)

Local and state governments offer the 457 plan.

Whatever you're doing, add to it. If your company sponsors a 401(k) or 403(b), make an appointment with the Human Resource office and sign up or increase the amount of your contribution as soon as you can. You can put up to a maximum of $10,000 a year directly from your paycheck into your retirement account. The benefits of saving pretax dollars are huge. Now with the twenty-eight percent tax bracket, that $10,000 contribution will be $2800 in tax savings. So the full annual contribution would really cost you only $7200. The same investing and selection of mutual funds as outlined in the book would apply inside the plan.

The problem is that time does not permit you to absorb and evaluate the vast amounts of information required to make astute investment decisions. Meeting your personal production schedules, sales, and service commitments must take priority. All too often, these problems ultimately push you, the plan participants, to choose expedient, short-term solutions that seem reasonable, but may not produce the results you desire.

The following investment-oriented steps are set forth to help you to accomplish your investment goals.

Participants normally have the right to move their funds in a 401(k) plan from one alternative to another periodically. One caution: By moving from equities to cash or fixed income and back, you unknowingly become your own personal market timer. (Aside from everything in the book about market timing, this type of activity also causes you to get "whipsawed" by market moves you may not understand, to the detriment of your long-term investment success.)

The best approach is to decide upon one strategy and stick with it. Work with your 401(k) plan's financial consultant and develop a personal strategy, in the form of a statement of investment objectives for each alternative, and commit to it in writing. Such a statement should articulate clearly what the fund may and may not invest in, the expected long-term goals (in terms of performance and volatility), and the general approach to be taken by the manager (whether a private investment manager or a mutual fund manager) in achieving those results.

Most 401(k) plans have a long-term, systematic manner of monitoring any plan's investment progress. You should inquire into how your assets are to be monitored. If mutual funds are used as an investment vehicle, then you should be provided performance results periodically. Otherwise, periodic meetings or telephone conferences with your financial consultant should be requested.

The kinds of questions that should form the basis of such meetings are:

1. Is your manager continuing to apply the style and strategy that you understood would be used in the management of your assets?
2. Do you find the reporting clear, logical, and understandable? Does it show clearly what your plan owns?

3. Do you feel comfortable that your overall communications with the financial consultant are good, and that your queries and needs are attended to promptly?
4. Is your 401(k) plan's performance roughly in line with the performance you expected? Or, is the fund apparently doing much better or much worse than you expected? Why is this the case? Is the explanation satisfactory?
5. If there are investment restrictions in your guidelines, are these being adhered to?

Your financial consultant can be called upon to meet with participants to explain the advantage of various investment alternatives, as well as how the plan has progressed. This, of course, would be at the option or request of the sponsoring company. As a participant, you should understand that, over long periods of time, common stocks — although more volatile — tend to produce overall returns almost twice as high as high quality bonds.

You may be able to run your own asset class strategy; an alternative is a balanced portfolio which may combine elements of cyclical stocks, large and small growth stocks and others, with good quality bonds (fixed income securities). It will seldom involve an element of market timing. Balanced portfolios are often used by major funds and charitable endowments, as well as by individuals. They provide great flexibility.

401(k) plans are much more attractive to many companies since the company's investment committee is not directly liable for any losses sustained by the plan. Many employees like the sense of control they get from a 401(k) plan. But serving as one's own money manager can also be overwhelming to people who have trouble managing their own checkbooks, let alone their financial future. Unfortunately, with so much at stake, many participants feel intimidated about making investment decisions. That is why the most popular choice in 401(k) plans are low risk, fixed-rate guaranteed investment contracts (GICs) offered by insurance companies.

Luckily for plan investors, back in the 1980s fixed-rate contracts were paying unusually high rates of around nine percent. But in the 1990s, interest rates came down. Participants coming out of a five-year, nine percent contract had to reinvest at lower rates, which means they are coming up short at retirement. Still, many investors who are given a choice with their retirement money prefer to play it safe with a fixed income. That's fine, if it's the only way you can sleep at night; but don't forget, there is a trade-off in results.

What Should a Participant Investor Be Aware of?

Faced with a number of investment decisions, an employee should get prepared:

> Step 1. The first step in the process of investing is the identification of investment goals.
>
> Step 2. Select and set appropriate risk parameters and choose an option to meet your financial needs.
>
> Step 3. Look at all the options — not just the guaranteed ones. Remember that, in fixed investment vehicles, low risk often means low return.
>
> Step 4. If provided, get investment counseling.
>
> Step 5. Monitor your investment manager's progress.

In most 401(k) plans, participants are offered short-term investment vehicles that neglect their long-term investment needs. This can spell trouble twenty years from now when many plan participants may learn, too late, the ruthless rules of investing.

The reality is that guaranteed fixed income investment contracts and market timing or daily switching produces, over the long run, only negligible investment returns. Unfortunately, this is what's being sold to the 401(k) investing public. *Warning*: The Pension Benefits Guaranty Corporation (PBGC) does not cover 401(k) plans. About forty percent of all money in 401(k) plans is invested in a product called a Guaranteed Insurance Contract (GIC), which is like a certificate of deposit issued by an insurance company. GICs offer a guaranteed yield. Most investors mistakenly think that their principal is guaranteed; what is actually guaranteed is the rate of interest for a set period of time. The principal is secured by the insurance company's general fund, which is used to secure all policies.

Many insurance companies have huge investments in non-investment grade junk bonds — eight to eleven percent of their portfolio is typical. If forced to liquidate today, one in five insurance companies would not have enough money to meet its obligations.

Not Being Properly Advised

It's a sad fact that most 401(k) participants are not being properly advised and cannot be expected to make appropriate investment allocations or choices. The feature of daily switching (a feature offered by 401(k) service providers which gives the participant the freedom to transfer between investment options on a daily basis) offers plan participants the greatest control over their assets.

Regulations Give No Guidance

Beyond the minimum requirement of providing a prospectus that offers the standard three investment choices, there is absolutely no incentive for employers to inform employees of investment options. This forces the employee participants to fend for themselves in rough investment seas. In most cases, participants act as their own asset allocators or market timers, deciding each quarter — or sometimes each day — how much money should be invested in each class.

What to Do

How can an employer with a 401(k) plan get the best ongoing investment advice?

- Have your plan reviewed for investment performance. Begin the year by having a qualified financial firm review your 401(k) plan.
- Request investment counseling regarding asset allocation appropriate to the participant's individual objectives, his or her retirement horizons, and his and her risk tolerance.
- Set up an educational program to acquaint participants with the capital markets and provide specific investment counseling regarding an appropriate mix of investments.
- Participants with long-term investment horizons, or younger participants, should be encouraged to invest to some extent in equities.

Pension Plans

In a defined benefit pension plan, the sponsoring company takes full responsibility for providing a guaranteed benefit for you as a participant. The sponsoring company shoulders all the investment risks and promises to make specific payouts. To many companies that have abandoned pension plans, retirement benefits generated from these plans didn't seem worth the extensive amount of government paperwork and the fiduciary risk that the sponsoring company had to shoulder.

Retirement Check Up

Pension miscalculations are a growing problem that affects people of all ages, not just retirement age. Any time someone changes jobs or takes a lump sum pension cash out, they're at risk. Women are especially vulnerable to pension mistakes because they tend to move in and out of the workforce more often than men. For the most part, pension mix-ups aren't intentional. Federal pension laws are incredibly difficult even for expert number crunchers.

How would you know if there was an error that had been compounding for many years? How can you ensure that you'll get what's rightfully yours when retirement arrives? It's up to you to keep track of your own pension. Know your rights and monitor your retirement plan before the "golden years" creep up on you. Learn the details. Ask for a summary plan description. This will show how your pension is calculated. If you're in a workplace 401(k), get a description of your program from the administrator of your benefits plan. Also, an individual benefit statement will tell you what your benefits are currently worth and how many years you've been in the plan. It may even include a projection of your monthly check.

Check for obvious errors such as wrong years of your service. If you're stashing money away in a 401(k), you'll get periodic statements just as you do with your checking accounts. Save all your statements. You should keep any pension documents your company gives you over the years. Also keep records of dates when you worked and your salary, since this type of data is used by your employer to calculate the value of your pension. Ask for professional help, if you're still thinking something might be wrong. Ask for the name of a qualified specialist in your area. Call the American Society of Pension Actuaries at 703-516-9300 or the National Center for Retirement Benefits at 800-666-1000.

Nine Common Pension Mistakes

Most of the time companies won't intentionally fudge; sometimes the blame can be on simple errors. Here's what to watch for:

1. The company forgot to include commission, overtime pay, or bonuses in determining your benefit level.

2. Your employer relied on incorrect social security information to calculate your benefits.
3. Somebody used the wrong benefit formula (i.e., an incorrect interest rate was plugged into the equation).
4. Calculations are wrong because you've worked past age sixty-five.
5. You didn't update your workplace personnel officer of important changes that would affect your benefits, such as marriage, divorce, or death of a spouse.
6. The firm's computer software is flawed.
7. The year 2000 computer problem is also something you should be aware of and consult with your pension administrator to make sure that their computer software doesn't lose your precious data.
8. The company neglected to include your total years of service.
9. Your pension provider just made a basic math mistake.

If you do not have a qualified retirement plan available, you should look to invest in a private IRA. With the new limits and options, you may find one that you qualify for. Be very careful to avoid the insurance salesman who sells the "private pension plans" as an alternative to qualified retirement plans. These are often a scam, and some major insurance companies are being sued for misleading sales practices relating to these plans.

Use your investments to make up the difference of social security and your retirement benefits.

Start by completing the form to request that the Social Security Administration send an accounting of your benefit payments, so you can know ahead of time how much you're going to be making when you retire. Also request from your company that same information regarding your pension plan, if you have one. Subtract the total of those two amounts from what you would anticipate needing in retirement and the difference is going to be your investment goal.

Last Notes on Retirement Planning

Since qualified plans all have contribution limits, what do you do if you have already contributed, or are contributing, the maximum amount into your retirement plans and will still have a shortfall?

Avoid any get-rich-quick plan or the *sure bets* — they probably are not what they appear to be. Believe it or not, millions of dollars are contributed every year to scams. What may appear as a great conversation piece at a cocktail party may very well put you in a position of not being able to afford to attend the next one.

After your qualified retirement plan is fully funded, you have two general options: investing in a taxable account or a tax-deferred account. Examples of taxable accounts are CDs, mutual funds, stocks (if traded), and bonds. Examples of tax-deferred vehicles would be fixed and variable annuities.

Some advisors include variable life as a tax-deferred vehicle for analysis purposes. If you *need* life insurance and are planning to invest the difference anyway, a versatile universal life (VUL) policy may make sense. If you do not need the life insurance, why pay for it, and in most cases, give a life insurance agent fifty percent commission or more on your contribution?

Variable annuities have expenses that mutual funds do not have and are also taxed differently. If you have less than ten years before you begin distributions, the cost and less favorable taxation of the annuity may negate the benefits of the tax deferral and the death benefit. You may have other sources of capital to use for retirement income, such as a 401k, that would enable you to continue to defer the use of the annuity for income and maximize the benefit of the variable annuity.

22 What Are Annuities?

Annuities are a popular retirement savings vehicle. But investors should consider their options and costs carefully before purchasing one. You won't get into too much trouble as long as you think of yourself as a sheep drinking from the wolves' stream. Just read the fine print.

Overview

In general, there are two types of annuities, fixed and variable. A fixed annuity provides a specific income for life. With a variable annuity, payouts are dependent on investment return, which is not guaranteed. Variable annuities offer the choice of several investment divisions such as stocks, bonds, and money market funds, which can cause the rate of return to fluctuate with market conditions.

In both fixed and variable annuities, you do not have to pay income tax on the accumulated earnings until payouts start. But you should keep in mind that withdrawals are taxable and, if you are under age $59^1/_2$, may be subject to a ten percent tax penalty.

Fixed Annuities

The word "fixed' is used to describe the type of annuity referred to by the interest rate paid by the issuing insurance company. The fixed annuity offers security in that the rate of return is certain. Typically, with a fixed annuity the insurance company declares a current interest rate and sets the interest rate. It promises to pay at a lower rate than the rate it expects to earn on its

148

investment. The difference in rates is sometimes referred to as the "spread." It allows the insurance company to recover its administration cost and profit.

The fixed aspect of the annuity also offers security in that the annuity holder does not take responsibility for making decisions about how the money should be invested. Also, the amount of the benefit that will be paid out of the annuity when the contract is annuitized is also fixed. The settlement options that the annuitant would receive from the insurance company would be the same each year during the annuitization phase. If the annuitant chooses a settlement option based on life expectancy, the same amount will come to that annuitant each month for the rest of his or her life without any investment decisions or risk on their part.

Variable Annuities

Variable annuities are often called "mutual funds with an insurance wrapper." A variable annuity combines the best aspects of a traditional *fixed annuity* (tax deferral, insurance protection for beneficiaries, tax timing, controlled income options) with the benefits of traditional mutual fund-type portfolios (flexibility in selecting how to invest funds, the potential for higher investment returns).

Let's say you are a thirty-five year-old online investor. If you took $10,000 out of your trading profits and invested it in a no-load, low cost variable annuity, and you got a boring return of twelve percent a year, by your sixty-fifth birthday, you could accumulate over $240,000. If you are able to add $5,000 a year all along the way, your $160,000 of total invested capital, compounding tax free, could balloon to over $1,282,558. If you continue working and don't retire until age seventy, your variable annuity could hold over $2,224,249. That's what's possible by investing in a variable annuity.

Variable annuity investors control their contract options. They dictate the amount, frequency, and regularity of their contributions, how their contributions are invested, and when the money is disbursed. You pay a premium to the insurance company, which then buys *accumulation units*, similar to mutual fund shares, in an investment fund. The IRS imposes no limits on the annual non-sheltered amount an individual may contribute to a variable annuity funded with after-tax dollars. In other words, you can put in as much money as you can afford. This is particularly important when it comes to supplementing retirement assets beyond the annual tax-free contribution limitation.

The variable annuity investor directs those funds in subaccount portfolios consisting of either stocks, bonds, or cash money market funds. Diverse investment options make it possible to structure an investment portfolio to meet a variety of needs, goals, and risk tolerances. These investments may be managed by a mutual fund company or by the insurance company. With the important advantage of tax-free rebalancing, investors can adjust their portfolios at any time. This allows an investor's advisor to carefully plan and manage the asset allocation strategy based on changing needs or market conditions, without having to worry about generating current tax.

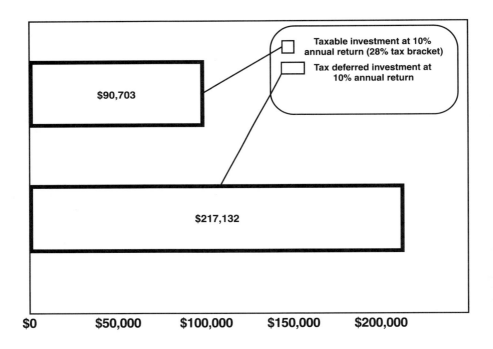

$1,200 annual investment over 30 years

Figure 22.1 Investing in a tax-deferred annuity vs. taxable mutual fund.

Unlike a mutual fund, an annuity does not pay out earnings or distribute any capital gains, so these are compounded on a tax-deferred basis. The ability to reallocate assets without current tax ramifications, combined with the tax-deferred compounding of potential earnings, makes variable annuities a highly competitive investment vehicle.

A variable annuity's rate of return is not guaranteed but, rather, is determined by the performance of the investments selected. As the value of the stocks in the portfolio varies, each unit will be worth more or less. Today's variable annuity managers, along with their affiliate mutual fund managers, seek diversification, consistent performance, and competitive returns by maximizing a portfolio's return and also minimizing the level of risk. Variable annuity investments are often balanced by investing a percentage of assets in the annuity fixed-income option to provide a less volatile investment return. These fixed annuity investments tend to smooth out extreme fluctuations; investors won't profit as much from a good year in the market with such an annuity, but neither will they suffer as much loss of income during a bad year.

Payouts from variable annuities reflect the investment experience of the underlying portfolios. The amount of variable payments is not guaranteed or fixed and may decline in periods of market decline. However, if the annuitant dies during the accumulation phase (that is, prior to receiving payments from the annuity), the designated beneficiary is guaranteed to receive the greater of the account's accumulated value, or the full amount invested less any withdrawals and applicable premium taxes. Some annuities also offer "enhanced death benefits," such as options that would enable a client to receive a step up every six years until age seventy-five, to lock in gains. Also, in most states, this built-in benefit generally bypasses the delays and costs of probate.

When withdrawals do begin, taxes are generally paid only on the amounts withdrawn that represent a gain at ordinary tax rates, while the remainder of the account value can continue to grow tax-deferred. However, if you take funds from the annuity before age $59^1/_2$, there is the additional ten percent IRS penalty on the withdrawal of any gain.

Most variable annuities offer a free annual withdrawal provision that gives you access of up to ten percent of the annuity value yearly without paying any surrender charges. Any distributions in excess of that ten percent are subject to the surrender charges. No-load variable annuities that do not impose a surrender charge are one hundred percent liquid but, like all annuities, may be subject to a ten percent federal penalty for withdrawal prior to age fifty-nine.

Despite their inherent advantages, all variable annuities are *not* created equal. They can vary widely in terms of costs and available investment options. Because of their insurance benefits, variable annuities generally cost more than traditional taxable investments, such as mutual funds. There may be front-end charges (loads), management fees, and sometimes back-end surrender charges for early withdrawals from the policy. These charges and the length of time they apply to the policy vary widely across the industry. The average policy probably has a six to seven percent first-year surrender charge that declines one percentage point per year. Some have "rolling surrender charges" which means that each investment you make has a new surrender charge schedule. An example would be if you invested $1000 every year, each $1000 contribution would have a new surrender charge schedule. I would avoid these if possible.

In addition to portfolio management fees, variable annuities charge a fee to cover the issuing insurance company's administrative costs and mortality and expense (M&E) charges. According to the 1997 *Morningstar Benchmarks*, annual M&E charges for the current industry average are around 1.3 percent and are increasing.

The higher the overall costs, the longer it takes for the benefit of tax deferral to compensate for those costs. A no sales-load, low-cost variable annuity can help shorten that break-even holding period. In general, variable annuities are designed to be held as long-term investment vehicles so a break-even of ten to fifteen years may be affordable for those investors with that type of time frame. Remember, time horizon is not measured by when you will retire, it is measured according to the time you would need to start withdrawals. Income distributions from a variable annuity are best used to supplement conventional retirement benefits or as a reserve until other payouts are exhausted.

A variable annuity receives varying interest on the funds placed inside the annuity, depending upon the choice of investment options. In addition, the holder of the variable annuity assumes the risk associated with the underlying investments done at the investment decision. Understanding how returns are credited on money invested in the framework of variable annuities can be a little more complicated than with a fixed annuity.

One of the main differences between a fixed annuity and a variable annuity is that the variable annuity is considered to be a security under federal law and therefore subject to a greater degree of regulation. Anyone selling the variable annuity must have acquired a securities license. Any potential buyer of a variable annuity must be provided with a prospectus — a detailed document that provides information on the variable annuity and the investment options.

In a variable annuity, the annuity holder may choose how to allocate premium dollars among a number of investment choices, including stocks, bonds, a guaranteed account, income, growth fund, and various funds called subaccounts. Any funds placed in the guaranteed account of a variable annuity are credited with a fixed rate of interest in much the same manner as funds in a fixed annuity contract. There's a guaranteed interest rate and a current interest rate, and the current rate changes periodically. If it drops below the floor set by the guaranteed rate, then the annuity holder receives at minimum the guaranteed rate.

The variable annuity typically offers the annuity holder several different subaccounts in which to invest all or a portion of the premiums paid into the annuity. The term "subaccount," "flexible account," and "flexible subaccount" are certainly interchangeable. When an annuity holder purchases a variable annuity, he determines what proportion of the premium payments, usually on a percentage basis, will be allocated or paid to the different variable subaccounts. Once a percentage is determined, it remains in effect until the annuity holder notifies the insurance company that he wishes to alter the allocation arrangement. Many variable annuities offer an option called "dollar cost averaging" which provides a method of systematic transfer of dollars from one fund to another inside the variable annuity.

In contrast to the fixed annuity option, an annuity holder who elects to receive all or part of the benefit payments under the variable option would receive a check for the same amount each month.

The accumulation phase is a period of time from the purchase of the annuity until the annuity holder decides to begin receiving payments from the annuity. It is during this period that the annuity builds up and accumulates the funds that will provide the annuity holder with future benefits. This works for both the fixed annuity and the variable annuity.

Deferred Annuities

Deferred annuities are the most popular. They allow people to accumulate money without paying current income tax on their earnings. This means that the amount can grow faster, due to the tremendous power of compound interest. Most deferred annuity contracts provide more flexibility concerning the timing of premium payments and benefit payouts.

A tax-deferred annuity is an interest-bearing contract between an investor and insurance company. When an investor purchases an annuity, the insurance company pays interest which is tax-deferred until withdrawal. You may withdraw the money at regular intervals or a specific period of time in a lump sum or through random withdrawals.

One feature of an annuity that is unique and is not found in any other investment vehicle is that the annuity provides a stream of income that an annuitant cannot outlive. Annuities offer protection against living too long. (This statement about living too long refers only to the person's financial situation.) Dollars inside the annuity remain tax-deferred until withdrawal, which is at the complete discretion of the owner of the annuity.

For example, if you have $10,000 to invest in a deferred annuity that is earning five percent a year, at the end of the first year your annuity will be worth $10,500. That full amount will be available to earn interest the following year. If, instead, you invest in a currently taxable investment that is also earning five percent, and your marginal tax rate is twenty-eight percent, at the end of the year only $10,360 will be available for reinvestment. The remaining $140 will be paid to the government for income tax on the $500 you earn. This may seem like a small sum of money, but if this continues for ten years, the difference between the values of the tax-deferred annuity and the currently taxable investment will be $2,046! (Of course, taxes must still be paid when the earnings inside the annuity contract are distributed. If the annuity is cashed in after ten years, the income tax would be $1,761, assuming a twenty-eight percent rate and no penalty taxes.)

Immediate Annuities

An immediate annuity is one that begins paying benefits very quickly, usually within one year of the time purchased. By nature, it is almost always a *single premium* purchase. The immediate annuity can be useful for an individual who has received a large sum of money and must count on these funds to pay expenses over a period of time.

Methods of Purchase

Single Premium Annuity

A single premium annuity is purchased with one premium. The single premium option may be used to purchase either a fixed annuity or a variable annuity. A single premium annuity requires an initial lump sum deposit (generally a minimum of $1,000 to $5,000) and does not accept any future contributions.

As an example, Bob Jones recently received a settlement from an insurance claim — a lump sum of $150,000. He does not need the money currently, so he uses the funds to purchase a single premium annuity for $150,000 and chooses to receive benefits at his retirement age by electing one of the income settlement options.

Other types of individuals might be athletes, actors, or artists, who receive a large payment at one time, they may want to purchase a single premium annuity that begins paying benefits when the person's career ends. Another example would be a business owner who's recently sold his company. If its an immediate annuity, benefit payments will usually begin within one year of the annuity's purchase. However, if the annuity is a deferred annuity, the annuity holder may delay the receipt of benefits for several years.

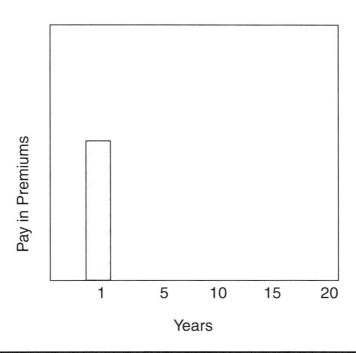

Figure 22.2 Single premium annuity accumulation phase.

Flexible Premium Annuity

A flexible premium annuity allows payments to be made at varying intervals and in varying amounts. Flexible premium annuities can accept future contributions and often require a smaller initial deposit. This type of annuity is usually used for accumulating a sum of money that will provide benefits at some point in the future. As with a single premium annuity, the flexible premium annuity can also purchase either a fixed or variable annuity.

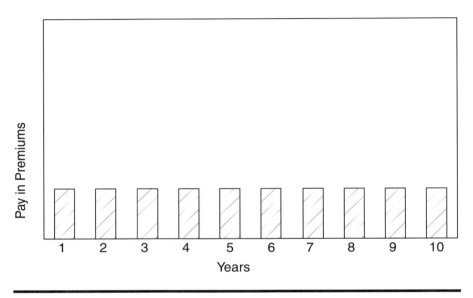

Figure 22.3 Flexible premium annuity accumulation phase.

Annuity Stages

There are two phases of an annuity:

1. The asset-building, or accumulation phase. A variable annuity is generally more appropriate for a customer with longer time horizons to allow a substantial accumulation of wealth through equity investments on a tax-deferred basis. In the accumulation phase, you buy units similar to that of mutual fund shares. But unlike a mutual fund, the annuity does not pay out income or distribute any capital gains, so you accumulate unit values over a period of years. These also grow tax-deferred, making the compound effect even more dramatic.

2. The payout, distribution, or benefit phase. The payout phase is when the insurance company starts making a series of payments consisting of principal and earnings for a defined period of time to the annuitant

or to the main beneficiary. Taxes are only assessed on the portion of each payment that comes from earned interest (except with qualified contracts).

Payout options include

- Lifetime income — the entire account value is converted to a monthly income stream guaranteed for as long as the annuitant lives.
- Lifetime income with period certain — income stream is guaranteed for a specified number of years, or for as long as the annuitant lives, whichever is longer.
- Refund life annuity — the entire account value is converted to a monthly income stream guaranteed for as long as the annuitant lives. If the annuitant dies prior to the principal amount being annuitized, the balance is paid to the beneficiary.
- Joint and survivor — income stream is guaranteed for as long as either annuitant lives (for example, you or your spouse).
- Fixed period certain — the entire account value is fully paid out during a specified period of time.
- Fixed amount annuity — equal periodic installments are withdrawn until the account balance is exhausted.

Unlike regular life insurance, which pays out a lump sum upon premature death, the lifetime payout option insures you against the danger of outliving your money. Once a guaranteed income option is elected, you cannot withdraw money or surrender the contract.

The single exception to this is the immediate annuity, which does not actually pass through an accumulation phase, but moves immediately after it is purchased into the annuitization phase.

Parties to an Annuity

Generally, there are four potential parties to an annuity contract: the owner, the annuitant, the beneficiary, and the issuing insurance company. The rights and duties of each of these entities will be discussed in a general overview. The owner is the person who purchases the annuity and the annuitant is the individual whose life will be used to determine how payments under the contract will be made. The beneficiary is the individual or entity that will receive any death benefits, and the issuing insurance company is the organization that accepts the owner's premium and promises to pay the benefits spelled out in the contract.

The most common situation involves only three parties, since the owner and the annuitant are most often the same individual. Thus, the three parties are the owner/annuitant, the individual or beneficiary, and the insurance company.

The Owner

Every annuity contract must have an owner. Usually the owner is a real person, but there's no qualification that the owner be a real person as there is with the annuitant. In most instances where the owner and the annuitant are the same person, the owner pays money in the form of premiums into the annuity during the accumulation phase.

Also, the owner has the right to determine when the annuity contract will move from the accumulation phase into the payout or annuitization phase and begin making payments. Most annuity contracts do not specify a maximum age past which annuity payments cannot be deferred. But in most annuities, the age will usually be well past retirement age.

The Annuitant

The annuitant is the individual whose life is of primary importance in affecting the timing and the amount of payout under the contract. In other words, the annuitant's life is the measuring life.* The annuitant, unlike the owner and the beneficiary of the annuity contract, must be a real person.

The Beneficiary

Similar to the conditions of a life insurance policy, in the annuity contract, beneficiaries receive a death benefit when the annuitant dies prior to the date upon which the annuity begins paying out benefits. In effect, the payment of the death benefit allows the owner to recover his investment and pass it along to the beneficiaries if the annuitant does not live long enough to begin receiving annuity contract benefits. The death benefit is equal generally to the value of the annuity contract at the time of death.

---

* See IRA, Section 72-S6.

Owner and Annuitant

Accumulation Phase

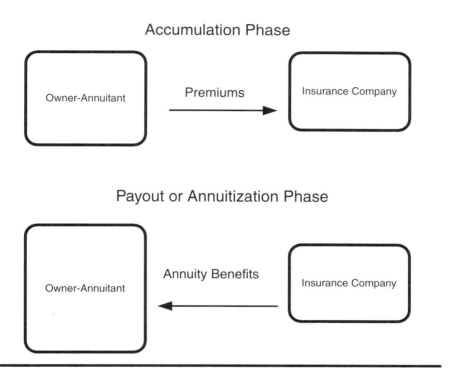

Payout or Annuitization Phase

Figure 22.4 Accumulation phase and annuitization phase.

The beneficiary has no rights under the annuity contract other than the right to receive payments of the death benefit. He or she cannot change the payment settlement options or alter the starting date of the benefit payments, nor make any withdrawals or partial surrenders against the contract. The owner, under most annuity contracts, has the right to change the beneficiary designation at any time. In a very general sense, the insurance company that issues the annuity contract promises to invest the owner's premium payments responsibly, credit interest to the funds placed in the annuity, and pay the contract death benefit in the event of the death of the owner prior to annuitization of the contract, and make benefit payments according to the contract settlement options selected by the contract owner.

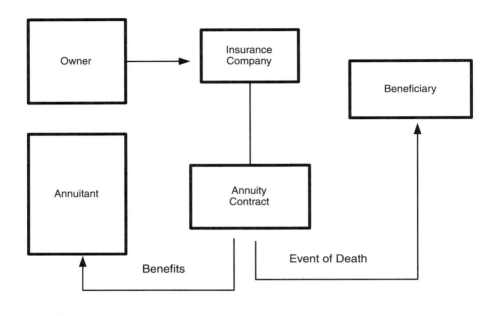

Figure 22.5 The relationship of various parties to the annuity contract.

The Internal Revenue Code requires that all annuities contain certain provisions in order to be eligible for the tax benefits associated with the annuity contract, but there is considerable variation between companies. For example, all companies have a maximum age beyond which they will not issue an annuity contract. If an individual is eighty years old, he or she will not be able to purchase an annuity contract from a company whose maximum age is say, seventy-five.

Financial strength and investment philosophy of the issuing company should be examined. To evaluate the financial strength, you could look at the AM Best companies, Moody's, Standard & Poor's, or Duff and Phelps. The rating services examine the items connected with the insurance company that are important in gauging the effectiveness and probability of the company's likelihood of performing in the future. It includes a list of information evaluating the company's profitability and capitalization and its liquidity. In addition, rating services examine the company's investment strategy and marketing philosophy, as well as its business practices and history.

Other Facts You Should Know

Settlement Options

A settlement option in the annuity contract is the method that the annuity owner can select to receive payments of benefits under the annuity contract. Most annuity contracts allow the settlement option to be changed with proper notice to the insurance company. Although not a complete list, following are the most common settlement options: life annuity, life with period certain guaranteed, refund life annuity, joint survivor annuity, fixed period annuity; and fixed amount annuity.

Maintenance Fees

The annual contract maintenance fee generally ranges from $25 to $40.

Insurance-Related Charges

Many fixed annuity contracts levy a charge against partial or full surrender of the contract for a period of years after the annuity is purchased. This charge is usually referred to as a surrender charge or a deferred sales charge. It can range from 0.5 percent to 1.5 percent per year of average account value. There are also no-load annuities that do not have surrender charges. The surrender charge is usually applicable to surrender made for an annuity for a certain number of years. Typically, a surrender chadrge is a percentage decreasing with each passing year similar to vesting.

For example, a fixed annuity contract might provide the following surrender charges:

> Year 1: surrender/withdrawal charges eight percent
> Year 2: seven percent
> Year 3: six percent
> Year 4: five percent
> Year 5: four percent
> Year 6: three percent
> Year 7: one percent

Loans

Most annuity contracts do *not* offer the option of taking a loan against the annuity value.

Death Benefits

There are certain standard provisions common to most annuity contracts. They require distribution after the death of the owner to be made in a particular manner as requested by the Internal Revenue Code.

If the annuitant dies, the value of the death benefit is the greater of the amount originally invested in the contract or the annuity's account value. The death benefit is guaranteed never to be lower than the total amount invested in the annuity. In this sense, annuities look a bit like life insurance.

Interest Rates

Typically, a fixed annuity contract will offer two interest rates: a guaranteed rate and a current rate.

The guaranteed rate is the minimum rate that will be credited to the funds in the annuity contract regardless of how low the current rate sinks or how poorly the insurance company fares. Typically, the guaranteed rate is three to four percent.

The current interest rate varies with insurance companies. The current rate may be seven percent and its guaranteed rate could be four percent. On the anniversary of the purchase of the annuity, the company notifies the owner of the new current rate. If, for some reason, the interest rate drops below the guaranteed rate, a bailout provision allows the contract holder to fully surrender the annuity contract and not incur any surrender charges under the annuity contract. The name for this is a "bailout provision" or "escape clause."

For example, an annuity offering a bailout clause allows the contract to be surrendered if the current interest rate drops one percent below the interest rate of the previous period. Assuming that the prior interest rates were 6.5 percent, if the current rate for the next period falls below 5.5 percent, the annuity holder could surrender the annuity contract completely and not be subject to any contract charges. The ten percent penalty tax on premature withdrawals may still apply to a surrender under the bailout provision.

Competitive Return

Fixed annuities offer a competitive interest rate because their rate is more closely tied to the medium- or long-term maturities rather than typically lower rates of short-term maturities associated with products like CDs. The current rate, which is actually the annualized rate, is usually guaranteed for one year, although other options may be available. At the end of the guaranteed period of the current or initial rate, the annuity will renew with a new rate that is the best rate the company can offer under the current economic conditions. The minimum guaranteed rate also applies, usually around three to four percent, which is the lowest rate possible regardless of where the current rates are, and that rate is also tax-deferred.

As we have discovered, because annuities have many different features, there are a number of factors to examine. For example, you should ask if there are penalties for early withdrawals. Are there graduated withdrawal charges over a period of years? How much can you withdraw at any one time without a penalty?

In addition, if you are considering the purchase of an annuity, you should ask:

- What is the current interest rate and how often does it change?
- What is the minimum interest rate guaranteed in the contract?
- Is there a "bailout option" that permits you to cash in the annuity, without withdrawal penalties (there may be tax penalties), if the interest rate drops below a specific figure?
- Are there front-end load charges or annual administrative fees? How much are they and how will they affect your return?

What Is a Subaccount?

A subaccount is a term that describes the mutual fund portfolio held inside a variable annuity.

Variable annuities offer anywhere from five to thirty-five subaccount investment options. Mutual fund account managers select individual securities inside the subaccounts; you then select the most appropriate subaccount based on the security selection for your portfolio. If this sounds exactly like a mutual fund, that's because it is. The same, or "clone" as they're commonly called, mutual funds tend to have the same managers inside variable annuity subaccounts, so the same criteria exist for choosing a mutual fund as for choosing a subaccount — and the same benefits also exist, such as professional money management, convenience, economies of scale, and diversification. Subaccount exchanges do not create taxable events and do not entail sales or transfer charges. Most companies do set limits, usually twelve, on the number of annual exchanges before a transfer fee is charged.

The variable annuity, however, gives the added benefit of tax-deferred wealth accumulation. Subaccounts usually include a list of the primary investment objectives, and it's relatively easy to determine what the fees are applied for. It is required for a subaccount to specify the primary group of securities held, and the issuing insurance or mutual fund company.

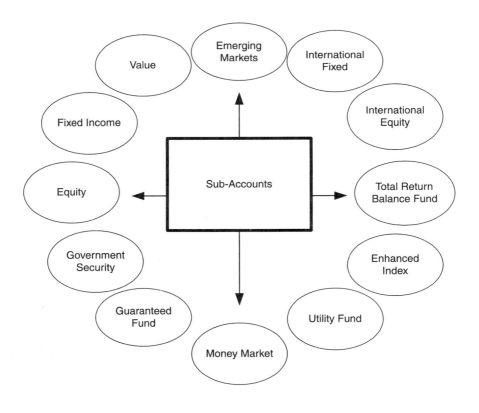

Figure 22.6 Typical variable annuity investment options.

The Investment Flow of a Subaccount

All investment funds flow through the insurance company in the various subaccounts, depending on your choices.

Each subaccount has a specific investment objective. Combined with other subaccounts, this gives you a chance for diversification and the ability to select different portfolios to meet asset allocation and diversification needs. Subaccount managers purchase stocks, bonds, or cash which is valued daily as an accumulation unit.

Accumulation units — shares — are purchased by the contract owner at accumulation unit value (AUV), which is very similar to the mutual fund equivalent known as net asset value (NAV), without commissions, in full and fractional units.

Types of Subaccounts

Subaccounts may be divided into several broad categories: asset classes seeking aggressive growth; asset classes seeking more stable growth; asset classes seeking low volatility utilizing fixed income bonds; a combination; and asset classes featuring money market rates. Inside each of these classes, categories are further broken down.

1. Fixed income accounts are established to decrease risk for those in need of meeting current income requirements. Fixed income subaccounts include government agencies, corporate rate bonds, high yield, foreign government corporate bonds, and certain fixed income choices.
2. Equity or stock investing would be in funds for growth of principal. Since variable annuities are long-term investments, the equity subaccounts will be most important to review.
3. Other asset classes could include cash and cash equivalents, which would be more short-term.

Table 22.1 illustrates the investment options available in a variable annuity offered to consumers through investment advisors. I have illustrated in the last column the type of asset class that is represented. Remember, asset classes are groups of stocks with similar attributes that behave similarly during changing economic conditions.

You still may have questions about subaccounts and mutual funds, how they work, and what makes up a mutual fund. As you read the next section,

Table 22.1 Subaccounts

Portfolio	Objective	Type of Investment	Asset Class Represented
Small cap value	Capital appreciation	Equity securities of small U.S. and foreign companies	U.S. small cap
Enhanced index	Total return modestly in excess of the performance of the S&P 500 Index	Primarily equity investments of large- and medium-sized U.S. companies	U.S. large cap
Domestic blue chip	Primarily long-term growth of capital; secondarily providing income	Common stocks of "blue chip" companies	U.S. large cap
Utility fund	High current income and moderate capital appreciation	Equity and debt securities of utility companies	Energy
Money fund	Current income with stability of principal and liquidity	High-quality money market instruments	Cash
High yield income bond fund	High current income and overall total return	Lower-rated fixed income securities	High yield fixed income
U.S. Government securities	Current income	U.S. Government securities	Short-term fixed income
Emerging markets	Capital appreciation	Equity securities of companies in countries having emerging markets	Emerging markets

Table 22.1 Subaccounts (Continued)

Portfolio	Objective	Type of Investment	Asset Class Represented
Growth equity	Capital appreciation	Primary equity securities of domestic	U.S. large cap
Domestic small cap	Capital appreciation	Primarily common stocks, convertibles and other equity-type securities with emphasis on small company stocks	U.S. small cap
International fund	Capital growth	Primarily equity securities of companies located outside the U.S.	U.S. large cap
Value fund	Primarily long-term capital appreciation; secondarily current income	Equity securities of medium- to large-sized companies, primarily in the U.S.	U.S. large cap value
International small cap	Long-term capital appreciation	Primarily equity securities of small and medium-sized foreign companies	International small cap
International equity	Capital appreciation	Equity securities of non-U.S. companies	International large cap
Small company growth	Capital growth	Equity securities of small-sized U.S. companies	U.S. small cap

think of a subaccount inside the variable annuity and a mutual fund as being the same thing. Although they are kept separate, and the fund within each cannot be commingled, for ease of understanding how these work, we will look at the predecessor to the subaccount, the mutual fund.

How Mutual Funds and Subaccounts Work

The manager of the mutual fund uses the pool of capital to buy a variety of stocks, bonds, or money market instruments based on the advertised financial objectives of the fund. The mutual fund manager uses the investment objectives as a guide when choosing investments. These objectives cover a wide range. Some follow aggressive policies, involving greater risk in search of higher returns. Others seek current income and little risk.

When you purchase mutual fund shares, you pay "net asset value," which is the value of the fund's total investment minus any debt, divided by the number of outstanding shares. For example, if the fund's investment value is $26,000, it has no debt, and there are 1000 shares outstanding, the net asset value (NAV) would be $26 per share. In a regular mutual fund, which includes thousands and often millions of shares, the NAV is calculated on a daily basis, with values moving up or down along with the stock or bond markets. The NAV is not a fixed figure because it must reflect the daily change in the price of the securities in the fund's portfolio. In contrast, a variable annuity issues shares at accumulation unit value (AUV). The only difference between the two is that inside a mutual fund you will sometimes pay higher than the NAV for shares that have front-end commissions and in annuities this is not an option.

Costs

It's simply common sense that lower expenses generally translate into higher overall returns. The goal of the smart investor is to keep his or her acquisition costs as low as possible. There are four basic kinds of costs.

Sales Charges

Sales charges (or loads) are commissions paid on the sale of mutual funds. All commissions used to be simply charged up front, but that's all changed. There are now several ways that mutual fund companies charge fees. This option has no front-end sales charges, but higher internal costs. If you decide to redeem your shares early, usually within the first five years, you pay a surrender charge.

Some sales charges, as in B-shares, are levied on the back end as a contingent deferred sales charge. The load is charged when you redeem shares in the fund. A customer who redeems shares in the first year of ownership would typically pay a five percent sales charge. The amount would drop by an equal amount each year. After six years, the shares would be redeemed without further charge. For large purchases, you should never purchase B-share mutual funds.

Class C shares typically have even higher internal expenses, but pay the selling broker up to one percent per year based on assets. This fee comes directly from your investment performance and is paid to the selling broker. C-shares may have no up-front fee, possibly a one percent deferred sales charge in year one (sometimes longer), and higher annual expenses (up to one percent extra per year).

No-load mutual funds do *not* mean *no cost.* Some no-load funds charge a redemption fee of one to two percent of the net asset value of the shares to cover expenses mainly incurred by advertising. Fee comparisons are particularly important. Every dollar charged comes directly from the performance of the subaccount. Remember to compare the proverbial apples to apples in this case, similar equities to equities subaccounts; and similar bonds to bonds subaccounts.

Operating Expenses

These are fees paid for the operational costs of running a fund. These costs can include employees' salaries, marketing and publicity, servicing the toll-free phone line, printing and mailing published materials, computers for tracking investments and account balances, accounting fees, and so on. A fund's operating expenses are quoted as a percentage of your investment; the percentage represents an annual fee or charge. You can find this number in a fund's prospectus in the fund expenses section, entitled "Total Fund Operating Expenses" or "Other Expenses."

A mutual fund's operating expenses are normally invisible to investors because they're deducted before any return is paid, and they are automatically charged on a daily basis. Beware though, a subaccount can have a very low management fee, but have exorbitant operating expenses. A fund that frequently trades will have more wire charges, for instance, than a fund that does not.

Transaction Charges

This is another term for execution costs. Total transaction costs (or the cost of buying and selling stocks) have three components: (1) the actual dollars paid in commissions, (2) the market impact — i.e., the impact a trade has on the market price for the stock, and (3) the opportunity cost of the return incurred by not executing the trade instantaneously.

For example, when an individual investor places an order to buy 300 shares of a $30 stock (a $9,000 investment), he or she is likely to get a commission bill for about $204, or 2.3 percent of the value of the investment. Even at a discount broker, commissions are likely to cost between $82 (0.9 percent) and $107 (1.2 percent). A mutual fund, on the other hand, is more likely to be buying 30,000 to 300,000 shares at a time! Their commission costs often run in the vicinity of one-tenth of the commission you would pay at a discount broker! Where commission might have been $0.35 a share, the mutual fund could pay only $0.05 a share or even less! The commission savings can (and should) mean higher returns for you as a mutual fund shareholder.

The Twenty Best Variable Annuities on the Market Today

The following variable annuities have no front-end load, below-average costs, a wide selection of mutual fund subaccounts with good performance, and are issued by insurance companies rated A (excellent), B (good), or C (fair) by Weiss Ratings. When selecting individual funds within these annuities, be sure to make comparisons based on the funds' total cost (insurance cost + annual expense).

The Twenty Best Variable Annuities

Name of Variable Annuity Name of Insurer (Phone Number)	Front- end Load	Surrender Charge	No. of Funds	No. of Strong Funds	Weiss Safety Rating
(1) Jack White Value Advantage Plus Fortis Benefits Insurance Co. (800-622-3699)	None	None	24	10	B+

The Twenty Best Variable Annuities (Continued)

Name of Variable Annuity Name of Insurer (Phone Number)	Front-end Load	Surrender Charge	No. of Funds	No. of Strong Funds	Weiss Safety Rating
(2) Vanguard Variable Annuity Plus Providian Life & Health Insurance Co. (800-523-9954)	None	None	9	5	B-
(3) Schwab Variable Annuity Great West Life & Annuity Insurance Co. (800-838-0650)	None	None	20	14	B+
(4) Janus Retirement Advantage VA Western Reserve Life Assurance of Ohio (800-504-4440)	None	None	9	5	B
(5) USAA Life Variable Annuity USAA Life Insurance Co. (800-531-6390)	None	None	7	5	A
(6) Providian Advisor's Edge VA Providian Life & Health Insurance Co. (800-866-6007)	None	None	17	10	B-
(7) Ameritas No-Load VA Ameritas Life Insurance Co. (800-255-9678)	None	None	10	4	A
(8) Touchstone Variable Annuity II Western-Southern Life Assurance Co. (800-669-2796)	None	None	7	5	B+

continued next page

The Twenty Best Variable Annuities (Continued)

Name of Variable Annuity Name of Insurer (Phone Number)	Front-end Load	Surrender Charge	No. of Funds	No. of Strong Funds	Weiss Safety Rating
(9) Pacific Mutual One VA Pacific Life Insurance Co. (800-722-2333)	None	None	13	6	A
(10) Guardian Value Guard II VA Guardian Insurance & Annuity Co. (800-221-3253)	None	0.5%	9	6	A
(11) T. Rowe Price No-Load VA Security Benefit Life Insurance Co. (800-469-6587)	None	None	7	5	C+
(12) Scudder Horizon Plan VA Charter National Life Insurance Co. (800-225-2470)	None	None	7	5	C
(13) Fidelity Retirement Reserves VA Fidelity Investments Life Insurance Co. (800-544-2442)	None	5% declining over 5 yrs	13	8	B
(14) AARP Variable Annuity American Maturity Life Insurance Co. (800-396-5552)	None	Rolling 5% declining over 5 yrs	9	7	B
(15) Ohio National Top Plus B (NQ) Ohio National Life Insurance Co. (800-366-6654)	None	6% declining over 6 yrs	13	6	B

The Twenty Best Variable Annuities (Continued)

Name of Variable Annuity Name of Insurer (Phone Number)	Front-end Load	Surrender Charge	No. of Funds	No. of Strong Funds	Weiss Safety Rating
(16) Best of America IV - Nationwide Nationwide Life Insurance Co. (800-848-6331)	None	Rolling 7% declining over 7 yrs	34	14	B+
(17) Hartford - The Director Hartford Life Insurance Co. (800-862-6668)	None	Rolling 6% declining over 7 yrs	10	6	B+
(18) Mass Mutual Panorama Plus Mass Mutual Life Insurance Co. (800-234-5606)	None	5% declining over 10 yrs	6	3	A-
(19) Security Benefit Variflex LS Security Benefit Life Insurance Co. (800-888-2461 x. 3112)	None	None	11	6	C+
(20) WRL Freedom Bellweth VA Western Reserve Life Assurance of Ohio (800-851-9777)	None	None	16	8	B

Note: In arriving at the above list of "best" variable annuities, mutual fund sub-account performance played an important role in the selection process. After all, a variable annuity can have low costs and a strong Weiss Safety Rating, while at the same time offering only mediocre fund performance. Likewise, when researching other variable annuities, you will want to include in your evaluation the performance of the funds in which you are interested.

Ten Unattractive Variable Annuities on the Market Today

On the whole, the variable annuities offered today are much better than those available only a couple of years ago. Nevertheless, the following variable annuities possessed one or more drawbacks that made them unattractive investment options at the time of this publication.

Ten Unattractive Variable Annuities

Name of Variable Annuity / Name of Insurer	Front-end Load	Surrender Charge	No. of Funds	No. of Strong Funds	Weiss Safety Rating	Primary Drawbacks
(1) PaineWebber Milestones B/D PaineWebber Life Insurance Co.	None	Rolling 5% declining over 5 yrs	9	3	D	High cost and weak rating
(2) American Skandia Advisor's Plan American Skandia Life Assurance	None	Rolling 7.5% declining over 7 yrs	28	18	D+	High cost and weak rating
(3) First Investors VA First Investors Life Insurance Co.	7.0%	None	10	4	C+	High load
(4) Principal Banker's Flex VA Principal Mutual Life Insurance Co.	7.0%	None	1	1	B+	High load and only one fund
(5) John Hancock Accommodator VA John Hancock Mutual Life Ins. Co.	8.0%	None	18	9	A-	High load

Ten Unattractive Variable Annuities (Continued)

Name of Variable Annuity Name of Insurer	Front-end Load	Surrender Charge	No. of Funds	No. of Strong Funds	Weiss Safety Rating	Primary Draw-backs
(6) United Investors Advantage II VA United Life & Annuity Ins. Co.	8.5%	Rolling deferred	11	6	C	High load
(7) Providian Life Prism VA - A units Providian Life & Health Insurance Co.	5.75%	None	6	4	B-	High load
(8) Golden America Fund for Life VA Golden American Life Insurance Co.	1.5%	None	1	1	C+	Load and only one fund
(9) Allmerica Variable Annuity Allmerica Financial Life Ins. & Annuity	None	7% declining over 9 yrs	3	1	C	Only three funds
(10) Farm Bureau Variable Annuity Farm Bureau Life Insurance Co.	None	6% declining over 6 yrs	6	1	A-	Poor per-forming funds

Note: The above list is intended to provide a sample of those variable annuities that contain one of more unattractive features. Exclusion from this list does not mean that a particular variable annuity is a good investment choice. Likewise, some of the insurance companies listed above offer several additional variable annuity policies that may be worthy of consideration.

Weiss Safety Ratings

The Weiss Safety Ratings assigned to the above insurance companies are defined as follows:

A. Excellent. The company offers excellent financial security. It has maintained a conservative stance in its investment strategies, business operations and underwriting commitments. While the financial condition of any company is subject to change, Weiss Ratings believes that the company has the resources necessary to deal with *severe* economic conditions.

B. Good. The company offers good financial security and has the resources to deal with a variety of adverse economic conditions. It comfortably exceeds the minimum levels for all of our rating criteria, and is likely to remain healthy for the near future. However, in the event of a *severe* recession or major financial crisis, Weiss Ratings feels that this assessment should be reviewed to make sure that the firm is still maintaining adequate financial strength.

C. Fair. The company offers fair financial security and is currently stable. But during an economic downturn or other financial pressures, Weiss Ratings feels the company may encounter difficulties in maintaining financial stability.

D. Weak. The company currently demonstrates what Weiss Ratings considers to be significant weaknesses which could negatively impact policyholders. In an unfavorable economic environment, these weaknesses could be magnified.

E. Very Weak. The company currently demonstrates what Weiss Ratings considers to be significant weaknesses and has also failed some of the basic tests that Weiss Ratings uses to identify fiscal stability. Therefore, even in a favorable economic environment, it is Weiss Ratings' opinion that policyholders could incur significant risks.

F. Failed. The company is under the supervision of state insurance commissioners.

+   The plus sign is an indication that with new data, there is a modest possibility that the company could be upgraded.

-   The minus sign is an indication that with new data, there is a modest possibility that the company could be downgraded.

Conclusion

The variable annuity appears to be the answer to the shortfall retirement problems of longer life expectancies and longer retirement periods. Why? Because current trends point to drastic reductions in expected pension benefits, both corporations and government are getting out of the retirement benefits business.

You Should Know

A variable annuity's rate of return is not guaranteed but, rather, is determined by the performance of the investments selected. As the value of the stocks in the portfolio varies, each unit will be worth more or less.

More and more variable annuity companies are offering asset class investing to provide a less volatile investment return. As we have already pointed out, these asset classes tend to smooth out extreme fluctuations; investors won't profit as much from a good year in the market with such an annuity, but neither will they suffer as much loss of income during a bad year.

Any distributions in excess of that ten percent are subject to the surrender charges. No-load variable annuities that do not impose a surrender charge are one hundred percent liquid but, like all annuities, may be subject to a ten percent federal penalty for withdrawal prior to age fifty-nine.

Warning

The higher the overall costs, the longer it takes for the benefit of tax deferral to compensate for those costs. A no sales-load, low-cost variable annuity can help shorten that break-even holding period. In general, variable annuities are designed to be held as long-term investment vehicles, so a break-even of ten to fifteen years may be affordable for those investors with that type of time frame. What does this mean?

History

Prior to the 1997 Taxpayer Relief Act, the break-even point for investors in the twenty-eight percent tax bracket (during both the accumulation and withdrawal phase of a variable annuity) was about twelve years. Today, the break-even period is extended to about eighteen years. (The break-even point means when you are better off in a variable annuity than investing in a mutual fund.) The mainstream media predicted the demise of the variable annuity because it was so long. But I would have to argue that the capital gains tax cuts won't have the effect that the media predicts.

Maximum advantage is centered around your ability to reduce your long-term capital gains tax to twenty percent while extending the maximum holding period to eighteen months.

Tax Changes

The tax changes have created a three-tiered schedule for taxing capital gains. If you hold an investment for less than twelve months and realize a gain when you sell, you will pay tax on the gain at your ordinary income tax rate (which now can be as high as 39.9 percent). If you sell a holding between twelve and eighteen months after buying it, gains will be taxed at the twenty-eight percent long-term capital gains rate. If you sell the holding after eighteen months, your gains will be taxed at twenty percent.

A client in the 39.9 percent tax bracket whose $100,000 investment of taxable dollars returns 10 percent, produces a $10,000 gain.

Gain taxed as ordinary income at 39.9%	$3,990 tax
Gain taxed at 28% capital gains tax rate	$2,800 tax
Gain taxed at 20% capital gains tax rate	$2,000 tax

Investors who realize their gains within the twelve- to eighteen-month window and pay the twenty-eight percent capital gains tax, have a thirty percent savings over the regular income tax rate at which short-term capital gains are taxed. If they hold investments for 18 months or longer, the twenty percent tax rate reduces the amount of federal taxes by almost fifty percent versus ordinary income tax rates.

This savings is predicated solely on not realizing the gain for a minimum of eighteen months. What's not talked about is that most stock market investing is influenced by institutional investors, not taxable investors. Most mutual funds managers employ very active day-to-day short-term trading to maximize total return. This approach will take away any advantage of the new lower capital gains tax rate and still leave their taxable investors exposed to nearly forty percent.

It's human nature. Mutual fund managers are going to try to get the highest returns because their jobs depend on it. They are judged quarter by quarter; not every eighteen months. If they can take a profit short-term, they will — which creates happy institutional investors and ordinary income to taxable investors. The last thing mutual fund managers are concerned about is whether they should hold a security for twelve months or eighteen months. So all cases being equal, we are right back where we started.

So What Do You Do Today?

Say you just received a lump sum of $500,000 and you invested it into a variable annuity and it grows to $1 million, you do not have to cash it all in and pay tax on the $500,000 of growth at one time. If you annuitize, that million dollars will be paid to you in monthly installments from a portion of the original $500,000 and a portion of the $500,000 gain. This means that taxes are paid at a lower rate. What's even better is that you do not have to keep track of when you bought which shares and how long you held them. That's a huge advantage.

What the Experts Say

Jeff Saccacio, partner-in-charge of the West Coast Personal Financial Services Practice for PricewaterhouseCoopers L.L.P., comments: "Assuming tax rates remain the same and that you are invested in an equity income type mutual fund, a large amount of your dividend income will be taxed at ordinary income rates. The alternative is to invest in a variable annuity product, which invests in the same type of mutual fund, but you are taxed later on the distribution."

■ This makes a big difference. If you get taxed now and you are in a high income tax state, you're going to pay anywhere between 46 and 48 cents out of every dollar, which gets taken right off the top before reinvestment. If you invest in a variable annuity product, that 46 to 48 cents doesn't get taken out until the annuity product pays out in the future. So, you get the benefit of compounding on what you otherwise would have paid in tax.

■ You will accumulate more overall, even though you will have to pay tax on the gains in the future. This is a simple present value calculation: that is, the present value of that future accumulation, vs. the present value of your earnings stream if you don't elect to use this deferral type, variable annuity product. The variable annuity works if you do not need access to your money right away, plus you have an emergency cash reserve, and your goal is to accumulate funds for retirement. A variable annuity provides you with a tax shelter on an accumulation basis.

■ If you have maxed out your 401k and you are cut off from contributing to a Roth IRA, you are left with the choice of after-tax contributions to your retirement plan, or after-tax contributions to an IRA, both of which are extremely limited. The logical choice would be to consider a variable annuity product which gives the sheltered growth benefits of a qualified plan.

Survey after survey reveals that building a retirement nest egg is the number one financial concern of most U.S. households. Since most people are concerned about outliving their retirement funds, accumulating money is only one side of the retirement coin. Positioning assets to provide sufficient income during retirement is equally critical.

The Most Overlooked Benefit Is the Death Benefit

No, this is not a sick joke. Obviously, no one can predict if you will die when the market is up or down. But, the *standard* death benefit provided by variable annuities guarantees that if the policyholder dies while still saving for retirement, his or her heirs will receive the greater of either the amount of money invested or the policy's value at the time of death. Many variable annuities go even further and offer *stepped up* benefits that actually lock in investment gains every year.

This means that if an investor buys a variable annuity today with $100,000, but when he dies it's only worth $80,000, the insurance company is obligated to pay the difference of $20,000. A variable annuity is, in effect, insuring the heirs against a market downturn, and you are paying for that benefit.

Should You Buy the Underlying Funds and Pay Taxes?

Whether the break-even point of a mutual fund and a mutual fund inside a variable annuity is five, ten, or eighteen years is virtually irrelevant. What you're interested in is what will save you time and still provide a high probability that you will retire comfortably. After all, you bought the variable annuity in order to accumulate assets *over and above* what you could place in your retirement account.

The primary goal of a retirement plan, of course, is to provide employees with an adequate amount of retirement income. Variable annuities were specifically created to satisfy that goal and are recognized by the IRS as a tax advantaged income vehicle.

What Can You Do to Become Better Informed?

Revisit your recent Monday *Wall Street Journals* and look at the variable annuities listed. Notice the subheadings which indicate names of insurance products and investment subaccounts. Instead of focusing only on past performance or unit price, look at the total expense column (the last column listed). Total expense includes management, operations, and insurance-related expenses. You will see that these costs wander all over the board, as high as 2.79 and as low as .79. Now check the prospectus of the annuity you are considering in order to uncover any up-front costs or surrender charges. Armed with this simple guide, you will be able to increase your returns by lowering your costs. Not all variable annuities are shown in the *Journal*, only ones that have three years of performance numbers are listed.

Best Advice: Cut Costs

There's a common-sense way to shorten that break-even period. Buy no-load or low-cost variable annuities. Obviously, higher fees counter the benefits of tax deferral. But despite their lower costs, no-load variable annuities aren't that popular, commanding only one percent of all variable-annuity assets. Why? Because many investors are willing to pay a load for the extra education and service that comes with the added cost.

Tax deferral offered by a variable annuity works over the long run. Maximize the rate of return of your variable annuity by lowering expenses. These should be held outside the variable annuity. Narrow your search by finding the annuity with the lowest marketing and administrative expenses that allows you to invest in asset classes.

Appendix

Directory of Variable Annuity Products Offered through Investment Advisors

Company	Variable Annuity Products	Primary Markets	Telephone
AAL Capital Management	AAL Variable Annuity	Consumer or Broker NQ, IRA	800-553-6319
Aetna Life Ins. & Annuity Co.	Aetna Marathon Plus Growth Plus Multi Vest Plan Variable Annuity Account C Variable Annuity Account D3	Consumer or Broker NQ, IRA, 401(k), TSA	800-367-7732
Aegon Financial Services Group – PL & H	Advisor's Edge Dimensional Marquee	Investment Advisor	800-797-9177
AIG Life Insurance Co.	AIG Life Insurance Variable Acct. I Alliance Gallery I Variable Annuity II	Consumer or Broker NQ, IRA	800-862-3984
Alexander Hamilton Life	Allegiance Variable Annuity	Consumer or Broker NQ, IRA	800-289-1776
Allianz Life Insurance Co.	Franklin Valuemark II	Consumer or Broker NQ, IRA	800-342-3863
Allmerica Financial Life	Allmerica Select Resource Allmerica Medallion Execannuity Plus Separate Account (A,B,C,G,H)	Consumer or Broker NQ, IRA, 401(k), TSA	800-669-7353

Directory of Variable Annuity Products Offered through Investment Advisors (Continued)

Company	Variable Annuity Products	Primary Markets	Telephone
American Enterprise Life	AE Personal Portfolio	Consumer or Broker NQ, IRA	800-333-3437
American General Life	Separate Account D Variety Plus	Consumer or Broker NQ, IRA	800-247-6584
American International Life	Variable Account A	Consumer or Broker	800-362-7500
American Life Insurance Co. of NY	American Separate Acct. No. 2	Consumer or Broker NQ, IRA	800-872-5963
American Partners Life Insurance	Privileged Assets Select Annuity	Consumer or Broker NQ, IRA	800-297-8800
American Republic Insurance Co.	Paine Webber Advantage Annuity	Consumer or Broker NQ, IRA	800-367-6058
American Skandia Life Assurance	Advisors Choice Advisor Design Advisors Plan Alliance Capital Navigator Galaxy Variable Annuity The Lifevest Select Stagecoach	Consumer or Broker NQ, IRA, 401(k)	800-704-6201
American United Life Insurance	AUL American Unit Trust	Consumer or Broker NQ, IRA	800-634-1629
Ameritas Variable Life Ins.	Overture Annuity II Overture Annuity III Plus	Consumer or Broker NQ, IRA	800-634-8353

continued next page

Directory of Variable Annuity Products Offered through Investment Advisors (Continued)

Company	Variable Annuity Products	Primary Markets	Telephone
Anchor National Life Insurance	American Pathway II ICAP II Polaris	Consumer or Broker NQ, IRA	800-445-7861
Annuity Investors Life Ins.	Commodore Mariner Commodore Nauticus VA Commodore Americus	Consumer or Broker NQ, IRA	800-789-6771
Banker Security Life Ins.	Centennial (P) Centennial (Q) The USA Plan (P) The USA Plan (Q)	Consumer or Broker NQ, IRA	
Canada Life Ins. of America	Trillium Varifund Annuity	Consumer or Broker NQ, IRA	800-905-1959
Century Life of America	Members Variable Life	Consumer or Broker NQ, IRA	
Charter National Life	Scudder Horizon Plan	Consumer or Broker NQ, IRA	800-225-2470
CNA	Capital Select Variable Annuity Capital Select Equity Index Annuity	Consumer or Broker NQ, IRA	800-262-1755
Conn. General Life Ins. CIGNA	CIGNA ACCRU Variable Annuity	Consumer or Broker NQ, IRA	800-628-2811
COVA Financial Services Life	COVA Variable Annuity	Consumer or Broker NQ, IRA	800-343-8496
Dreyfus	Dreyfus/Trans- america Triple Advantage	Consumer or Broker NQ, IRA, 401(k)	800-258-4260

Directory of Variable Annuity Products Offered through Investment Advisors (Continued)

Company	Variable Annuity Products	Primary Markets	Telephone
Equitable Life Assurance Soc.	Accumulator Equi-Vest Equi-Vest Personal Ret Program Income Manager Accumulator Income Manager Rollover Momentum Momentum Plus Rollover IRA	Consumer or Broker NQ, IRA, 401(k), TSA	800-628-6673
Equitable Life of Iowa	Equi-Select	Consumer or Broker NQ, IRA, TSA	800-344-6864
The Hartford	The Director The Director I Dean Witter Select Dimensions	Consumer or Broker NQ, IRA 401(k)	800-862-6668
IDS	Flexible Portfolio Annuity IDS Life Flexible Annuity Symphony	Consumer or Broker NQ, IRA	800-437-0602
Farm Bureau Life Ins. Co.	Farm Bureau Life VA	Consumer or Broker NQ, IRA	800-247-4170
Fidelity Inv. Life Ins. Co.	Fidelity Retirement Reserves	Consumer or Broker NQ, IRA	800-544-2442
Fidelity Standard Life	Fidelity Standard Life Separate Acct.	Consumer or Broker NQ, IRA	800-283-4536

continued next page

Directory of Variable Annuity Products Offered through Investment Advisors (Continued)

Company	Variable Annuity Products	Primary Markets	Telephone
First Allmerica Fin Life	Allmerica Select (NY) Delaware Medallion (NY) Execannuity Plus (NY)	Consumer or Broker NQ, IRA	
First Investors Life Ins.	Execannuity Plus (NY)	Consumer or Broker NQ, IRA	800-832-7783
1st Providian Life & Health	Vanguard Variable Annuity Plan (NY)	Consumer or Broker NQ, IRA	800-523-9954
First Sunamerican Life	First SunAmerica ICAP II (NY) First SunAmerica Polaris	Consumer or Broker NQ, IRA	800-996-9786
First Transamerica Life	Dryfus/Transamerica Triple Advantage	Consumer or Broker NQ, IRA	800-258-4260
First Variable Life Ins. Co.	Vista Annuity/ Capital Five VA Capital No Load Annuity	Consumer or Broker NQ, IRA	800-228-1035
Fortis Benefits Ins. Co.	Fortis Masters VA Fortis Opportunity VA Fortis Value Advantage Plus VA Fortis Benefits Ins. Co.	Consumer or Broker NQ, IRA	800-800-2638

Directory of Variable Annuity Products Offered through Investment Advisors (Continued)

Company	Variable Annuity Products	Primary Markets	Telephone
General American Life	G.T. Global Allocator General American Step Acct. Two	Consumer or Broker NQ, IRA, TSA	800-233-6699
Glenbrook Life & Annuity	AIM Lifetime Plus VA STI Classic VA	Consumer or Broker NQ, IRA	800-776-6978
Golden American Life Ins.	Fund For Life Golden Select (2D) Golden Select DVA Plus	Consumer or Broker NQ, IRA	800-243-3706
Great American RSV Insurance	Great American RSV VA Acct. C Great American RSV VAE	Consumer or Broker NQ, IRA	317-571-3700
Great Northern Ins. Annuity Corp.	Paragon Power Portfolio VA	Consumer or Broker NQ, IRA	800-455-0870
Great West Life & Annuity	Future Funds Series Account Maximum Value Plan (MVP)	Consumer or Broker NQ, IRA	800-468-8661
Guardian Ins. & Annuity	Guardian Investor Value Guard II	Consumer or Broker NQ, IRA	800-221-3253
Integrity Life Insurance Co.	Grandmaster II Pinnacle	Consumer or Broker NQ, IRA, TSA	800-325-8583
ARM Financial Group	OMNI New Momentum		
John Hancock	Accumulator Accommodator 2000 Independence Independence Preferred Declaration	Consumer or Broker NQ, IRA	800-732-5543

continued next page

Directory of Variable Annuity Products Offered through Investment Advisors (Continued)

Company	Variable Annuity Products	Primary Markets	Telephone
Jackson National Life	JNL Perspective	Consumer or Broker NQ, IRA	800-873-5654
Jefferson-Pilot Life	Alpha Alpha Flex Jefferson-Pilot Separate Acct. A	Consumer or Broker NQ, IRA	910-691-3448
Kemper Investors	Kemper Advantage III Kemper Passport	Consumer or Broker NQ, IRA	800-554-5426
Keyport Life Insurance	Keyport Preferred Advisor Preferred Advisor	Consumer or Broker NQ, IRA	800-367-3654
Life Insurance Co. of Virginia	Common-wealth Variable Annuity Plus	Consumer or Broker NQ, IRA	800-352-9910
Lincoln Benefit Life	Investors Select Investors Select Variable Annuity	Consumer or Broker NQ, IRA	800-865-5237
Lincoln National Life	American Legacy American Legacy II American Funds	Consumer or Broker NQ, IRA, 401(k), TSA	800-443-8137
Lutheran Brotherhood	LN Variable Annuity Multifund	Consumer or Broker NQ, IRA, 401(k), TSA	800-421-9900
	LB VIP Variable Annuity	Consumer or Broker NQ, IRA	800-423-7056
Manufacturers Life	Lifetrust 1 Lifestyle Fixed	Consumer or Broker NQ, IRA	800-827-4546

Directory of Variable Annuity Products Offered through Investment Advisors (Continued)

Company	Variable Annuity Products	Primary Markets	Telephone
MFS Sun Life of Canada	MFS Regatta Gold MFS Regatta Compass-3	Consumer or Broker NQ, IRA, 401(k)	800-752-7216
MassMutual	Flex Extra Flex Extra (2) Lifetrust Panorama Panorama Plus Panorama Premier	Consumer or Broker NQ, IRA, 401(k), TSA	413-788-8411
MBL Life Assurance Corp	Dreyfus Series 2000 Dreyfus Series 2000 (2) Mutual Benefit VAC Acct.-2 Mutual Benefit VAC Acct.-3 Seligman Mutual Benefit Plan	Consumer or Broker NQ, IRA	
Merrill Lynch Life Ins. Co.	Portfolio Plus Retirement Plus (A) Retirement Plus (B)	Consumer or Broker NQ, IRA	800-535-5549
MetLife	The Preference Plus Account	Consumer or Broker NQ, IRA	800-553-4459
Midland National Life	Separate Account C	Consumer or Broker NQ, IRA	800-638-5000
Minnesota Mutual Life	Megannuity Multioption Flexible Annuity	Consumer or Broker NQ, IRA	800-443-3677
MML Bay State Life Ins.	Lifetrust 1	Consumer or Broker NQ, IRA	800-272-2216

continued next page

Directory of Variable Annuity Products Offered through Investment Advisors (Continued)

Company	Variable Annuity Products	Primary Markets	Telephone
Monarch Life Insurance Company	Milestone	Consumer or Broker NQ, IRA	
Mony Life Ins. Co. of America	Keynote Moneymaster Valuemaster	Consumer or Broker NQ, IRA	800-487-6669
Mutual of America Life	Mutual of America Separate Acct. 2	Consumer or Broker NQ, IRA	800-463-3785
National Integrity Life	Grandmaster (NI) Grandmaster II (NI) Pinnacle	Consumer or Broker NQ, IRA, 401(k), TSA	800-433-1778
Nationwide	Best of Americas Vision Best of America III Best of America IV DCVA DCVA - TSA Fidelity Advisor Classic Fidelity Advisor Annuity Select MFS Spectrum Multi-Flex Nationwide Variable Account 3 NEA Valuebuilder Annuity Nationwide Life & Annuity VA (A) One Investors Annuity	Consumer or Broker NQ, IRA, 401(k), TSA	888-867-5175

Directory of Variable Annuity Products Offered through Investment Advisors (Continued)

Company	Variable Annuity Products	Primary Markets	Telephone
New York Life	Facilitator (I) Facilitator (II) Lifestages NYLIAC VA I NYLIAC VA II (Qualified)	Consumer or Broker NQ, IRA, 401(k)	212-576-6569
New England Mutual Life	Zenith Accumulator	Consumer or Broker NQ, IRA, 401(k), TSA	
North American Security Life	Venture Venture Vision	Consumer or Broker NQ, IRA	800-334-4437
Northbrook Life Ins. Co.	Dean Witter Variable Annuity	Consumer or Broker NQ, IRA	800-654-2397
Northern Life	Northern Life Advantage	Consumer or Broker NQ, IRA, TSA	800-870-0453
Northwestern Mutual Life	NML Variable Annuity Acct. C	Consumer or Broker NQ, IRA	
Northwestern National Life	Northstar NWNL Variable Annuity Select Annuity II Select Annuity III	Consumer or Broker NQ, IRA	800-621-3750
Ohio National Life Insurance Co.	Top A (A) Top A (B) Top Plus (B)	Consumer or Broker NQ, IRA	800-366-6654
Pacific Corinthian Life	Pacific Corinthian Variable Annuity	Consumer or Broker NQ, IRA	619-452-9060

continued next page

Directory of Variable Annuity Products Offered through Investment Advisors (Continued)

Company	Variable Annuity Products	Primary Markets	Telephone
Pacific Mutual Life	Pacific Select Variable Annuity Pacific Select Variable Annuity One Pacific Portfolios	Consumer or Broker NQ, IRA	800-722-2333
Paine Webber Life Insurance	Paine Webber Milestones B Paine Webber Milestones D	Consumer or Broker NQ, IRA	800-552-5622
Penn Insurance & Annuity	Pennant	Consumer or Broker NQ, IRA	800-548-1119
Penn Mutual Life Insurance	Diversifier II	Consumer or Broker NQ, IRA	800-548-1119
PFL Life Insurance	Endeavor Variable Annuity Fidelity Income Plus	Consumer or Broker NQ, IRA	800-525-6205
Phoenix Home Mutual	Big Edge Big Edge Choice Big Edge Plus Templeton Investment Plus	Consumer or Broker NQ, IRA	800-243-4361
Principal Mutual Life Insurance	Pension Builder Plus Principal Variable Annuity	Consumer or Broker NQ, IRA	800-986-3343
Protective Life Insurance Co.	Protective Variable Annuity	Consumer or Broker NQ, IRA	800-456-6330

Directory of Variable Annuity Products Offered through Investment Advisors (Continued)

Company	Variable Annuity Products	Primary Markets	Telephone
Provident Mutual Life & Annuity	Market Street VIP Market Street VIP (2) Options VIP	Consumer or Broker NQ, IRA	610-407-1717
Providian Life & Health	Marquee Variable Annuity Providian Prism The Advisors Edge	Consumer or Broker NQ, IRA	800-866-6007
Pruco Insurance Co. of NJ	Discovery Select Discovery Plus (NJ)	Consumer or Broker NQ, IRA, 401(k)	201-802-6000
Prudential Insurance Co.	Variable Investment Plan Discovery Plus Discovery Select	Consumer or Broker NQ, IRA, 401(k)	800-445-4571
Putman	Capital Manager	Consumer or Broker NQ, IRA	800-225-1581
SAFECO Life Insurance Co.	Spinnaker Q & NQ Flex Spinnaker Plus Mainsail SAFECO Resource Acct. A SAFECO Resource Acct. B	Consumer or Broker NQ, IRA, 401(k), TSA	800-426-6730
Schwab	Schwab Variable Annuity	Consumer or Broker NQ, IRA	800-838-0650

continued next page

Directory of Variable Annuity Products Offered through Investment Advisors (Continued)

Company	Variable Annuity Products	Primary Markets	Telephone
Security Benefit Life	Parkstone Variable Annuity SBL Variable Annuity Acct. III SBL Variable Annuity Acct. IV Variflex LS Variflex T. Rowe Price Variable Annuity	Consumer or Broker NQ, IRA, 401(k), TSA	800-888-2461 800-541-8803
Security First Life Ins.	Flexible Bonus Investors Choice Strive	Consumer or Broker NQ, IRA	800-284-4536
Security Life of Denver	Exchequer Variable Annuity	Consumer or Broker NQ, IRA	800-933-5858
Sun Life Assurance of Canada	MFS Regatta Gold MFS Regatta Compass 3 Compass 2	Consumer or Broker NQ, IRA	800-752-7216
TIAA	College Retirement Equities Fund	Consumer or Broker NQ, IRA, TSA	800-842-2776
Templeton	Templeton Imm. Variable Annuity	Consumer or Broker NQ, IRA	800-292-9293
Touchstone	Touchstone Variable Annuity Touchstone Variable Annuity II	Consumer or Broker NQ, IRA, 401(k)	800-669-2796

Directory of Variable Annuity Products Offered through Investment Advisors (Continued)

Company	Variable Annuity Products	Primary Markets	Telephone
Transamerica Occidental Life Ins. Co.	Schwab Investment Advantage Dryfus/Trans- amer Triple Advantage	Consumer or Broker NQ, IRA	800-258-4260
Travelers	Universal Annuity Vintage Portfolio Architect	Consumer or Broker NQ, IRA, 401(k), TSA	800-334-4298
Union Central Life Insurance	Carillon Account	Consumer or Broker NQ, IRA	800-825-1551
United Companies Life Insurance	Spectraselect	Consumer or Broker NQ, IRA	800-825-7568
United Investors Life	Advantage II	Consumer or Broker NQ, IRA	800-999-0317
United of Omaha Life Ins. Co.	Ultrannuity Series V	Consumer or Broker NQ, IRA	800-453-4933
USAA Life Insurance Co.	USAA Life Variable Annuity	Consumer or Broker NQ, IRA	800-531-6390
Vanguard (Providian Life & Health)	Vanguard Variable Annuity	Consumer or Broker NQ, IRA	800-522-5555
Variable Annuity Life Ins.	Portfolio Directory 2 Independence Plus Portfolio Director Portfolio Director 2	Consumer or Broker NQ, IRA	800-228-2542

continued next page

Directory of Variable Annuity Products Offered through Investment Advisors (Continued)

Company	Variable Annuity Products	Primary Markets	Telephone
Western Reserve Life	Janus Retirement Advantage WRL Freedom Attainer WRL Freedom Bellwether WRL Freedom Conqueror C.A.S.E Reserve Variable annuity Meridian/INVES CO Sector VA	Consumer or Broker NQ, IRA, 401(k), TSA	800-443-9974 ext. 6510

23 Social In-Security

Social Security cannot continue to exist in its present form. So what's new? Neither can Medicare, Medicaid, or Welfare.

Our generation has literally been cast adrift in an economic and financial ocean. While there are tools available to help people meet their long-term investment objectives, most Americans don't know how to use those tools. Unfortunately, this suggests that even though most Americans are trying desperately to meet their objectives, they won't be able to do so. By first understanding how the economic system works and the tools available, you will be able to fashion a financial plan to achieve your goals. But before you can even begin to set out on the voyage, you've really got to understand the boat.

Social Security can be likened to a giant pension fund that we all pay into. Theoretically, the assets taken in will grow to fund the liabilities that the fund will have down the road when you retire. However, Social Security was not originally set up to be a retirement plan. It was meant to be a safety net, a last resort.

Social Security originated in 1936 during the depression years. Working people would pay a small portion of their wages into the social security system with the idea that the current working population would support the retirees of that time. So money went in and right back out again. It worked because in 1937, the first full year of operation, there were 33 workers for every one retiree. The annual contribution of a working person was only $30.00, so the system was workable. The problem is that, given the demographics of the following years including the slowing down of the birth rate and the fact that wages grew more slowly, strains on the system started to build.

In 1960, there were 15 workers for every one person retired. It's estimated that in the year 2029, there will be two and a half workers for every one person retired. You can see that something has to give.

But there is some good news!

Before you buy an expensive insurance policy, remember to check into your Social Security benefits. Obtain estimates of your future benefits based on what you have been credited for and what you will be credited for by the time you reach retirement age.

We don't want to debate whether Social Security will be here or not. We could have the same debate about your insurance company. What we discovered was that if one of us was to die today each of his or her children and spouse would get almost $900 a month; and if one of us were to become disabled, he or she would get over $800 a month. When we figured the cost of how much insurance it would take to duplicate those benefits, Social Security looks very good. A policy that would give you a $2,100 monthly death benefit for your family would cost you a small fortune.

The point is that you may not even need expensive life insurance — and you don't even know it. You can take the money you would save and invest it in a mutual fund instead of contributing it to an insurance company's coffers. Table 23.1 shows how Social Security benefits are calculated.

You can send the form shown as Figure 23.1 to your nearest Social Security Office or to:

Social Security Administration
Wilkes-Barre Data Operations Center
P.O. Box 20
Wilkes-Barre, PA 18711-2030
Or Social Security HCDP://www.ssa.gov

The next Section is called "House Cleaning." It covers all the other little things you need to do to put your investment plan in place, including a chapter on "Do-it-Yourself Online." We'll discuss other types of nonliquid assets, plus the crucial qualifications you should look for in a financial advisor or broker.

There's also a chapter in this section for those of you who still want to buy an individual stock from time to time, on how to analyze an investment and how to read a boring prospectus. Finally, we pull it all together with a "Quick Start Plan" to get you going safe and smart, plus an investment calendar with important dates and a schedule to keep you on track. This last section will help make investing much less mysterious — and even user friendly.

Table 23.1 How Social Security Income Builds

Your Age in 1988		Annual Social Security Benefit, Based on Earning in 1987 of:				
		$20,000	$25,000	$30,000	$35,000	$45,000
25	Individual	11,796	13,548	14,568	15,600	17,652
	Couple	17,688	20,316	21,852	23,400	26,472
35	Individual	10,896	12,540	13,476	14,436	16,296
	Couple	16,344	18,804	20,208	21,648	24,444
45	Individual	9,972	11,496	12,360	13,104	14,412
	Couple	14,952	17,244	18,540	19,656	21,612
55	Individual	9,048	10,344	10,920	11,352	12,036
	Couple	13,572	15,516	16,380	17,028	18,048
65	Individual	8,100	9,216	9,564	9,792	10,056
	Couple	12,144	13,824	14,340	14,688	15,084

Note: These figures represent the approximate yearly income from Social Security benefits for a single person and, on the following line, for a nonworking spouse of the same age, when they become eligible for full Social Security benefits at age 65 to 67. All of the amounts in the table are Social Security Administration projections in 1988 dollars, based on continuous employment throughout an adult lifetime.

Request for earnings and benefit estimate statement

1. Name shown on your Social Security card:

First	Middle Initial	Last

2. Your Social Security number as shown on your card:

|__|__|__| - |__|__| - |__|__|__|__|

3. Your date of birth:

_____
     Month   Day   Year

4. Other Social Security numbers you have used:

|__|__| - |__|__| - |__|__|__|__|

|__|__| |__|__| |__|__|__|__|

5. Your Sex: ☐ Male ☐ Female

6. Other names you have used (including a maiden name):

First	Middle Initial	Last

7. Show your actual earnings for last year and your estimated earnings for this year. Include only wages and/or net self-employment income covered by Social Security.

8.

    A. Last year's actual earnings:
        $ |__|__|__| |__|__|__| |__|__|
        Dollars only

    B. This year's estimated earnings:
        $ |__|__|__| |__|__|__| |__|__|
        Dollars only

8. Show the age at which you plan to retire:

|__|__|__|

(Show only one age)

9. Below, show the average yearly amount that you think you will earn between now and when you plan to retire. Your estimate of future earnings will be added to those earnings already on our records to give you the best possible estimate.

Enter a yearly average, not your total future lifetime earnings. Only show earnings covered by Social Security. Do not add cost-of-living, performance or scheduled pay increases or bonuses. The reason for this is that we estimate retirement benefits in today's dollars, but adjust them to account for average wage growth in the national economy.

However, if you expect to earn significantly more or less in the future due to promotions, job changes, part-time work, or an absence from the work force, enter the amount in today's dollars that most closely reflects your future average yearly earnings.

Most people should enter the same amount that they are earning now (the amount shown in 7B).

Your future average yearly earnings:

$ |___|___|___| , |___|___|___| . |___|___|
Dollars only

10. Address where you want us to send the statement:

Name
_____

Street Address (Include apt. No., P.O. Box, or Rural Route)
_____

City   State   Zip Code
_____

I am asking for information about my own Social Security record or the record of a person I am authorized to represent. I understand that if I deliberately request information under false pretenses I may be guilty of a federal crime and could be fined and/or imprisoned. I authorize you to send the statement of earnings and benefit estimates to the person named in item 10 through a contractor.

_____
Please sign your name (Do not print)

_____   _____
Date   (Area Code) Daytime Telephone No.

ABOUT THE PRIVACY ACT
Social Security is allowed to collect the facts on this form under Section 205 of the Social Security Act. We need them to quickly identify our record and prepare the earnings statement you asked us for. Giving us these facts is voluntary. However, without them we may not be able to give you an earnings and benefit estimate statement. Neither the Social Security Administration nor its contractor will use the information for any other purpose.

Figure 23.1 Request for earning and benefit estimate statement.

SUMMARY

Contents

24 Do it Yourself — Online

W arning! While the Internet offers tremendous opportunities, it also is a spawning ground for investment fraud. Just apply what you have learned about investing and always ask, "Why am I getting such a great deal?"

If you do find you've been duped, the net makes it easier to go for help. Investors can e-mail complaints to the Office of Investor Education and Assistance at (Help@sec.gov). Complaints and inquiries numbered 600 during the second half of 1996, then ballooned to 5,000 inquiries in 1997. Total complaints and questions through all media for 1996 totaled over 44,000, according to the Commission's 1996 annual report. The office evaluates the complaints and if there is fraud, they refer it to the Division of Enforcement, which can be reached at (enforment@sec.gov). There is also the National Fraud Information Center (www.fraud.org).

Financial Planning on the Internet

Think of the Web as a gigantic computerized *Yellow Pages* with colorful graphics and links that, at the click of a mouse, let you connect with websites containing related information. You'd have to go to the library and search through dozens of books and periodicals to get the same information.

Back to the Last Phases of Our Simple Plan

Louis Schiff, founder, and Doug Gerlach, senior editor, of the Armchair Millionaire website were asked to help after you've set the book down. Louis Schiff is an advocate of a methodology called "common sense saving and investing" and he has a great website. He also understands asset class investing.

They have a five-step plan to financial freedom. Their website will teach you great savings methods in the first four steps. The fifth step is when you begin to implement the plan. They recommend a basket of index funds, tell you how to approach a broker, fill out applications, and answer confusing and intimidating questions that are more designed for the broker than the investor — they've got a whole community of regular people who have already gone through it.

They will help define common sense saving and investing. Investing experience is not unlike other consumer experiences. When you buy a television, you compare remote controls, prices, and features and choose the one that fits your bill, whereas, in investing, people seem to choose investments with their eyes closed and then cross their fingers. That doesn't have to be the case. You can actually make consumer-style investment decisions based on a fair comparison of features.

Each of the five steps is very understandable. But if you don't understand it, don't do it. Every component of the plan is useful in and of itself. It's not like the whole plan hangs together or falls apart. Probably the one most crucial component you will learn about is the power of compounding. Other than that, each piece can be considered on its own merit.

One of the qualities that makes their website different from others is that its main function is financial planning. When they do deal with the process of investing, they put a strong focus on the planning part. What stocks, mutual funds, or bonds do you actually buy? It's the fifth step, but not the only step. There are important things you can do before you actually make the decision about what you're buying.

Even if you simply choose a product like fixed income CDs or a savings account, steps one through four, which are savings techniques, are so powerful that you will really be far ahead of the game. If you only follow steps one to four, you'll start saving regularly and putting money away for the long term. Then, when you are ready for step five — to invest in the stock market — you're there.

If you just follow their advice and use index funds, seven out of ten times you'll make the right decision. Being in the market as a whole is a very valuable place to be. Virtually everything you do in investing involves looking at history and then projecting to the future.

Schiff and Gerlach also follow the rules of diversification, which makes an index fund choice so appropriate. When you diversify, you're essentially spreading risk, and that definitely can kill some of that exciting individual stock buzz — the American dream of picking the next Microsoft, IBM, or Yahoo. There are great stories about people who invested in IBM, Sears & Roebuck, or Coca Cola fifty years ago. But that's not too far off from betting on the lottery. You're just hoping that a lot of things that are statistically against you are going your way.

They are launching a model portfolio as we are writing this book. It will be one-third S&P 500, which represents seventy percent of the publicly traded stock market, one-third in the Russell 2000, taking advantage of the phenomenon of the small company (which is that small companies gain faster than the average large cap), and one-third in the Morgan Stanley EFA, Europe-Australia-Far East fund. They're making a bet there that the blue chip stocks around the globe have value and are strategically important and are growing. Historically, when it comes to diversification, that pays off. Investing in the large caps in America, especially the biggest, is practically like investing in a mutual fund.

Through their website, they're trying to get more people to understand investing is a psychological process. Why should anyone listen to these guys? The answer is, there is a certain amount of strength in numbers when it comes to investing. When people see other people doing it, they feel as if there must be some legitimacy to the style or the idea. You can actually see and meet the people who are doing it. You can talk to them. In particular, you can see how they're applying it in their own personal way. They address more lifestyle-oriented goals: sending kids to college and saving for retirement. And you can do this in the comfort of your own home.

The user becomes a member of the Armchair Millionaire Investor Club. An investing club is a great idea and people who join clubs are having a great time. There are many people who don't have time to go to meetings, even once a month. They bring you together for chats and message boards, special guests, special features, new tools, or special deals they've arranged with the sponsors. Anything they think will help you better apply common sense saving investment methodology. It takes 45 minutes to go through it once and get a sense of it and it doesn't cost anything.

They have a message board called "There's no Such Thing as a Dumb Question." Why? Because everyone was a beginner when they started investing. And they know that you are going to have questions. They answer lots of questions on the site in the articles that are published and on the five steps.

The Web is seeing an explosion of women's participation online; even a simple question has no gender associated with it, and the answers are given with respect and thoughtfulness. They don't know whether a person is tall, short, fat, skinny, male, or female. There is no race, color, creed, or religion. Armchair Millionaire is a website, but the Web is the best place to be.

The theories you will learn at the site are not new. Even before the Web, Compuserve users were practicing this in a small, significant way. It's powerful. Historians may look back on this time period and say, "Something about investing changed in the middle of the 1990s." It has a lot to do with technology, the Web, and the sharing of information.

It's an environment in which people are trying all sorts of things and learning so much so fast. This coincides with the rise of 401(k) programs in America and the sunset of the pension program and lifetime employment idea. It's a powerful movement taking place that has absolutely required that investors take on the responsibility and education themselves.

Due Diligence

The way to do your due diligence is to educate yourself. Once you open an account with a brokerage firm, you can use the Internet for trading as well as research. After you log on with your account number, the online brokerage firm will give you a password. You can check your investments and you can create a watch list of investments of your own. Investing online is covered by the same rules as regular investing. After you have opened an account, it's easy to bring up your portfolio online. It takes a matter of seconds to value your holdings. You could customize the look of your portfolio and you could even have a message alert you when there's a news flash on one of your holdings.

Self-directed investors or delegators will appreciate being able to view several different brokerage firms or mutual fund families on the same screen. In less than five minutes, someone can see how all their investments are doing.

On the Web, you are free to try many different suppliers, programs, services, and brokers. And you are free to change your mind. It's a new world; one in which public retailing, free trials, and competition among various investment software products and services will inevitably bring down prices.

Beware: there is a lot of free stuff for investors on the Internet. Some of it is wonderful, but you are probably not going to strike it rich just by picking up a hot stock tip from a newsgroup or downloading some minimalist investment free-ware.

Online Trading

Online trading has exploded over the past year as investors are becoming more self-sufficient and comfortable using their computers for investing. That's great for all the technically inclined folks, but is it right for you? It's great to be able to access your account information at a moment's notice. We like the idea of using an online brokerage account, but we also realize that some people prefer to deal with a real person when they are placing trades.

When shopping around for an online discount broker, you should ask plenty of questions about its customer service department. Sure, online brokerage accounts are becoming easier to use and are providing more and more information, but you need to know how you can access your account information if you can't get online for some reason and need to make a transaction. Will a "live" broker be accessible to you if you need to place a trade?

If you're comfortable with your computer and you don't really need to hear that voice on the other end of the phone, we recommend that you go with a discount broker and trade online.

Online Offerings

Wirehouses are beginning to offer online trading in order to retain clients.

It should come as little surprise that in this era of do-it-yourself investing, Internet-based trading firms are flourishing. This new breed of brokerage, having grown from a mere handful a few years back to more than seventy brokerage firms today, has been luring a growing number of investors by drastically slashing the commissions that clients pay to make transactions.

Last year, the number of Americans investing over the Internet grew 120 percent to 3.3 million, according to Credit Suisse First Boston. Online transactions grew 181 percent to 26 million.

The real challenge that full-service firms face is how to offer online service to clients at competitive prices. The average full-service commission for purchasing 3,000 shares at $10 is $672.59 — more than four times the average discount brokerage commission of $145.05 on the same trade, according to Credit Suisse First Boston. Full-service firms can't offer $10 trades over the Internet, because their cost structure isn't set up to do that. They have to offer the convenience of online trading without creating internal warfare.

Despite these wirehouses' ventures into Internet trading, many analysts say their actions serve defensive purposes only. Major firms are not seeking to grab a share of the online firms' clients, analysts say, but are simply trying to keep their own clients.

Most of the people attracted to deep-discount trading left full-service brokerage firms a long time ago.

Here's a round-up of what's being offered in online trading at full-service brokerages.

PaineWebber

PaineWebber is beginning a pilot test later this year, and is planning to offer online trading to all of its clients shortly thereafter. The service will be offered in a fee-based structure, most likely through PaineWebber's wrap account, called Premier Asset Account. Fees for trading are based on a client's assets under management.

Merrill Lynch

Merrill Lynch is offering online trading as part of the Merrill Lynch Online account. Still, Merrill has repeatedly stated that it will not discount commissions, and that online trading will be part of an account whereby a customer must still utilize a broker. In fact, according to a company spokesperson, online transactions will be paid on the same grid and in the same manner as regular trades. As with other innovations in the brokerage industry, many of the brokerage firms are closely watching the reaction of Merrill brokers and clients to the new service, analysts say.

Salomon Smith Barney

Salomon Smith Barney offers online trading through Salomon Smith Barney Access, as well as charts, news, and commentary from analysts online.

Prudential Securities

Prudential Securities is currently beta-testing its new online trading service, called PruTrade, with approximately 200 investors. A company spokesperson says the firm is still looking at various price models. Prudential plans to offer the service fully to clients some time later this year.

Morgan Stanley Dean Witter

Although MSDW offers discount online trading through its newly acquired Discover Brokerage Direct (formerly Lombard Brokerage), online trading is not available to Dean Witter retail clients. Insiders say the firm purchased the discounter to attract do-it-yourselfers not interested in full-service brokerage.

Brokers say that MSDW is planning to offer clients online trading eventually, but that the service is a long way off.

Active Online Websites

- Schwab — www.schwab.com (With over $160 billion in assets, they are by far the leader online in discount trading.)
- DLJ Direct — www.dljdirect.com
- Web Street Securities — www.webstreetsecurities.com
- E*Trade — www.etrade.com
- Waterhouse — www.waterhouse.com
- Quick & Reilly — www.quick-reilly.com

Online Danger

There are ads all over the Internet where you can buy all the shares of stock you want for six bucks. Most people don't keep their finances in perspective. They point, click, and sell; point, click, and buy and try to trade on short-term profits — and we know that ninety percent of the people who do that are going to lose. But that is what is advertised: the perception that through trading, an investor makes big profits. How many trades do people make in a year on average? I've probably purchased two different classes in the last twelve months. The last time I sold anything was probably ten years ago.

What you can do on the Internet, definitely and decisively, is immerse yourself in the established subculture of computerized investing. You can learn what's available before purchasing packaged software or subscriptions and see which techniques and services can help you win at your chosen game. Here are some good places to start:

> THE ARMCHAIR MILLIONAIRE — http://armchairmillion-aire.com. Offers a five-step plan: pay yourself first; dollar-cost averaging; compound interest; pay lower taxes; and build your plan.

BETTERINVESTING — www.betterinvesting.org/clubs/13.html. For those of you who want to hear and share in other investors' experiences.

BLOOMBERG — www.bloomberg.com. For news and updated market information.

EDGAR — http://www.sec.gov/edaux/current.html. The Securities and Exchange Commission owns the largest of all financial databases, including all companies reporting to the SEC. Here you can pick up and read all filings (of quarterly earnings, for example) made by companies within, say, the preceding two days. It's especially helpful for locating current balance sheets. Online earnings releases often exclude this information. Data you may download from popular sources aren't as fresh.

INVESTOGUIDE — www.investoguide.com. It is a massive site with free e-mail and newsletters.

INVESTORAMA — www.investorama.com. A description of thousands of links to investor sites.

INVESTOOLS — http://www.investools.com. This site is a free-sample heaven. It's great for reading investment resources like investment newsletters, opinion pieces, helpful lists of money managers and advisers, and books and periodicals. Read a back issue or free-sample newsletter before deciding to subscribe.

LOMBARD INSTITUTIONAL BROKERAGE — http://www.lombard.com. Without even opening an account, you can freely sample the range of services available on line for this brokerage's customers. They are very good indeed and include delayed quotes and charts. Account holders can get real-time quotes, see displays of their portfolios and transactions and, of course, place trades. At this site, you can chart 7,000 stocks and 61,000 options, free of charge. The charts are excellent, although they are screen displays only. Nevertheless, it is an outstanding facility and, no doubt, option traders camp out at Lombard's website. It is currently one in the top five percent of the most-visited Internet sites.

THE MOTLEY FOOL — http://fool.web.aol.com/fool_mn.htm. Go straight to a feature called the Fool Portfolio. This thing returned sixty-eight percent in 1995, putting it ahead of most mutual funds in the top ten. This site is essentially an advertisement for the immensely popular Motley Fool service on America Online. But the underlying philosophy is rock solid and deeply conservative in tone. Fools or not, this is a good place to look for information on high-yielding Dow stocks.

PAWWS FINANCIAL NETWORK — http://www.pawws.com This is a no-nonsense site with a sampling of many different useful commercial services. We liked the realistic and matter-of-fact tone of the site, which is essentially a multipage catalog. It covers a wide spectrum and will give you a good idea of the services available on the Web. PAWWS provides access to three affiliate brokers: National Discount Brokers (NDB), Jack White & Co., and the Net Investor. Each offers special incentives to online traders. NDB will trade any Nasdaq stock for a flat fee of just $20. Jack White offers a ten percent discount. The Net Investor features a free package of online news, research, and analysis worth $50 per month.

SILICON INVESTOR — http://www.techstocks.com. This is a big, well-focused site that concentrates on digital, electronics and communications technology. It has detailed data on nearly 250 stocks and maintains indices on four of the technology groups: communications, software, computers and peripherals, and semiconductors. The service has quick-look fact sheets on individual stocks, newsgroups, detailed data, quotes, and charts. You can compare a stock's performance with that of its group, find out what other investors are thinking about it, and check the company's own news and news releases. Silicon Investor is a good place to learn what the day's big moves have been.

TIPNET — http://www.telescan.com/home.htm. This is a sampler of the full-blown financial software and services supermarket available via the Telescan Investor's Platform, or TIP. It presents, in one place, the technical screening, portfolio, and quotes-retrieval software regarded by computerized investors as essential tools. TIPnet also provides direct access to important services like Zacks and Standard & Poor's MarketScope.

ZACKS INVESTMENT RESEARCH — http://aw.zacks.com. Probably the most powerful force driving the price of high-visibility stocks is this: the revisions in earnings estimates issued by the 2,500 analysts working at 210 brokerage firms. One could earnestly argue that earnings, not estimates, move stock prices. But the estimates are the earliest news the market gets, and wow, does it ever react to this news!

Please note: For security-sensitive investment services, like stock trading through a broker and personal-portfolio displays over the Internet, you should use "secure aware" software. This security requirement is met only by Netscape.

Let Your Computer Be Your Broker

Charles Schwab sells company reports for as little as $3. Services also give you an up-to-date picture of your holdings — some in so-called "real time" so you can find the last bid price on your Intel stock — and others are updated a few times a day.

Still, no hacker can transfer assets out of your account — additional, offline security procedures prevent it.

Like full-service brokerage houses, the online trading companies carry SIPC (Securities Investor Protection Corporation) coverage, which will replace up to $500,000 in losses — including up to $100,000 cash — if the brokerage goes bankrupt.

Pay a visit to the Gómez Advisors website (www.gomezadvisors.com). This Boston firm ranks online trading services according to cost, ease of use, customer confidence, on-site resources (quotes, news, advice, recommendations and screening tools). Gómez also scores the firms according to their appropriateness for four kinds of investors: life goal planner, serious investor, hyperactive trader, and one-stop shopper. From the Gómez site, you can visit other sites.

Financial Management Software

Financial management software can help you get organized while letting you indulge your passion for computing. Microsoft, Intuit, and Meca Software, the companies that make the most popular financial planning programs, are all offering brand-new editions. They automatically update your portfolio, balance your checkbook and will sort your spending into categories.

Microsoft Money '98 Financial Suite ($29.95; $54.95 for the deluxe version) includes a goal planner that allows you to monitor your progress toward long-term goals — say, retirement in Provence. You can also use the program to connect to the Microsoft Investor website.

Intuit's Quicken ($39.95 basic; $59.95 deluxe; and $89.95 for Suite '98, a program that includes a special retirement planner) gives you a jazzier version of the goal planner. It automatically calculates how quickly your savings program will get you to Provence. The Deluxe version lets you connect to Quicken's website (www.quicken.com).

Financial Planning

> Deloitte & Touche (www.dtonline.com), the accounting firm, provides financial planning and retirement advice.
>
> Fidelity Investments (www.fidelity.com) recommends Fidelity products to use for a variety of financial problems.
>
> FinanCenter/Smartcalc (www.financenter.com) will calculate your car and mortgage payments and show you how much you need to save in order to retire.
>
> Intuit (www.intuit.com) offers samples of its financial management software programs Quicken and TurboTax.

Investing

Among general information sites providing research, tips, and market updates, a few of our favorites are:

> Morningstar, Inc. (www.morningstar.net), the Chicago mutual funds research company, offers one of the most useful sites on the Web, including exhaustive information on more than 6,500 individual mutual funds as well as financial news and columns.
>
> The Motley Fool (www.motleyfool.com) offers irreverent investing advice and comment, along with lively lunchtime and evening news updates on the state of the financial markets.
>
> The Street.com (www.thestreet.com) provides quirky commentary on stocks, interest rates, and the economy. After a two-week free trial, subscriptions cost $9.95 a month for access to the website and a daily morning bulletin.
>
> IBC Financial Data (www.ibcdata.com) lists money market funds and bond funds with data on their historic performance.
>
> Invest-o-rama (www.investorama.com), from the National Association of Investment Clubs, provides links to more than 2,000 investment-related sites and offers analysts' consensus reports on thousands

of individuals stocks, as well as tips on how to set up and run an investment club.

Microsoft Investor (www.investor.msn.com) contains data on thousands of individual stocks and mutual funds and makes recommendations. Subscriptions are $9.95 a month.

Mutual funds Interactive (www.fundsintractive.com) offers news and views about mutual funds.

Nest Egg (www.nestegg.com), sponsored by Investment Dealer's Digest, provides news on mutual funds and stocks and can help you calculate your ideal rate of retirement saving.

William F. Sharpe (www.sharpe.stanford.edu), the Stanford University finance professor, is online offering insights on foreign and domestic markets.

Zacks Investment Research (www.zacks.com) provides a database of 5,000 companies and a screen for variables including price earnings ratios, projected profits, dividends and capitalization. Subscription is $150 a year.

Tax Help

The two most popular tax-software offerings are *TurboTax* and its Macintosh cousin, *MacinTax* by Intuit, and Kiplinger Tax Cut by Block Financial Software. In addition to their other features, both allow you to transfer data from other financial management software into relevant tax deduction or expense categories.

TurboTax ($35; $50 for the deluxe version) takes you through an interview process that includes a "refund monitor" that automatically changes your bottom line every time you make an entry. You don't have to look at intimidating forms because the program enters the data in the proper categories and does the calculations for you. After the interview, TurboTax checks for omissions and flags deductions that you may have forgotten. You can see for yourself whether you've gone overboard in making claims. When it finishes, it pumps out tax forms — or submits them electronically to the IRS.

Kiplinger Tax Cut ($20; $25 for a state version) does everything TurboTax does and also displays lines of the tax form as you answer its questions. TurboTax prints or files the forms electronically.

Summary

There are currently over two hundred mutual fund sites on the World Wide Web; and because this is an advantage for mutual fund companies, it's growing rapidly. The web offers cost savings in the distribution of information and the handling of transactions. For the first time investor, the web offers convenient up-to-the-minute information and account security. Just keep in mind that the fund families with the highest level of assets under management compose the bulk of websites.

25   **Your Investment Plan**

Before you consider hiring someone to assist you, take some time and write out an investment plan. It will enable you to clearly communicate your long-term financial goals and objectives, and will serve as a guideline to help implement the investment strategy. An advisor will call this an investment policy statement, but it's the same thing.

This plan will give you a way of evaluating how you and your advisor are doing. You need a way to assess if you are on track with your investments. It also protects you from seat-of-the-pants revisions to an otherwise sound investment plan. This document will help you create a set of expectations. You can compare this to a business plan. Very few successful businesses have started and succeeded without one.

Having and using this in written form compels you to become more disciplined and systematic, increasing the probability of success.

There are six steps to writing your own Investment Plan.

1. Set long-term financial goals and objectives. Long-term goals can be anything from early retirement to purchasing a new home. One of the most common goals I see is to be financial independent. What that often means to most first time investors is that their investment portfolio will provide them with the income necessary to maintain their quality of life. This is just as important for those who are still working as those already retired.

    Your goals: _____

    _____

2. Establish your expected time horizon. You have to determine your investment period. The minimum expected investment period must be at least five years for any portfolio containing equity securities. For any portfolio with less than a five-year time horizon, your portfolio should be in a core savings or comprised predominantly of fixed investments. This five-year minimum investment period is critical. The investment process must be viewed as a long-term plan for achieving the desired results. One-year volatility can be significant for many equity asset classes, as seen in the appendix. However, over a five-year period, the range of returns is greatly reduced.

   Your time period: _____

3. Determine the rate of return objective. In getting started, you should write down a range of returns that would be acceptable. In John Bowen's *The Prudent Investor's Guide To Beating The Market* the author has identified the specific return risk profiles of each optimized model portfolio. We have reproduced these in Table 25.1. You can use these ranges of returns for each risk level as the framework to determine your return expectation for your portfolio as well as the component asset classes. The range should be consistent with the weighted average expected rate of return of your portfolio asset classes over the last twenty years. Don't just look at the last five years. That is likely to be an unusual period. You also want to examine some difficult market periods like the 1973 to 1974 time frame to see if you can stay the course.

   Your return expectation: _____

4. Define the level of risk you are willing to accept. Along the road to reaching your financial goals, there are going to be bumps caused by the downturn in various markets. It is important for you to understand the amount of risk you are willing to tolerate during the investment period. In designing a portfolio, you must determine the absolute loss you are willing to accept in any one-year period without terminating the investment program.

   The level of risk you are willing to accept (standard deviation):

   _____

Table 25.1 Expected Returns Standard Deviation

Asset Class	Expected Return (%)	Standard Deviation (%)
Money Market	4.90	3.30
Fixed Income	6.70	3.90
U.S. Large	13.60	20.30
U.S. Small	19.40	38.50
International Large	13.60	20.30
International Small	19.40	38.50
Emerging Markets	16.00	29.00

5. Select the asset classes to be utilized to build your prospect's portfolio. In Part III, you will find the list of all the different asset classes that you might want to consider in your portfolio.

   Asset Classes: _____

   _____

   _____

6. Rebalancing. A financial advisor can help you create a measuring benchmark to review investment portfolio performance. If goals and objectives have been clearly defined, it becomes much easier to determine how the portfolio is performing relative to these goals and objectives.

You should familiarize your investment advisor with this plan and see if this is something they can assist you in implementing. The written plan will enable you to better define your investment expectations and put you in a position to decide how best to implement an asset class portfolio.

Are you a trustee of a retirement plan? This investment plan can assist you. If you have no interest in this, skip to the next section.

If you are trustee and subject to the following guidelines, the written investment policy statement creates a road map for plan fiduciaries to meet the legal requirements of the "prudent-investor" rules. The written plan also provides standards against which the trustee can be judged. The written investment policy statement must be clear and specific enough to be a working document. Broad-based generalities will not serve as investment objectives. Being specific is the key to providing a proper working investment plan.

The American Law Institute, Restatement of The Law Third, Prudent Investor Rules, instructs trustees and courts that:

1. Sound diversification is fundamental to risk management and is therefore ordinarily required of trustees.
2. Risk and returns are so directly related that trustees have a duty to analyze and make conscious decisions concerning the level of risk appropriate to the purposes, requirements, and circumstances of the trust.
3. Trustees have a duty to avoid fees, transaction costs, and other expenses that are not justified by needs and realistic objectives of the trust's investment program.
4. Fiduciary duty of impartiality requires a balancing of elements of return between current income and the protection of purchasing power.
5. Trustees may have the duty as well as the authority to delegate as prudent investors would.

If you represent a corporate pension plan or other plan governed by the Employee Retirement and Income Securities Act (ERISA), you must diversify your plan's assets unless it is clearly prudent not to do so. The Department of Labor states that a fiduciary can be held personally liable for breach of violation of these responsibilities, even to the extent of having to restore lost profits to the plan. ERISA was enacted to protect the interests of participants in employee benefit plans from abuses and discriminatory practices.

The scope and complexity of ERISA has led to a widespread lack of understanding of its basic principles and a commensurate lack of understanding of liabilities that trustees may be subject to. Compliance with the ERISA rules has been a major concern of trustees and plan sponsors since this landmark legislation was passed in 1974. These rules, governed by the Department of Labor (DOL), impose heavy responsibilities on any persons involved in the management of employee benefit plans.

ERISA provides a federal standard of conduct to be followed and observed concerning the management of retirement fund assets. A fiduciary not acting in accordance with the precepts of ERISA can not only be subjected to personal liability, but could subject the plan under management to loss of its tax-free status.

ERISA outlines the following broad areas which set the standards of fiduciary conduct in administering a plan. In essence, anyone who exercises any authority over management, administration, or disposition of assets, or renders advice, will be held as a fiduciary.*

The scope of fiduciary responsibility is actually much wider than is generally recognized because the definition of "fiduciary" is so broad. A trustee not only has a duty to become familiar with and to follow standards set in ERISA, but also to seek outside assistance when appropriate. To be considered a fiduciary, one must have an element of authority or control over the plan, including plan management, administration, or disposition of assets. Obviously, trustees, plan officers, and plan directors fall under this definition, but so do persons who are delegated duties by named fiduciaries. "Named" fiduciaries are those listed in the plan documents as having responsibility for plan management. Others, such as corporate officers, directors, and shareholders, may also exert enough control to be deemed fiduciaries. To the extent that plan sponsors, consultants, and/or advisors influence or maintain discretionary authority over plan management or investments, they are also fiduciaries.

It is important to note that if trustees or named fiduciaries properly select and appoint a qualified money manager, they will not have a co-fiduciary responsibility for acts and omissions of the adviser, unless they knowingly participate in or try to conceal any such acts or omissions.

The fiduciary's duties must be discharged solely in the interest of plan participants and their beneficiaries. The Prudent Expert Rule defines the standard of competence to which a fiduciary will be held responsible with respect to plan investment decisions. ERISA states that a fiduciary must discharge his duties "with the care, skill, prudence and diligence under the circumstances then prevailing that a prudent person acting in a like capacity and familiar with such matters would use in the conduct of an enterprise of a like character with like aims." In other words, fiduciaries may be held to the same level of skill as that of a professional money manager in making investment decisions. It is important to remember that pension dollars belong to employees and beneficiaries, not the sponsoring company. Hence, ERISA may hold fiduciaries to as high a standard as that of a professional investment expert.

Penalties may be imposed for up to six years after the fiduciary violation, or three years after the party bringing suit had knowledge of the breach. A willful violation carries personal criminal penalties of up to $5,000 ($100,000 for corporations) and up to one year in prison.

---

* Section 404(a)(1)(b) of the Internal Revenue Code.

Civil actions can be initiated by plan participants, beneficiaries, other fiduciaries, and the Department of Labor. Losses to the plan as well as profits made from the improper use of plan assets must be restored to the plan. Failure to disclose information to plan participants can result in a daily penalty of $100. The Department of Labor can also remove the fiduciary and take control over plan assets.

It is critical to bear in mind that the fiduciary's responsibilities are ongoing, and liability may exist even when professional advisors are hired and subsequently breach their fiduciary duties or fail to meet plan goals. In other words, delegation alone will not protect a fiduciary; a system of delegation and oversight will. The process of monitoring should mirror the plan's funding and investment objectives.

26 How to Analyze an Investment — What to Watch Out For!

The fastest way to lose your money is to follow a trend. We have said throughout this book that you can't beat the stock market by buying and selling hot stock picks. While you shouldn't be discouraged from buying and holding an individual stock long term, especially in the company you work for, your core investment strategy shouldn't include the growth of that stock. You might invest in an individual company, hold it for years and the company could go bankrupt. No one can predict the future, but if you built your core investment program with asset class mutual funds, your program would still be in place.

One of our associates once placed a huge order of an individual stock. It was General Electric, 55,000 shares and it amounted to over $3,000,000. The stock was part of an estate left to a university. What was amazing was the person who left it was not from a rich family or the head of a company, but a secretary to a bank president. Years ago, her employer gave her shares of Utah Construction Company as part of her bonus and told her to hold onto it. She kept accumulating the shares and the stock split over 1,200 times before General Electric bought the company.

There are three basic concepts that Wall Street uses to analyze an investment — technical, fundamental, and trend analysis.

Technical analysis is essentially the making and interpreting of stock charts. The people who swear by technical analysis are often referred to as "technicians" or "chartists." The chartists believe that the market is only ten percent logical and 90 percent psychological, so the charts are like a crystal ball to them. But ninety percent of Wall Street security analysts consider themselves fundamental.

Technicians deal with charts, and patterns from the past. They analyze current price movements and chart patterns, then relate them to price movements and patterns from the past. By applying mathematical charting methods from the past to the present, they draw conclusions about future buying and selling. The problem with technical analysis is that it ignores the all-important cultural factors. If human activities really could be reduced to mathematical patterns, we'd be writing a book about technical analysis. But of course, they can't, so we aren't.

Fundamental analysis looks at all the known facts about a particular investment, including external factors that technical analysis often overlooks. These external factors include cultural and political trends, general investment areas and industry groups, the future of inflation and interest rates, and investment cycles. Internal factors include earnings-per-share, the track record of management, the price/earnings ratio, any new technical breakthroughs, cost of production, valuable contracts, and worker morale.

Here are the basic points of fundamental analysis:

1. Management. One of the key factors is the ability and integrity of a company's management. In the preceding chapter, we suggested that you get in touch with the people whom the managers have supplied as references.
   a. Do the managers own stock in the company they are managing — and how much? If they don't invest in their own offering, you'd be foolish to do so. (Be wary of "dilution." You can find information about dilution in the prospectus under the heading, "Dilution." If you find dilution, it might be wise to investigate further. Dilution is not evidence of fraud or wrong-doing, but it is a red flag. A high degree of dilution is almost always a bad sign.)
   b. Compare management compensation to similar companies. Some American managers tend to be grossly overpaid in comparison to their foreign counterparts.
   c. Experience. In general, you should look for management with at least ten years experience in the business.
2. Size. Look at the size of the company. This appears in the balance sheet. The smaller the size, the more risk involved.
3. Good balance sheet. Look at the company's debt. This is also in the balance sheet. Preferred stocks and debentures — "senior" securities

— are just another form of debt, so be on the lookout for them. In the 1980s, with seemingly unlimited credit available, many companies were restructured. Some of these companies, with their attendant heavy debt loads, will be at a competitive disadvantage against high-quality growth companies carrying relatively light debt. Those companies with sizable debt service obligations will be focused on short-term cash flow (profits, rather than market share gain). A focus on short-term cash flow can be inimical to strategic planning.

4. Dominance. Look for companies with limited competition.
5. Return on equity. The return on equity tells an investor how efficiently his money is being used. A minimum of fifteen percent is recommended.
6. Reasonable price/earnings ratio. The higher the P/E ratio, the higher the risk. We recommend companies with a P/E ratio at, or below, the current market multiple. A good benchmark is the S&P 500, which carries a P/E of 13 times.
7. Simplified annual report. The simpler the better, no CPA gobbledy-gook.

The Stock Market

Okay, if you still insist on wanting something to watch, here's an indicator we pay attention to.

In trying to guess what the stock market's going to do, most investors don't look past short-term indicators. But as you've been reading, consistent results come from a long-term holding strategy. So what can you watch that may indicate the future of the stock market? Well, nothing gives you a better long-term indicator of economic health than the relationship of a country's spending patterns to its deficit.

The national deficit is one of the least understood economic concepts, yet it's one of the best indicators of long-term economic health. You may be wondering, *who owns the national debt?* The media has led many to believe the Japanese do. *Wrong!* According to Dr. Bob Goodman, Ph.D., senior economic advisor for Putnam Investments, over eight percent of the total outstanding national debt is owned by Americans in the form of bonds. Americans consider the bonds they buy as assets, not liabilities — and eighty percent of the interest on the national debt goes right back to Americans as income upon which they pay taxes.

Next concern: the size of the deficit. It's not so much the actual size of the debt that is critical, but rather whether our economy is growing faster than the debt is accumulating. That's what you want to focus on. Think in terms of your own income. As long as your income is growing faster, relative to your debt, you're going to come out ahead even if your debt grows.

The total government debt just after World War II, 60 years ago, was around $120 billion, while our annual gross domestic product (GDP) was $100 billion. Our government, therefore, owed 1.2 years' worth of GDP. Today our debt is $5 trillion, 40 times higher than after WWII, but our GDP is now over $7 trillion, so the national debt represents only 70 percent of the GDP. That's only 70 percent of a year's income vs. 120 percent back in 1946. It's important to watch where the ratios are and if they're going down — which they have been.

Today our government is taking in more than it's spending. Recently the Congressional Budget Office estimated that the total federal budget surplus should amount to around $1.55 trillion over the next decade. That's how much more the government expects to take in from taxes than what it expects to spend on government services. That's an annual surplus of over 60 billion dollars. While that money may burn a hole in the government's pocket, one way or another, it's a good long-term indicator to watch.

The general trend in the stock market for the past 60 years has been up. At times during that upward march there will be downturns — and that's inevitable and normal. A 200 point drop on the Dow today at 9000 is a drop less than two percent, and that shouldn't scare anyone into selling funds. Instead of panicking when the stock market drops, you should hold on for the long term. Take advantage of the dips by adding to your holdings.

For more information, read John Maynard Keynes' 1936 book, *The General Theory of Employment, Interest and Money.*

27 Other Types of Asset

We're not suggesting these for the first time investor, but you should know what they are and how they work.

What are *hard assets*? Hard assets are sold as defensive type investments and would do best during bear markets or during times of high inflation, neither of which we are in. They are also not liquid, which means you may have a hard time getting your money out if you needed it.

All tangibles are inflation hedges. Their value tends to flourish during times of soaring inflation and volatile interest rates languish when the economy is stable. Owners can make money on their investments only when they sell, with some exceptions in real estate. Investors should plan to hold their assets for the long term, sometimes as long as ten to twenty years. However, to compensate for their lack of liquidity, tangibles appreciate tax free during the years you hold them.

Each tangible investment offers some advantages and disadvantages. Real estate can be good for the investor who wants to build personal financial security while curbing the tax bite, or for the investor who has little or no capital and who is seeking a tax-deductible shelter for other income.

Real Estate

During the 1970s, when inflation was rampaging in a way the U.S. had never before experienced, real estate investment became the darling of investors and speculators alike. Interest rates lagged behind the inflationary upticks, mortgage money was available, and repayment could be made in ever-cheaper dollars. In fact, tax savings subsidized out-of-pocket costs.

Euphoric investors caught the scent of fast profits and snapped up properties regardless of costs, and often regardless of quality. The prevailing wisdom dictated that inflation would inevitably push prices higher, and another investor would willingly pay an even fatter price later on. This delivered nice capital gains to countless sellers. In those glorious days, everyone investing in real estate became an instant financial genius.

Of course, the bubble burst, as it always does. The real estate frenzy slowed to a crawl in the early 1980s, as inflation fell. Prices remained high, but there were precious few buyers.

Real Estate Syndication

On the surface, real estate syndication looks like an ideal vehicle for those who'd like to join the parade but don't care for hands-on exposure. Such deals *need* inflationary pressures to boost profits at resale. Many never pan out.

The syndicator generally assumes the role of "general partner," meaning he or she manages the properties, collects rent, and eventually sells them. Theoretically, the general partner's risk is unlimited, but the general partner usually puts no cash into the project and receives an acquisition fee, often a management fee, a share of the cash flow from the properties, and a share of any capital gains realized at sale.

Real Estate Investment Trusts

Real estate investment trusts (REITs) are like a mutual fund of real estate investments. A typical REIT invests in different types of property, such as shopping centers, apartments, and other rental buildings.

REITs are a specialized form of equity that allows investors to own a portion of a group of real estate properties, although most investors think of them as an alternative to bonds. REITs have become increasingly popular over the past decade. Granted special tax status by the Internal Revenue Service, REITs pay out at least ninety-five percent of their earnings in the form of dividends to shareholders, often offering healthy dividend yields of the same magnitude as bonds. Even better, as REITs acquire more property and increase the value of the properties they own, the value of the equity increases as well, providing a nice total return.

REITs trade as securities on the major stock exchanges. You can research and purchase individual REITs. Even better is to buy a mutual fund that invests in a diversified mixture of REITs. Some real estate writers have criticized REITs. REITs are a good alternative for people who want to invest in real estate without all the hassles and headaches that come with directly owning and managing rental property. You can easily buy REITs in a retirement account investment (you can't do so with rental properties). For more information on REITs, check the website of the National Association of REITS (NAREIT).

Futures

Most futures transactions involve exchange of contracts on goods not yet produced. Originally, all commodities were agricultural products. Today, they include currencies, petroleum, metals, cotton, and lumber.

Stock Derivatives: Options and Futures

Options and futures are "derivative" securities, meaning their value is "derived" from that of another security or commodity. Options and futures both are very risky because they often carry an incredible amount of leverage. For instance, each options contract on an individual stock controls one hundred shares of that stock for a fraction of the stock's current value. This can make for huge upward moves, but this is offset by the risk of losing one hundred percent of the money put into the option. If an investor owns an option and the underlying stock is not within the given price range within the given time period, the option expires worthless.

Collectibles, Art, and Antiques

Art, antiques and collectibles constitute a rather difficult sector of the investment world, because of the lack of liquidity and the subjective nature of this type of investment.

Investment Gemstones

To look at a gem is to know its worth. For centuries, people have understood that the beauty and rarity that separate precious stones from mere rocks also make them real stores of value. Boasting a track record of appreciation that spans all of recorded history, gems have been a "given," set against the variable of myriad failed get-rich-quick investment vehicles.

Investment-grade gemstones may be diamonds, other precious stones, such as emeralds or rubies, or semiprecious stones, perhaps topaz or tourmaline. These stones will always have some intrinsic worth, but that does not mean that the changing demands of the marketplace will not influence their price. The markets for both diamonds and colored stones can and do fluctuate dramatically, following swings in the overall economy and the weighting of supply and demand. Like most tangibles, gems tend to flourish during periods of soaring inflation and volatile interest rates, and languish in stability.

The effects of this kind of speculative fever took center stage during the last bout with inflation during the late 1970s and early 1980s. Investors scurrying to find investments capable of retaining their worth sent the price of a one-carat flawless diamond from $20,000 in 1979 to more than $60,000 by 1980. By 1981, when inflation began to cool, the same stone commanded only $16,000. The 16.9 percent compounded annual rate of return generated by diamonds during the high-flying inflationary years from 1976 to 1980 plummeted to zero during the disinflation of 1982 to 1984.

These blips in the performance of gems cannot detract from their long-term potential — and that is what the investor must keep in view. For example, even with these sharp declines, certain diamonds enjoyed a price increase of 1,100 percent from 1970 to 1983, while rubies rose 650 percent during the same period and blue sapphires advanced 300 percent.

By definition, a mineral must posses beauty, rarity, durability, and be in demand in order to be considered a gem. While rarity and durability are fairly easy to determine, judgments about beauty and demand are much more arbitrary. Discovery of new gem deposits also influences the market. As a result, gems are subject to fads, and tend to rise and fall according to the current vogue.

Diamonds account for about eighty percent of all gemstones sold today. For that reason, they remain the blue chip investment among precious stones. The problem again is there is no efficient market for diamonds. Warning! This whole area requires a lot of study and should be at the top of your investment pyramid.

Suggested Reading

- *Gemstone Investing Fact Sheet*, Federal Trade Commission (free), Room 130, Sixth Street and Pennsylvania, N.W., Washington, D.C., 20580.

- *How to Buy and Sell Gems,* by Benjamin Zucker, Times Books, 3 Park Avenue, New York, NY 10016. (This book is available in most libraries, but is now out of print.)
- *Colored Stone Aesthetics,* by John Rouse, Ge-Odyssey Gem Publications, 7271 Garden Grove Boulevard, Garden Grove, CA 92641.
- *The Gemstone Identifier,* by Walter Greenbaum, Acro Publishing, 215 Park Avenue South, New York, NY 10003.

Numismatic Coins

These are defensive instruments.

Tangibles have risks, as do all investments. The main point to remember about tangible investments is that they are risky and may not be a wise choice for the first time investor.

28 | How to Read a Prospectus

A jargon-filled mutual fund prospectus may not be enthralling, but it's a must-read for would-be first time investors. It describes investment objectives, strategies, and risks, and it's required by the federal government as a protection for investors. Any misstatements or omissions can lead to stiff penalties, hence the tendency for legalese.

Start by identifying the type of asset class mutual fund you are interested in and request a prospectus by calling or writing the fund, or asking a broker or financial planner. When you get it, check the date to make sure it is current — such documents must be updated at least once a year.

Here's what to look for in a mutual fund prospectus:

Minimums — If the minimum amount required to open an account is too high for you, read no further.

Investment objective — At the core of the prospectus is a description of the fund's investments and the portfolio manager's philosophy. The objective should outline what types of securities the fund buys and the policies regarding the quality of those investments. If the fund has more than twenty-five percent of its assets in one industry or holds bonds rated below investment quality, these policies must be included in the prospectus. A global equity fund, for example, earns a high level of total return through investments in world capital markets. A typical balanced fund strives to obtain income equally with capital growth, whereas the investment objective of a long-term municipal bond fund is to preserve capital by seeking a high level of interest income exempt from federal income tax.

Performance — This bottom-line information on how funds have fared over the last decade shows you what you would have earned in per-share dividends and capital gains distributions, and any increase or decrease in the value of that share during the year. The portfolio turnover rate reveals how actively the fund trades securities. The higher the turnover, the greater the fund's brokerage costs.

Risk — Different investors can tolerate different risk levels. In this section of the prospectus, the fund should describe the potential for risk. For instance, a fund that invests in only one portion of the economy may offer greater risk than a highly diversified fund, while a fund that invests in well-established companies may be less risky than one that favors start-up companies. Other risks are associated with certain types of funds or securities. Bond funds are susceptible to interest rate changes, while fixed-income savings and investment vehicles are subject to inflation risks.

Fees — Management and accounting fees and the cost of printing and mailing reports to shareholders are internal charges that should be evaluated. Generally, a company that keeps its expenses — excluding sales fees — at one percent or less of its assets is considered a low-cost fund. A fund whose expenses are above 1.5 percent of its assets is viewed as high-cost. Fees are required to be summarized in a table in the front of the prospectus. Other charges to consider are minimum fees for subsequent investments or fees for switching from one fund to another in the same family.

Management — When you're putting money in a mutual fund, you're paying for professional management. Consider the fund's managers to evaluate investment philosophy and to find out whether the portfolio is managed by an individual or committee.

Services — This section will tell you if features such as check-writing or automatic investing are available.

Buying or selling shares — Information detailing how to get in and out of a fund and whether there's a charge for redeeming shares.

Additional information, such as securities in the fund's portfolio at the end of its fiscal year, is included in a Statement of Additional Information, also called Part B of the prospectus. Funds must provide this information free on request.

Other tools to evaluate mutual funds include news accounts and the fund's annual report. Make sure you are comparing *apples* to *apples*. Magazines measure funds during different time periods and use different criteria, which could affect a fund's ranking.

The good news is that a movement is afoot to simplify the language used in prospectuses. The Securities and Exchange Commission has recommended the creation of a clearly written one-page summary to accompany these documents. The new rules are targeting the fund booklets. Hopefully, by the time you're reading this book, the Securities Exchange Commission and the mutual fund companies will have adopted their new language called "plain English." The SEC has adopted rules that will force mutual funds to ditch the legalese and translate their prospectuses — the disclosure booklets most people toss in the trash unread — into easily understood language.

Also, fund companies may distribute a streamlined profile that includes a mutual fund's vital statistics. This is a victory for the consumer, at least for those who care enough to follow through and do their homework. Both documents will contain a ten-year bar chart, a fund performance, a table comparing performance to market index, and a description of the risk involved in the investment. A three- to six-page profile also will summarize the fund's fees, risks, and investment objectives at the beginning of the document.

There's one significant difference between the two new documents. Fund companies had to begin distributing the plain English prospectuses in 1998, which was good news. With more than the estimated six thousand mutual funds to choose from, many investors feel overwhelmed when comparing possible investments.

A survey by the Investment Company Institute, the mutual fund industry's trade group, discovered that only half of the fund shareholders consult a prospectus before investing.

Now, for you Internet investors whose printers have been clogged after trying to download a twenty-page prospectus, this should be a relief. Soon you will be able to make side-by-side comparisons of different funds. Information will be more visible in a shorter document available online.

29 How to Pay for Your Children's College!

The best way to pay for college is to motivate your kids to achieve a high grade point average for scholarship eligibility. Begin searching the Internet for grants and scholarships when your children first start high school. Find an advocate or counselor at their school who can alert and steer them toward scholarships. Many states have college fee waiver programs for children and dependents of service-connected or service-related disabled veterans. Did you know if you earned a Purple Heart for wounds received in combat your children can attend any California university or state college for free? That's a major savings. Most of these college fee waiver programs are not public knowledge, so it takes a little research that is well worth it. Check with your state Veterans' Affairs office if you believe you may be eligible.

In addition to scholarships, grants, or waivers you may still need extra money. Providing a college education today (and, even more so, tomorrow) can cost as much as buying a house. It's going to require some careful advance planning. (For more information, call the Federal Student Aid information Center, 800-333-4636.)

There has been a shift in the balance in federal aid to students. This trend does not seem likely to reverse anytime soon. Moreover, with government assistance to higher education being cut back and current tax law changes, it will become increasingly difficult for schools to raise money from private sources. Thus, planning for college costs means planning to hit an even higher target.

A college cost worksheet has been provided at the end of this chapter, designed to help you set up a personalized action plan for meeting your family's

236

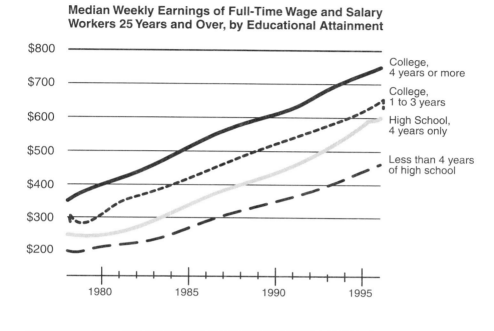

Median Weekly Earnings of Full-Time Wage and Salary Workers 25 Years and Over, by Educational Attainment

Figure 29.1 The value of education.

educational costs. When you complete it, you will have the basic information you need to plot your course.

How to Meet the Cost

Step 1 — Estimate how much you will need. To estimate total college costs, complete step 1 of the worksheet below. The annual average increase in school costs may turn out to be higher or lower than the six percent projected.

Step 2 — Find the future value of your current savings. To estimate how compounding can increase the value of your current savings by the time your child enters college, complete step 2 of the worksheet.

Step 3 — Before you become unduly alarmed over the gap between your savings and the amount of money you will need, remember that there are a wide variety of financial and student aid programs

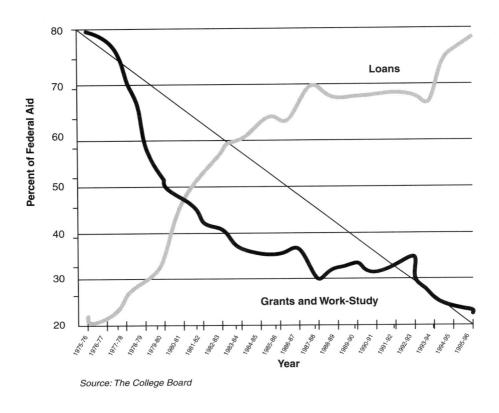

Source: The College Board

Figure 29.2 The shifting balance in federal student aid, 1975 to 1995.

available. Each school has its own way of deciding whether a student qualifies for aid, and the federal government has its own criteria for awarding federal grants. Table 29.2 will give you a rough idea how much help you may be eligible for today. If you expect to finance some of your educational costs through outside sources, complete step 3 of the worksheet.

Step 4 — Complete steps 1 through 3 of the worksheet. If line 10 shows that you will have expenses that won't be covered either by your current savings or by outside aid, you will need to add to your savings between now and when your child enters school. To estimate how much you will need to save each month to reach your target amount, complete step 4 of the worksheet.

Table 29.1 Projected Total Four-Year Costs of Attending College

Year Student Will Begin College	Public College	Private College	Savings Compounding Factor (see Step 2)	Monthly Investment Factor (See Step 4)
1998	$48,377	$98,015	2.00	158.48
1999	$51,279	$103,895	2.16	184.17
2000	$54,356	$110,129	2.33	211.98
2001	$57,617	$116,737	2.52	242.11
2002	$61,074	$123,741	2.72	274.74
2003	$64,739	$131,166	2.94	310.08
2004	$68,623	$139,036	3.17	348.35
2005	$72,741	$147,378	3.43	389.79
2006	$77,105	$156,220	3.70	434.68
2007	$81,731	$165,594	4.00	483.29
2008				
2009				
2010				
2011				
2012				
2013				
2014				
2015				

To determine the four-year cost of attending college, find the year your student will be starting college in the left column. Then read across the column to find the projected total costs (including tuition, room and board, books, and other expenses) for a student entering college in that year.

Chart assumes 6% annual increases of college costs. The savings compounding factor and monthly investment factor assume 8% pre-tax return on all investments. Based on 1998–1999 costs projected by the American Council on Education.

Step 5 — Now you know how much money you will need to invest. But which investment should you choose? Your time horizon, more than any other factor, should dictate your choice because it is intimately linked to investment risk and return. Table 29.3 shows appropriate investment strategies based on your time horizon.

The College Board publishes the latest cost figures each fall in the *College Cost Book*. To obtain a current catalog or for more information, call (212)

Table 29.2 How Much Will Financial Aid Cover Today? Estimated Percentage of Average 1998–99 Private College Costs Paid for by Financial Aid

Total Family Assets[a]	Annual Family Pre-Tax Income		
	$20,000	$40,000	$60,000
$40,000	94%	61%	15%
60,000	90%	52%	6%
80,000	86%	43%	0%
100,000	81%	34%	0%

Note: The percentage of college costs covered by financial aid is based on approximate expected parental contributions toward 1998–99 college expenses (for a family of four) from *Peterson's College Money Handbook* and assume an average 1998–99 college cost of $12,500.

[a] Includes equity in home (estimated value of home less unpaid mortgage).

Table 29.3 Timing is the Key to Your Investment Strategy

Years Until Student Begins School	Appropriate Risk/Reward Level	Investment Strategy
>5	High	Invest in an index mutual fund to build maximum assets and outpace inflation of educational costs. Don't worry now about short-term ups and downs — time will tend to smooth them out. Long-term growth should be your primary goal, and the longer your time horizon, the more aggressive you can be.
3–5	Moderate	Choose a more conservative growth and income stock fund or higher yield bond fund to continue building assets while reducing overall price volatility.
0–2	Low	Switch to a taxable or tax-exempt money market or short-term bond fund which earns safe, steady income and will provide easy access to your money when you need it.

713-8150 or write: College Board Publications, P.O. Box 886, New York, NY 10101-0886.

Two other excellent sources on financial aid are: *Don't Miss Out, the Ambitious Student's Guide to Financial Aid,* published by Octameron Press, P.O. Box 3437, Alexandria, VA 22302 or call (703) 828-1882; and Peterson's *1989 College Money Handbook,* available at your local bookstore. Or, for a free copy of T. Rowe Price's Asset Mix Worksheet call (800) 638-5660.

The best way to pay for college is to start now teaching your kids how to invest and get motivated and helping them find scholarships, college aid, and grants. Use the new educational IRA. One easy way to make contributions is through an automatic investment plan. Investments grow tax-deferred. Earnings are withdrawn tax-free if they are used to pay for college costs, and the beneficiary has until age 30 to do so. Anyone, including non-relatives, can invest money for a child. The only drawbacks are, contributions are not tax-deductible and educational IRAs are not available to high-income individuals or couples. And there is a ten percent penalty if the child doesn't go to college. The good news is you can transfer the account to a younger sibling who does.

College Cost Worksheet

Facts You Will Need	Student Data	Special Instructions
Step 1		
1. Student's name	1. _____	
2. Year student will start college	2. _____	
3. Student's total 4-year college expenses	3. _____	(3) Using Table 29.1, find the year student will start college, then read across to find corresponding cost figure.
Step 2		
4. Amount you have already saved for college expenses	4. _____	
5. Savings Compounding	5. _____	(5) In Table 29.1, read across from the year the student will start college to find the appropriate Savings Compounding Factor. This multiplier estimates how much your savings could grow by the time the student enters college.
6. Estimated value of your savings by the time student starts college	6. _____	(6) Multiply Line 4 by Line 5.
7. Remaining expenses not covered by your current savings	7. _____	(7) Subtract Line 6 from Line 5. If you have no current savings, enter amount from Line 3.
Step 3		
8. Amount of total expenses (Line 3) which may be met through financial aid and/or loans, gifts, or other outside sources	8a. _____	(8a) Use Table 29.2 to estimate the percent of financial aid you could expect today, based on your current income and assets. Multiply this percent by Line 3 and enter result on Line 8a.
	8b. _____	(8b) Enter dollar amount of any loans, gifts, or other outside sources on Line 8b.

College Cost Worksheet (Continued)

Facts You Will Need	Student Data	Special Instructions
9. Estimated total dollar amount from outside sources	9. _____	(9) Add Line 8a to Line 8b. (Enter zero on Line 9 if you do not expect help from any outside sources.)
10. Net expenses not covered by current savings or outside sources	10. _____	(10) Subtract Line 9 from Line 7.
Step 4		
11. Monthly Investment Factor: this will help you estimate how much you will need to put away in equal monthly installments to meet total expenses	11. _____	(11) In Table 29.1, read from the year student will start college to find the appropriate Monthly Investment Factor.
12. Amount you should invest each month until September of the year this student starts college	12. _____	(12) Divide Line 10 by Line 11.

Source: T. Rowe Price Associates, Inc.

30 Putting It All Together

Taking Small Steps

We've come a long way since the first chapter. We hope you see that successful investing is clearly within your reach. For women especially, we hope you will follow the action steps in the last half of the book, and, if you are having trouble, find a female advisor or broker. She will be more likely to listen, develop a relationship with you, and not be so inclined to push you into immediate action. That's often not what a women wants or needs. When women feel pushed, they tend to feel distrust, misled, and upset. If you hire a male advisor, find one who is going to listen, relate, and not push you too quickly into action. Men do what they do. Women do what they do.

Whatever gender you are, investing is about balance and understanding. Relying on financial direction, advice, and guidance from a trusted professional advisor is vital to your success. But, ultimately, it is you, after you have determined your needs and specified your goals with the assistance of an advisor, who must choose to implement a recommended investment strategy or financial plan. And it is you who must choose the investments that are best for you. Here are simple steps, small steps, to help you take action today.

Step One — Get Started!

1. Know what you want; be more specific as you get clearer.
2. Focus your mind on getting what you want.
3. Believe you can have it.
4. Take action.

5. Realize you have the power to change.

Step Two — Rewrite Your Beliefs About Money to Make Them Positive

Examine your old belief system. Your thoughts affect your actions, your perceptions, and your experience. Your thoughts control your experience of reality.

Your fears may bind and temporarily cripple you, but they don't have to stop you! From a different point of view, look at yourself in relationship to money. Change "I'm too busy to learn about or make investments" to "The time I spend on investing will pay off."

Clarify what you want, and make a commitment to achieve it by a certain date. There is power in knowing where you are going and when you expect to get there.

Step Three — Develop Trust of Your Intuition and Inner Knowing

Love money! This is a hard one for some, but it works. Whatever you love is drawn to you and you to it. Break up your old beliefs that money is the root of all evil and all that stuff. Rewrite: *Money gives my family happiness and stability.*

Focus on investments and take action. Remember, we are designed for self-healing. Think of a cut on your skin; your body intuitively knows how to heal.

A meditation: Close your eyes and imagine money all around you. Now, invite it inside of you. Imagine wealth going into your body, feel it, and believe it is attached to you.

Step Four — Complete the Financial Quiz

The financial personality quiz in Chapter 4 will help you determine your personal financial needs and place your financial goals in realistic time frames. An investment plan must be matched to your own personality, fears, needs, and wants. Defining these in writing will help you get a clear picture of your situation and prepare you to consult with your advisor.

Step Five — Plan

Now, it's time to plan. By now, you should have a pretty good understanding of investments and your own needs. It's time to ask a professional for advice. Ask for investment recommendations from the professionals you are considering so you can compare these against what you have learned in this book, and see if they seem to fit your needs.

Step Six — Establish Time Horizons

Set time horizons that match the investment and the eventual use of the money. If money needs to be available in less than two years, use certificates of deposit, savings accounts, and money market accounts.

For three- to five-year time horizons or longer, there are many possibilities, including stock mutual funds, bonds, and variable annuities. Stocks, whether in a mutual fund or variable annuity, should only be considered for this long-term horizon because the stock market goes down one year in every four, and no one has ever been able to predict accurately which year it will decline. If you have short-term money in stocks and you need to withdraw it during a down year, you will take a loss.

Step Seven — Start Slow, But Start Now

The idea is not to jump in and invest in everything at once. Get your plan completed, then take one or two components of your plan and start investing. Then build on your plan as time goes on and you feel more confident.

Step Eight — Determine the Amount of Risk You Can Take

You should determine the level of risk with which you are comfortable. For example, a three percent loss may be tolerable, while a twelve percent decline in a single year may be too aggressive for you. Don't set yourself up for failure. Recognize that there are going to be down years in all investments, except fixed annuities, and you need to be ready to ride through those years. You must accept some degree of risk or you will never stay ahead of inflation and enjoy financial security. It's a matter of trying to decide in advance of investing how much risk you can handle.

Step Nine — Set Realistic Targets

Set realistic targets and match your expectations with the appropriate investments. Ask to see different mixes of investment products that have the highest probability of meeting your target rates of return and the various amounts needed to invest at those rates. Comparing different mixes will help you anchor your expectations in reality.

Step Ten — Diversify

Investing in a wide range of investments that tend to move in very different cycles lowers risk. The theory is simple: if one asset class goes down, another asset class goes up. By varying the ratio of investments in the different asset classes, an advisor can gauge the degree of risk assumed.

Step Eleven — Don't Buy from Advertisements

Don't buy mutual funds just because they look good in magazine ads. These high advertised returns were usually made during the 1980s. Most people have no knowledge of how performance returns are reported and the risks associated with the stock market. It is not a good strategy to see a fifteen percent advertised average annual total return for one year by a mutual fund company, mentally compare it to your current bank's two percent, then make your decision.

Step Twelve — Don't Panic

Don't panic and sell if stock prices go down. In fact, it's wise to expect fluctuations and ride them out. Use a drop in the market as an opportunity to average your cost downwards. If you buy good companies with low debt and compound earnings, drops in market value of the stocks will only be temporary.

Step Thirteen — Copy the Investment Masters

Read true accounts of successful investors, not get-rich-quick books. An excellent book is *New Money Master*, by John Train. Talk to successful people you know and ask questions. You will be surprised how open truly successful people often are.

Step Fourteen — Invest in Stocks

In the 1990s, we have seen an explosive advance in bond and stock prices, perhaps unprecedented in this century. Following one of the most prolonged bull markets in history, the '90s may see an even more spectacular advance in the stock market! Look for value. Companies that compound their rate of return each year and have little debt are good bets. Buy companies you know will be around. According to a University of Michigan study, if you missed just twenty of the biggest days of the 1982 to 1987 bull market (twenty days represents one percent of this time period), your compounded annual return was cut in half, from twenty-six percent to thirteen percent. If you missed the forty biggest gain days, your annualized return dropped to 4.3 percent. The secret to controlling the thermostat in investments is echoed in my grandmother's words: "Stop running around, sit still, and you'll cool off. The thermostat works just fine." It's the same when it comes to investing. Don't let sudden drops or rises in the stock market cause you to react in panic or to get greedy. Just keep a long-term perspective, expect your investments to fluctuate in value, and don't be adjusting your investment portfolio at every turn. The thermostat of the stock market works just fine without your fiddling.

Stocks are the only financial assets that have exceeded inflation through long periods of time. The tendency is to be underexposed or not have enough stocks in a portfolio to create meaningful growth.

Step Fifteen — Hire an Advisor to Guide You

Choose, as your financial advisor, a person you feel confident about and with whom you can communicate. Don't settle for the first person you come across. Look around, ask questions. Your advisor should clearly put your needs first, and treat your money and you with consideration and respect.

Invest with professional management. Most people need some help with their investment decisions. They don't have the time or expertise to go it alone. If you are starting out small, mutual funds can be your best bet. They reduce investment risk by diversification and still offer professional money management.

Step Sixteen — Taxes

If you are in a high tax bracket, using investments that reduce or defer taxes is wise. But avoid allowing your desire to pay fewer taxes weigh too heavily in your investment selection process. An investment should be evaluated first for its ability to increase in value or generate income. If you are satisfied with an investment's value irrespective of its tax advantages, then tax advantages are a welcomed bonus.

Step Seventeen — Set up a Retirement Account

If you are investing long-term, first use retirement accounts offered through your employment — 401(k)s, pension and profit share plans, SEPs — and personal individual retirement accounts (IRAs). Put as much money as you can afford into these types of accounts because of their tax-deferral features and because you can deduct from your taxes your portion of the contributions to these accounts. For example, if you are in the twenty-eight percent tax bracket and are eligible for an IRA, you can invest $2,000 and receive a tax deduction. This deduction is equivalent to the government putting $560 (twenty-eight percent of $2,000) into your account. Where else can you get an instant twenty-eight percent return?

Congratulations, you've done it! You've made it through the book and have hopefully started your investment program.

Sources

For some of the best books around, try the following:

1. *Making the Most of Your Money* by Jane Bryant Quinn (New York: Simon & Schuster, 1997).
2. Jeremy Siegels' *Stocks For the Long Run* (New York: McGraw-Hill, 1998).
3. Just about anything from Peter Lynch
4. *Personal Finance for Dummies* by Eric Tyson (excellent) (Foster City, CA: IDG Books Worldwide, 2000).
5. *Common Sense Mutual Funds* by John C. Bogle (New York: John Wiley & Sons, 1999).
6. *The Whiz Kid of Wall Street's Investment Guide: How I Returned 34 Percent on My Portfolio, and You Can, Too* by Matt Seto, with Steven Levingston (Morrow, William & Co., 1997).
7. *The Intelligent Investor* by Benjamin Graham; *The Battle for Investment* by Gerald Lobe (New York: Harper Collins, 1997).
8. *A Random Walk Down Wall Street* by Michael Burton G. Malkiel (New York: Norton, 2000).
9. Charles Schwab's *Guide to Financial Independence* (New York: Crown Publishers, 1998).
10. *Independently Wealthy (How to Build Financial Security in The New Economic Era)* by Robert Goodman, Ph.D., senior economic advisor for Putnam Investments and the author of a new book. (New York: John Wiley & Sons).

Recommended reading about asset class investing:

> *Asset Allocation: Balancing Financial Risk* by Roger C. Gibson (New York: McGraw-Hill, 2000).
> *The Prudent Investor's Guide to Beating the Market* by John J. Bowen, Jr. (New York: McGraw-Hill, 1997).

For information on mutual funds, *Morningstar Mutual Funds* is the absolute best — it costs about $400 plus per year. For more information, call 800-735-0700 or you can write to Morningstar at 225 West Wacker Drive, Chicago, IL 60606 or visit their site: www.morningstar.net.com. *Morningstar* is published every two weeks and it itemizes each mutual fund, performance, risk, portfolio operating history, and distribution information. It offers interviews with fund managers and gives advice on buying or avoiding particular funds.

Standard & Poor's *Stock Guide for Quick Review* — again, that volume used to belong on every broker's desk. Its twelve page publication called *Outlook* comes out weekly. It gives a ranking of the major companies' potential quality. An annual subscription to Outlook costs about $300. You can reach Standard & Poor's at 800-221-5277, 65 Broadway, New York, NY 10006, or online at www.stockinfo.standard&poor.com.

For those who want to start or join an investment club, you can contact the National Association of Investment Corporations (NAIC) 248-583-6242, 71 W. 13 Mile Road, Madison Heights, MI 48071.

Glossary

Accumulated Value: The value of all amounts accumulated under the contract prior to the annuity date.

Accumulation Unit: A measure of ownership interest in the contract prior to the annuity date.

Administrative Fee: An annual fee, usually 0.15 percent or less of the daily subaccount asset value, charged to reimburse administrative expenses.

Advisor: One who gives investment advice in return for compensation.

Aggressive Growth: High risk/reward investments, funds, or securities classes.

Analysis: Process of evaluating individual financial instruments (often stock) to determine whether they are an appropriate purchase.

Analysts: Those on Wall Street who study and issue reports on securities.

Annual Insurance Company Expenses: Annuity contracts include charges for insurance companies' annual expenses. In addition to the asset management fees, there are three other annual charges: annual policy fee, mortality and expense risk, and administrative fee.

Annual Interest Income: The annual dollar income for a bond or saving account is calculated by multiplying the bond's coupon rate by it's face value.

Annual Policy Fee (Maintenance Fee): An annual fee, usually $50.00 or less, is charged for the maintenance of the annuity records. The fee pays accounting, customer reporting, and other general expenses associated with financial record-keeping requirements.

Annualized Return: The total return on an investment or portfolio over a period of time other than one year, restated as an equivalent return for a one-year period.

Annuitant: The person whose life is used to determine the duration of any annuity payments and upon whose death, prior to the annuity date, benefits under the contract are paid.

Annuitant's Beneficiary: The person(s) to whom any benefits are due upon the annuitant's death prior to the annuity date.

Annuity: An annuity is a contract between an insurer and recipient (annuitant) whereby the insurer guarantees to pay the recipient a stream of money in exchange for premium payment(s).

Annuity Date: The date on which annuity payments begin. The annuity date is always the first day of the month you specify.

Annuity Payment: One of a series of payments made under an annuity payment option.

Annuity Payment Option: One of several ways in which withdrawals from the contract may be made. Under a fixed annuity option the dollar amount of each annuity payment does not change over time. Under a variable annuity option the dollar amount of each annuity payment may change over time, depending upon the investment experience of the portfolio or portfolios selected. Annuity payments are based on the contract's accumulated value as of ten business days prior to the annuity date.

Annuity Unit Value: The value of each annuity unit which is calculated each valuation period.

Asset Allocation: The decision as to how a customer should be invested among major asset classes in order to increase expected risk-adjusted return. Asset allocation may be two-way (stocks and bonds), three-way (stocks, bonds, and cash), or many-way (i.e., value mutual funds, growth mutual funds, small mutual funds, cash, foreign mutual funds, foreign bonds, real estate, and venture capital).

Asset Class: Assets composed of financial instruments with similar characteristics.

Asset Class Investing: The disciplined purchase of groups of securities with similar risk/reward profiles. This strategy is based on valid academic research and its results are predictable rather than random.

Asset Class Funds: Funds composed of financial instruments with similar characteristics. Unlike managers of index funds, asset-fund managers actively manage costs when buying and selling for funds.

Asset Mix: Investable asset classes within a portfolio.

Average Daily Trading: The average daily trading is the number of shares of stock traded in the preceding calendar month, multiplied by the current price and divided by twenty trading days.

Average Return: the measure of price of an asset, along with its income or yield on average over a specific time period. The arithmetic mean is the simple average of the returns in a series. The arithmetic mean is the appropriate measure of typical performance for a single period.

Back-End Load: A fee charged at redemption by a mutual fund or a variable annuity to a buyer of shares.

Bailout Rate: This feature is offered on some annuities and allows the customer to surrender the annuity with no penalty if the interest rate falls below a certain floor.

Balanced Index: A market index that serves as a basis of comparison for balanced portfolios. The balanced index used in the *Monitor* is comprised of a sixty percent weighting of the S&P 500 Index and a forty percent weighting of the SLH Government/Corporate Bond Index. The balanced index relates unmanaged market returns to a balanced portfolio more precisely than either a stock or a bond index would alone.

Balanced Mutual Fund: This term can be applied to any kind of portfolio that uses fixed income (bonds) as well as equity securities to reach goals. Many "boutique" investment managers are balanced managers, because it permits them to tailor the securities in a portfolio to the specific clients' cash flow needs and objectives. Balanced portfolios are often used by major mutual funds. They provide great flexibility.

Basis Point: One basis point is one hundredth of a percentage point, or 0.01 percent. Basis points are often used to express changes or differences in yields, returns, or interest rates. Thus, if a portfolio has a total return of ten percent versus seven percent for the S&P 500, the portfolio is said to have outperformed the S&P 500 by 300 basis points.

Bear Market: A prolonged period of falling stock prices. There is no consensus on what constitutes a bear market or bear leg. SEI, one of the most widely used performance measurement services, normally defines a bear market or bear leg as a drop of at least fifteen percent over two back-to-back quarters.

Beginning Value: The market value of a portfolio at the inception of the period being measured by the customer statement.

Benchmark: A standard by which investment performance or trading execution can be judged. The most widely used performance benchmark is the total return of the S&P 500.

Beneficiary: Similar to the beneficiary of a life insurance policy, the annuity contract beneficiary receives a death benefit when another party to the annuity contract dies prior to the date upon which the annuity begins paying out benefits.

Beta: Beta is the linear relationship between the return on the security and the return on the market. By definition, the market usually measured by the S&P500 Index has beta of 1.00. Any stock or portfolio with a higher beta is generally more volatile than the market, while any with a lower beta is generally less volatile than the market.

Bond Rating: Method of evaluating the possibility of default by a bond issuer. Standard & Poor's, Moody's Investors Service, and Fitch's Investors Service analyze the financial strength of each bond's issuer, whether a corporation or a government body. Their ratings range from AAA (highly unlikely to default) to D (in default). Bonds rated B or below are not investment grade—in other words, institutions that invest other people's money may not under most state laws buy them.

Bonds — Long-term, Short-term and High Yield: Debt instruments that pay lenders a regular return. Short-term bonds are five years or less. High yield bonds pay lenders a higher rate of return because of perceived risk.

Book-to-Market Ratio: Size of company's book (net) value relative to the market price of the company.

Broker: An individual with a Series 7 license entitled to buy and sell securities, especially stock, on behalf of clients and charge for that service.

Broker Dealer: A firm employing brokers among other financial professionals.

Bull Market: A prolonged period of rising stock prices. SEI, one of the most widely used performance measurement services, normally defines a bull market or bull leg as a rise of at least fifteen percent over two back-to-back quarters.

Business Day: A day when the New York Stock Exchange is open for trading.

Call Option: A call option gives the investor the right, but not an obligation, to buy a security at a pre-set price within a specified time. A "put" gives the investor the right to sell a security at a pre-set price within a specified time. Calls and puts are therefore essentially bets on whether the underlying security will rise or fall in price. Index option holders gain or lose in proportion to changes in the values of the new indexes, which in turn reflect the net asset value performances of the securities that comprise the indexes.

Cap: small cap, large cap: the stock market worth of an individual equity.

Capital Appreciation or Depreciation: This is an increase or decrease in the value of a mutual fund or stock due to a change in the market price. For example, a stock that rises from $50 to $55 has capital appreciation of ten percent. Dividends are not included in appreciation. If the price of the stock fell to $45, it would have depreciation of ten percent.

Capital Preservation: Investing in a conservative manner so as not to put capital at risk.

Commission: A transaction fee commonly levied by brokers and other financial middlemen.

Compound Annual Return: Geometric mean is another expression for compound annual return. The geometric mean is more appropriate when one is comparing the growth rate for an investment that is continually compounding.

Compounding: The reinvestment of dividends, and or interest and capital gains. This means that over time dividends and interest and capital gains grow exponentially; for example, a $100 earning compound interest at ten percent a year would accumulate to $110 at the end of the first year and $121 at the end of the second year, etc., based on the formula: compound sum = principal (1+ interest rate) number of periods.

Conservative: This is a characteristic relating to a mutual fund, a stock, or an investment style. There is no precise definition of the term. Generally, the term is used when the mutual fund manager's emphasis is on the below-market betas.

Contract Anniversary: Any anniversary of the contract date.

Contract Date: The date of issue of a contract.

Contract Owner: The person or persons designated as the contract owner in the contract. The term shall also include any person named as joint owner. A joint owner shares ownership in all respects with the contract owner. Prior to the annuity date, the contract owner has the right to assign ownership, designate beneficiaries, make permitted withdrawals and exchanges among subaccounts and guaranteed rate options.

Contrarian: An investment approach characterized by buying securities that are out of favor.

Core Savings Strategy: A core savings strategy is the home of your safe dollars that provides you overall financial security. A long-term commitment of savings not to be touched except in an emergency.

Correction: A correction is a reversal in the price of a stock, or the stock market as a whole, within a larger trend. While corrections are most often thought of as declines within an overall market rise, a correction can also be a temporary rise in the midst of a longer-term decline.

Correlation: A statistical measure of the degree to which the movement of two variables is related.

Coupon: This is defined as the periodic interest payment on a bond. When expressed as an annual percentage, it is called the coupon rate. When multiplied by the face value of the bond, the coupon rate gives the annual interest income.

CPI: This acronym stands for the Consumer Price Index, maintained by the Bureau of Labor Statistics, which measures the changes in the cost of a specified group of consumer products relative to a base period. Because it represents the rate of inflation, the CPI can be used as a general benchmark for gauging the maintenance of purchasing power.

Currency: A nation's paper notes, once redeemable but not now.

Currency Risk: Possibility that foreign currency one holds may fall in value relative to investor's home currency, thus devaluing overseas investments.

Current Return on Equity (ROE): A ratio that measures profitability as the return on common stockholders' equity. It is calculated by dividing the reported earnings per share for the latest twelve-month period by the book value per share.

Current Yield: This is a bond's annual interest payment as a percentage of its current market price. The current yield is calculated by dividing the annual coupon interest for a bond by the current market price. The coupon rate and the current yield on a bond are equal when the bond is selling at par. Thus, a $1,000 bond with a coupon of ten percent that is currently selling at $1,000 will have a current yield of 10.0 percent. However, if the bond's price drops to $800 the current yield becomes 12.5 percent.

Death Benefit: The greater of either the contract's accumulated value on the date the company receives due proof of death of the annuitant or the adjusted death benefit. If any portion of the contract's accumulated value on the date proof of the annuitant's death is received is derived from the multi-year guaranteed rate option, that portion of the accumulated value will be adjusted by a positive market value adjustment factor, if applicable.

Deferred Annuity: This is an annuity whose contract provides that payments to the annuitant be postponed until a number of periods have elapsed; for example, when the annuitant attains a certain age.

Deviation: Movement of an instrument or asset class away from the expected direction. In investment terminology, most often associated with asset class analysis.

Dissimilar Price Movement: The process whereby different asset classes and markets move in different directions.

Diversification: In broad terms, a first-time investor may diversify his or her investments among mutual funds, real estate, international investments, and money market instruments. A mutual fund may diversify by investing in many companies in many different industry groups. Diversification also can refer to the way large sponsors reduce risk by using multiple mutual fund styles.

Dividend: The payment from a company's earnings normally paid on common shares declared by a company's board of directors to be distributed pro rata among the shares outstanding.

Dollar Cost Averaging: a system of buying stock or mutual funds at regular intervals with a fixed dollar amount. Under this system an investor buys by the dollar's worth rather than by the number of shares.

Dow Jones Industrial Average (DJIA): A price-weighted average of thirty leading blue-chip industrial stocks, calculated by adding the prices of the thirty stocks and adjusting by a divisor, which reflects any stock dividends or splits. The Dow Jones Industrial Average is the most widely quoted index of the stock market, but it is not widely used as a benchmark for evaluating performance. The S&P 500 Index, which is more representative of the market, is the benchmark most widely used by performance measurement services.

Efficiency: The process of generating maximum reward from funds invested across a spectrum of asset classes.

Efficient Frontier: The point where the maximum amount of risk an investor is willing to tolerate intersects with the maximum amount of reward that can potentially be generated.

Emerging Growth Fund: This applies to new companies that may be relatively small in size with the potential to grow much larger.

Emerging Growth Mutual Fund: Here, a mutual fund manager is looking for industries and companies whose growth rates are likely to be both rapid and independent of the overall stock market. "Emerging," of course, means new. This implies such companies may be relatively small in size with the potential to grow much larger. Such stocks are generally much more volatile than the stock market in general and require constant, close, attention to developments.

Emerging Markets: Countries beginning to build financial marketplaces with appropriate safeguards.

EPS (Earnings per Share) Growth: This is the annualized rate of growth in reported earnings per share of stock.

Equities: Stocks. Equity mutual funds are made up of many individual stocks. A stock is a right of ownership in a corporation.

Excellent/Unexcellent Companies: Companies with either high (excellent) or low (unexcellent) stock market performances.

Exchange: One exchange will be deemed to occur with each voluntary transfer from any subaccount or general account guaranteed option.

Exchange Privilege: This is a shareholder's right to switch from one mutual fund to another within one fund family and is often done at no additional charge. This enables investors to put their money in an aggressive growth-stock fund, for example, when they expect the market to turn up strongly, then switch to a money market fund when they anticipate a downturn.

Execution Price: The negotiated price at which a security is purchased or sold.

Expected Return: Calculated as the weighted average of possible returns, where the weights are the corresponding probability for each return.

Expected Return: A tax term that means the expected amount to be received under an annuity contract, based on the periodic payment and the annuitant's life expectancy when the benefits begin.

Expenses: Cost of maintaining an invested portfolio.

Fee-Based: Describes a manager, advisor, or broker whose charges are based on a set amount rather than transaction charges.

Fee-Only: Describes a manager, advisor, or broker who charges an investor a pre-set amount for services.

Financial Advisor/Planner: One who helps an investor with a wide variety of financial and investing issues, including retirement, estate planning, etc. Often licensed and working for a larger financial entity.

Fixed Annuities: The word *fixed* is used to describe the type of annuity referred to by the interest rate paid by the issuing insurance company on the fund's place in the annuity. The fixed annuity offers security in that the rate of return is certain. Typically, with a fixed annuity the insurance company declares a current interest rate and sets the interest rate.

Fixed-Income Mutual Funds: Mutual funds that invest in corporate bonds or government-insured mortgages, T-Bills, Treasury bonds. If they own any stocks at all, these are usually preferred shares. Fixed income mutual fund managers have a broad range of styles, involving market timing, swapping to gain quality or yield, setting up maturity ladders, etc. A typical division of the fixed income market is between short (up to three years), intermediate (three to fifteen years), and long (fifteen to thirty years).

Forecasts: Predictions of analysts, usually associated with stock picking and active money management.

401(k): Section of the Internal Revenue Code. In its most simple terms, a 401(k) plan is a before-tax employee saving plan.

Free Look: Most annuity contracts provide a ten- to fifteen-day period after contract delivery when the owner can return the annuity and receive a full refund of the premium.

Front-End Load: A fee charged when an investor buys a mutual fund or a variable annuity.

Fundamentals: This word refers to the financial statistics that traditional analysts and many valuation models use. Fundamental data include stock, earnings, dividends, assets and liabilities, inventories, debt, etc. Fundamental data are in contrast to items used in technical analysis — such as price momentum, volume trends, and short sales statistics.

Fund Ratings: Evaluation of the performance of invested money pools, often mutual funds by such entities as Chicago-based Morningstar.

Fund Shares: Shares in a mutual fund.

Guaranteed Interest Rate: In a fixed annuity, the minimum interest rate that is guaranteed by the insurance company to be credited each year to the cash value.

General Account: The account that contains all assets other than those held in separate accounts.

Global Diversification: Investing funds around the world in regions and markets with dissimilar price movement.

Guaranteed Rate Options: The one-year guaranteed rate option and the multi-year guaranteed rate option.

Hot Tip: Slang for an individual investment, often a stock, that is apparently poised to rise (but may not).

Income Growth Mutual Fund: The primary purpose in security selection here is to achieve a current yield significantly higher than the S&P 500. The stability of the dividend and the rate of growth of the dividends are also of concern to the income buyer. These portfolios may own more utilities, less high tech and may own convertible preferreds and convertible bonds.

Index Fund: An index mutual fund is a passively managed portfolio designed and computer controlled to track the performance of a certain index, such as the S&P 500. In general, such mutual funds have performance within a few basis points of the target index. The most popular index mutual funds are those that track the S&P 500, but special index funds, such as those based on the Russell 1000 or the Wilshire 5000, are also available.

Indexing: Disciplined investing in a specific group (asset class) of securities so as to benefit from its aggregate performance.

Individual Investor: Buyer or seller of securities for personal portfolio.

Inflation: A monetary phenomenon generated by an overexpansion of credit which drives up prices of assets while diminishing the worth of paper currency.

Institutional Investor: Corporation or fund with market presence.

Interest: The rate a borrower pays a lender.

Interest-Rate Guarantee: A guarantee that the renewal rate will never fall below a particular level. Typical policies today have a four percent to five percent guarantee.

Intrinsic Value: This means the theoretical valuation or price for a stock. The valuation is determined using a valuation theory or model. The resulting value is compared with the current market price. If the intrinsic value is greater than the market price, the stock is considered undervalued.

Investing: A disciplined process of placing money in financial instruments so as to gain a return.

Investment Advisor: *See* Advisor.

Investment Discipline: A specific money strategy one espouses.

Investment Guru: A money manager or analyst, often employed by Wall Street, and commonly looked on as having special insight into the market. *See* Noise.

Investment Objective: The money goals one wishes to reach.

Investment Philosophy: Strategy justifying short- or long-term buying and selling of securities.

Investment Policy: An investment policy statement forces the investor to confront risk tolerance, return objectives, time horizon, liquidity needs, the amount of funds available for investment, and the investment methodology to be followed.

Investment Policy Statement: Embodies the essence of the financial planning process. It includes: (1) assessing where you are now, (2) detailing where you want to go, and (3) developing a strategy to get there.

Investment Wisdom: Process of understanding valid academic research concerning asset allocation.

Investor Discomfort: Realization that risk is not appropriate and reward is not predictable in a given portfolio.

IPOs: Initial public offerings, the sale of stock in a company going public for the first time.

Joint Owner: The person or persons designated as the contract owner in an annuity contract. A joint owner shares ownership in all respects with the contract owner.

Liquidity: Ability to generate cash on demand when necessary.

Load Funds: A mutual fund that is sold for a sales charge (load) by a brokerage firm or other sales representative. Such funds may be stock, bond, or commodity funds, with conservative or aggressive objectives. The stated advantage of a load fund is that the salesperson will explain the fund to the customer and advise him or her when it is appropriate to sell as well as when to buy more shares.

Lump Sum Distribution: Single payment to a beneficiary covering the entire amount of an agreement. Participants in Individual Retirement Accounts, pension plans, profit-sharing, and executive stock option plans generally can opt for a lump sum distribution if the taxes are not too burdensome when they become eligible.

Management Fee: Charge against investor assets for managing the portfolio of an open- or closed-end mutual fund, as well as for such services as shareholder relations or administration. The fee, as disclosed in the prospectus, is a fixed percentage of the fund's asset value, typically one percent or less per year.

Margin: A loan often offered to investors by broker-dealers for the purpose of allowing the investor to purchase additional securities. In a down market, margin loans can be called and portfolios liquidated when the value of the loan threatens to exceed the value of the portfolio.

Market: In investing terms: a place where securities are traded. Formerly meant a physical location but now may refer to an electronic one as well.

Market Bottom: The date that the bear leg of a market cycle reaches its low, not identified until some time after the fact. In the peak-to-peak cycle ended September 30, 1987, the market bottom came on August 12, 1982, when the S&P 500 closed at 102.42, down 27.1 percent from its previous bull market peak. The most recent bear leg ended on December 4, 1987, when the S&P 500 closed at 223.9. Market bottoms can also be defined as the month- or quarter-end closest to the actual bottom date.

Market Capitalization: The current value of a company determined by multiplying the latest available number of outstanding common shares by the current market price of a share. For example, on December 29, 1989,

IBM had about 590 million shares outstanding and the stock closed at $94.13. Thus, its market capitalization was $55 billion. Market cap is also an indication of the trading liquidity of a particular issue.

Market Timing: This is defined as the attempt to base investment decisions on the expected direction of the market. If stocks are expected to decline, the timer may elect to hold a portion of the portfolio in cash equivalents or bonds. Timers may base their decisions on fundamentals (e.g., selling stocks when the market's price/book ratio reaches a certain level), on technical considerations (such as declining momentum or excessive investor optimism), or a combination of both.

Market Value: The market or liquidation value of a given security or of an entire pool of assets.

Matrix Pricing: As an example of this technique, consider an asset class fund that is limited to securities with maturities of two years or less. The manager will extend maturities when there is a reward for doing so (when the yield curve is steep), and will hold short maturities when longer maturities do not provide additional expected return (when the yield curve is flat or inverted).

Maturities: Applies to bonds: the date at which a borrower must redeem the capital portion of his loan.

Model Portfolio: A theoretical construct of an investment or series of investments.

Modern Portfolio Theory: In 1950, Professor Harry Markowitz started to build an investment strategy that took more than thirty years to develop and be recognized as modern portfolio theory; he won the Nobel Prize for his work in 1990.

Money Market Fund: Money market fund managers invest in short-term fixed instruments and cash equivalents. These instruments make up the portfolio and their objective is to maximize principal protection. Even though these accounts have short-term (one-day) liquidity, they typically pay more like 90- to 180-day CDs versus passbook or one-week CDs.

Municipal Bonds: Fixed income securities issued by governmental agencies.

Mutual Fund: A pool of managed money, regulated by the Securities and Exchange Commission, in which investors can purchase shares. Funds are not managed individually as they may be by a private money manager.

Mutual Fund Families: A mutual fund sponsor or company usually offers a number of funds with different investment objectives within its family of funds. For example, a mutual fund family may include a money market fund, a government bond fund, a corporate bond fund, a blue chip stock fund, and a more speculative stock fund. If an investor buys a fund in the family, he or she is allowed to exchange that fund for another in the same family. This is usually done with no additional sales charge.

National Association of Securities Dealers, Inc. (NASD): The principal association of over-the-counter (OTC) brokers and dealers that establishes legal and ethical standards of conduct for its members. NASD was established in 1939 to regulate the OTC market in much the same manner as organized exchanges monitor actions of their members.

Net Asset Value (NAV): This is defined as the market value of each share of a mutual fund. This figure is derived by taking a fund's total assets (securities, cash, and receivables), deducting liabilities, and then dividing that total by the number of shares outstanding.

Net Trade: Generally, this is an over-the-counter trade involving no explicit commission. The investment advisor's compensation is in the spread between the cost of the security and the price paid by the customer. Also, a trade in which shares are exchanged directly with the issuer.

Noise: Information about investing that is not supported by valid academic research.

No-Load Funds: Mutual fund offered by an open-end investment company that imposes no sales charge (load) on its shareholders. Investors buy shares in no-load funds directly from the fund companies, rather than through a broker, as is done in load funds. Because no broker is used, no advice is given on when to buy or sell.

Nominal Return: This is the actual current dollar growth in an asset's value over a given period. See also total return and real return.

Nonqualified Contract: An annuity that is not used as part of, or in connection, with a qualified retirement plan.

Operating Expenses: Cost associated with running a fund or portfolio.

Optimization: A process whereby a portfolio, invested using valid academic theory in various asset classes, is analyzed to ensure that risk/reward parameters have not drifted from stated goals.

Outperform: Any given market that exceeds expectations or historical performance.

Over-the-Counter: A market made between securities dealers who act either as principal or broker for their clients. This is the principal markets for U.S. government and municipal bonds.

Owner's Designated Beneficiary: The person to whom ownership of an annuity contract passes upon the contract owner's death, unless the contract owner was also the annuitant — in which case the annuitant's beneficiary is entitled to the death benefit. (Note: this transfer of ownership to the owner's designated beneficiary will generally not be subject to probate, but will be subject to estate and inheritance taxes. Consult with your tax and estate advisor to be sure which rules will apply to you.)

Packaged Products: Specific types of products underwritten and packaged by manufacturing companies that can be bought and sold directly through those companies. Packaged products are not required to go through a clearing process. Packaged products include mutual funds, unit investment trusts (UIT), limited partnership interests, and annuities.

Partial Liquidity: Most annuities allow policy holders to withdraw up to ten percent a year of their account value without a penalty or surrender charge.

Payee: The contract owner, annuitant, annuitant's beneficiary, or any other person, estate, or legal entity to whom benefits are to be paid.

Percentage Points: Used to describe the difference between two readings that are percentages. For example, if a portfolio's performance was 18.2 percent versus the S&P 500's 14.65, it outperformed the S&P by 3.6 percentage points.

Portfolio: A separate investment series of the funds. Portfolio will also be used to refer to the subaccount that invests in the corresponding portfolio.

Portfolio Turnover: Removing funds from one financial instrument to place in another. This process can be costly.

Price/Earnings Ratio (P/E): This may be defined as the current price dividend by reported earnings per share of stock for the latest twelve-month period. For example, a stock with earnings per share during the trailing year of $5 and currently selling at $50 per share has a price/earnings ratio of ten.

Principal: The original dollar amount invested.

Prospectus: The document required by the Securities and Exchange Commission that accompanies the sale of a mutual fund or annuity outlining risks associated with certain types of funds or securities, fees, and management. At the core of the prospectus is a description of the fund's investment objectives and the portfolio manager's philosophy.

Put: A put gives the investor the right to sell a security at a pre-set price within a specified time.

Qualified Contract: If an annuity contract is part of an employee benefit plan and has met certain requirements it is "qualified" under the Internal Revenue Code. The contributions made into a qualified contract are income tax deductible to the employer making the contribution and certain nondiscrimination requirements are met.

Quality Growth Mutual Fund: This term implies long-term investment in high quality growth stocks, some of which may be larger, emerging companies while others may be long-established, household names. Such a portfolio may have volatility equal to or above that of the overall market, but less than that of an "emerging growth" portfolio.

Quartile: A ranking of comparative portfolio performance. The top twenty-five percent of mutual fund managers are in the first quartile, those ranking from twenty-six to fifty percent are in the second quartile, from fifty-one to seventy-five percent in the third quartile, and the lowest twenty-five percent in the fourth quartile.

Rate of Return: The profits earned by a security, measured as a percentage of earned interest and/or dividends and/or appreciation.

Ratings: Performance and creditworthiness measurement of funds and corporations generated by Lipper, Moodys, Morningstar, and others.

Real Return: This is the inflation-adjusted return on an asset. Inflation-adjusted returns are calculated by subtracting the rate of inflation from an asset's apparent, or nominal, return. For example, if common stocks earn a total return of 10.3 percent over a period of time, but inflation during that period is 3.1 percent, the real return is the difference: 7.2 percent.

Rebalancing: A process whereby funds are shifted within asset classes and between asset class to ensure the maintenance of the efficient frontier. *See* Optimization.

Reinvested Dividends: Refers to dividends paid by a particular mutual fund that are reinvested in that same mutual fund. Some mutual funds offer automatic dividend reinvestment programs. In the complex equation theoretically used to determine the performance of the S&P 500, each company's dividend is reinvested in the stock of that company.

REITs: Real estate investment trusts: bundled, securitized real estate assets often trading on the New York Stock Exchange.

Relative Return: The return of a stock or a mutual fund portfolio compared with some index, usually the S&P 500. For example, in 1989, American Brands had a total return of 12.2 percent in *absolute* terms. In isolation, that sounds good. After all, the historical annualized return on common stocks has been 10.3 percent. But because the S&P 500 had a return of 31.7 percent in 1989, American Brands underperformed the index in *relative* terms by −19.5 percentage points. Thus, its relative return was −19.5 percentage points.

Renewal Rate History: A bank should be able to supply you with a copy of their renewal rates, to see how their rates have held after the initial rate guarantee period.

Risk: The uncertainty of future rates of return, which includes the possibility of loss. This variability or uncertainty causes "rational" investors to expect higher returns on investments where the actual timing or amount of payoffs is not guaranteed. A mutual fund portfolio has two types of risk. The first, called market risk, captures the amount of portfolio variability caused by events that have an impact on the market as a whole.

Risk-Free Rate of Return: The return on an asset that is considered virtually riskless. U.S. Government Treasury bills are typically used as the risk-free asset because of their short time horizon and the low probability of default.

Risk Systematic: Potential for predictable, quantifiable loss of funds through the application of valid academic research to the process of disciplined asset-class investing.

Risk Tolerance: Investor's innate ability to deal with the potential of losing money without abandoning investment process.

Risk Unsystematic: Associated with investment in an undiversified portfolio of individual instruments through active management.

ROI: Return on investment, the amount of money generated over time by placement of funds in specific financial instruments.

Rule of 72: The rule is to divide the number 72 by the compound interest rate you have chosen. The result is the number of years it takes your money to double.

S&P 500: The performance benchmark most widely used by sponsors, managers, and performance measurement services. This index includes 400 industrial stocks, 20 transportation stocks, 40 financial stocks, and 40 public utilities. Performance is measured on a capitalization-weighted basis. The index is maintained by Standard & Poor's Corporation, a subsidiary of McGraw-Hill Inc.

S&P Common Stock Rankings: The S&P rankings measure historical growth and stability of earnings and dividends. The system includes nine rankings: A+, A, and A–, above average; B+, average; B+, B–, and C, below average; NR, insufficient historical data or not amenable to the ranking process. As a matter of policy, S&P does not rank the stocks of foreign companies, investment companies, and certain finance-oriented companies.

Securities: A tradable financial instrument.

Securities and Exchange Commission (SEC): The keystone in the regulation of securities markets. It governs exchanges, over-the-counter markets, broker-dealers, the conduct of secondary markets, extension of credit in securities transactions, the conduct of corporate insiders, and principally the prohibition of fraud and manipulation in securities transactions. It also has the power to interpret, supervise, and enforce the securities laws of the U.S.

Securities Investor Protection Corporation (SIPC): This is a government-sponsored organization created in 1970 to insure investor accounts at brokerage firms in the event of the brokerage firm's insolvency and liquidation. The maximum insurance of $500,000, including a maximum of $100,000 in cash assets per account, covers customer losses due to brokerage house insolvency, not customer losses caused by security price fluctuations. SIPC coverage is conceptually similar to Federal Deposit Insurance Corporation coverage of customer accounts at commercial banks.

Security Selection: The process of picking securities, especially stocks, for investment purposes.

Separate Account: The separate account is independent of the general assets of the company. The separate account invests in the portfolios.

Shares: Specific portions of tradable equity, a share of stock. It generally refers to common or preferred stocks.

Single Premium Deferred Annuity: An annuity purchased with a lump-sum premium payment which earns interest for a period of years before the payout period begins.

Speculator: One who uses an active management style to invest, without regard to the fundamentals of the security.

Standard Deviation: Volatility can be statistically measured using standard deviation. Standard deviation describes how far from the mean historic performance has been, either higher or lower. Mean is simply the middle point between the two historic extremes of the performance of the investment you are examining. The standard deviation measurement helps explain what the distribution of returns likely will be. The greater the range of returns, the greater the risk. Generally, the current price of a security reflects the expected total return of its investment and its perceived risk. The lower the risk, the lower the return expected.

Stock: A contract signifying ownership of a portion of a public or private company.

Stock Picker: Someone who is actively trying to select companies whose equity may rise in the short or long term.

Strategic Asset Allocation: Determines an appropriate asset mix for a customer based on long-term capital market conditions, expected returns, and risks.

Subaccount: That portion of the variable annuities separate account that invests in shares of the funds' portfolios. Each subaccount will only invest in a single portfolio.

Surrender Charge: A charge made for a withdrawal from (in excess of ten percent per year), or surrender of, an annuity contract before the annuity starting date; often scales down over time.

Surrender Value: The accumulated value, adjusted to reflect any applicable market value adjustment for amounts allocated to the multi-year guaranteed rate option, less any early withdrawal charges for amounts allocated to the one-year guaranteed rate option, less any amount allocated to the guaranteed equity option, less any premium taxes incurred but not yet deducted.

Systematic Withdrawal Plan: A program in which shareholders receive payments from their mutual fund investments at regular intervals. Typically, these payments are drawn first from the fund's dividends and capital gains distribution, if any, and then from principal as needed.

Tactical Allocation: Investment strategy allocating assets according to investor expectations of directions of regional markets and asset classes.

Tax-Efficient Fund: Money pool which makes no taxable distributions to investors.

Technical Analysis: Any investment approach that judges the attractiveness of particular stocks or the market as a whole based on market data, such as price patterns, volume, momentum, or investor sentiment, as opposed to fundamental financial data, such as earnings dividends.

Time Horizon: The amount of time someone can wait to generate or take profits from an investment.

Time-Weighted Rate of Return: The rate at which a dollar invested at the beginning of a period would grow if no additional capital were invested and no cash withdrawals were made. It provides an indication of value added by the investment manager, and allows comparisons to the performance of other investment managers and market indexes.

Total Return: A standard measure of performance or return including both capital appreciation (or depreciation) and dividends or other income received. For example, stock A is priced at $60 at the start of a year and pays an annual dividend of $4. If the stock moves up to $70 in price, the appreciation component is 16.7 percent, the yield component is 6.7

percent, and the total return is 23.4 percent. That oversimplification does not take into account any earnings on the reinvested dividends.

Trading Costs: Fees or commissions paid to move money from financial instrument to another.

Transaction Costs: Another term for execution costs; fees or commissions generated and paid in the management of a portfolio. Total transaction costs (or the cost of buying and selling stocks) have three components: (1) the actual dollars paid in commissions; (2) the market impact — i.e., the impact a manager's trade has on the market price for the stock (this varies with the size of the trade and the skill of the trader); and (3) the opportunity cost of the return (positive or negative) given up by not executing the trade instantaneously.

Treasury Bills: A U.S. financial security issued by Federal Reserve banks for the Treasury as a means of borrowing money for short periods of time. They are sold at a discount from their maturity value, pay no coupons, and have maturities of up to one year. Because they are a direct obligation of the federal government they are free of default risk. Most Treasury bills are purchased by commercial banks and held as part of their secondary reserves. T-bills regulate the liquidity base of the banking system in order to control the money supply. For example, if the authorities wish to expand the money supply they can buy Treasury bills, which increases the reserves of the banking system and induces a multiple expansion of bank deposits.

Turnover: Turnover is the volume or percentage of buying or selling activity within a mutual fund portfolio relative to the mutual fund portfolio's size.

12b-1 Mutual Fund: Mutual fund that assesses shareholders for some of its promotion expenses. These funds are usually no-load, so no brokers are involved in the sale to the public. Instead, the funds normally rely on advertising and public relations to build their assets. The charge usually amounts to about one percent or less of a fund's assets. A 12b-1 fund must be specifically registered as such with the Securities and Exchange Commission, and the fact that such charges are levied must be disclosed.

Underperform: Securities or markets that do not meet expectations.

Value Added: These are returns over and above those of the stock market.

Value Mutual Fund: In this instance, the mutual fund manager uses various tests to determine an intrinsic value for a given security, and tries to purchase the security substantially below that value. The goal and hope are that the stock price in the fund will ultimately rise to the stock's fair value or above. Price to earnings, price to sales, price to cash flow, price to book value, and price to break-up value (or true net asset value) are some of the ratios examined in such an approach.

Value Stocks: Stocks with high book to market valuations — i.e., companies doing poorly in the market that may have the potential to do better.

Variable Annuities: Insurance-based investment products, which like other forms of annuities allow for growth of invested premiums to be free from taxation until withdrawals are made from the contract. Unique to variable annuities are several forms of investment alternatives that vary in their potential for both reward and risk. Variable annuity choices are broad enough that an investor can employ either an aggressive or conservative approach, or a combination of both, while enjoying the benefits of tax-deferred growth. Guarantee of principal from loss upon death of the owner is covered by a death benefit provision.

Variable Annuity Accumulation and Distribution Phases: There are two phases of the "life" of an annuity. The initial phase is the accumulation phase. This is the period in which contributions are made, either as a lump-sum or in systematic payments. The contributions are invested in either a fixed or variable annuity. The assets compound tax-deferred until the contract owner makes the decision to distribute (distribution phase) the assets, either in a lump sum or systematically.

Volatility: The extent to which market values and investment returns are uncertain or fluctuate. Another word for risk, volatility is gauged using such measures as beta, mean absolute deviation, and standard deviation.

Weighting: A term usually associated with proportions of assets invested in a particular region or securities index to generate a specific risk/reward profile.

Yield (Current Yield): For stocks, yield is the percentage return paid in dividends on a common or preferred stock, calculated by dividing the indicated annual dividend by the market price of the stock. For example, if a stock sells for $40 and pays a dividend of $2 per share, it has a yield of five percent (i.e., $2 divided by $40). For bonds, the coupon rate of interest divided by the market price is called current yield. For example, a bond selling for $1,000 with a ten percent coupon offers a ten percent current yield. If the same bond were selling for $500, it would offer a twenty percent yield to an investor who bought it for $500. (As a bond's price falls, its yield rises, and vice versa.)

Yield Curve: A chart or graph showing the price of securities (usually fixed income) through time. A flat or inverted yield curve of fixed income instruments is thought by many to be an indicator of recession. This is because those who borrow at the far end of the curve usually pay more for their money than those who borrow for only a little while. When the yield curve is flat or inverted this means there is little demand for long-term money and this can be interpreted as a signal that there is little demand in the economy for the products that long-term borrowing would generate.

Yield to Maturity: The discount rate that equates the present value of the bond's cash flows (semiannual coupon payments, the redemption value) with the market price. The yield to maturity will actually be earned if (1) the investor holds the bond to maturity and (2) the investor is able to reinvest all coupon payments at a rate equal to the yield to maturity. When a bond is selling at par, the yield to maturity and the coupon rate are equal.

Index

A

AAA through BBB bonds, 84–85
Account, separate, 268
Accumulated value, 252
Accumulation phase, of variable annuity, 156, 159, 271
Accumulation units, 149, 252
Administrative fee, 252
ADV form, 104–105
Advisors, see Financial advisors/planners
Aggressive growth, 252
Aggressive growth funds, 55–56
AIMR Performance Presentation Standards, 116–118
Allocation
    asset, see Asset allocation
    tactical, 269
Allowances, for children, 128
American Institute of CPAs, 26
American Stock Exchange (AMEX), 76, 77
Analysis, 224–227, 252
    fundamental, 225–226
    stock market, 226–227
    technical, 269
Analysts, 252
Anniversary, contract, 256
Annual insurance company expenses, 252
Annual interest income, 252
Annualized return, 252
Annual policy fee (maintenance fee), 161, 252
Annuitant, 158, 253
Annuitant's beneficiary, 253

Annuitization phase, of annuity, 156–157, 159
Annuity (annuities), 148–196, 253
    as compared with mutual funds, 150
    deferred, 150–154, 257
    directory of variable offerings, 182–196
    fixed, 148–149, 259
    immediate, 154
    important facts, 177–181
    operation of, 168–170
    overview of, 148
    parties to, 157–160
    purchase methods, 154–156
    single premium deferred, 268
    stages (phases) of, 156–157, 159
    subaccounts of, 163–167, 269
    terminology of, 161–163
    variable, 149–153, 271
        ten unattractive, 173–175
        twenty best, 170–173
    Weiss Safety Ratings, 175–176
Annuity date, 253
Annuity payment option, 253
Annuity unit value, 253
Antiques, 230
Appreciation, capital, 255
    versus income, 17–18
Art investments, 230
A-shares, 45
Asset allocation, 8–9, 101–102, 253
    strategic, 269
Asset allocation funds, 58
Asset class, 253
Asset class investing, 253

273

Relative value managers, 110–111
Reliability, of financial advisor/planner
       types, 24–26
Renewal rate history, 267
Retail mutual funds, 61
Retirement, 133–201, see also Retirement
       strategies
   check-up on plans for, 145–147
   investment strategy for, 90–91
   savings required for $1 million at 65, 134
   tax equivalent yield, 133–135
Retirement expense calculation, xv
Retirement income and annual savings goal
       calculation, xvii
Retirement income calculation, xvi
Retirement planning, steps of, xiii–xviii
Retirement strategies, 135–147
   annuities, 148–196
      as compared with mutual fund, 150
      deferred, 150–154
      directory of variable offerings,
         182–196
      fixed, 148–149
      immediate, 154
      important facts and warnings,
         177–181
      operation of, 168–170
      overview, 148
      parties to, 157–160
      purchase methods, 154–156
      stages (phases) of, 156–157, 159
      subaccounts, 163–167
      terminology of, 161–163
      variable, 149–153
      Weiss Safety Ratings, 175–176
   individual retirement account (IRA),
       137–138
      educational, 138
      Roth, 138–139
   for self-employed, 139–140
      Keogh, 139–140
      simplified employee pension (SEP)
         plan, 140
   Social Security, 197–201
   at work
      401(k), 18, 140–144, 249, 260, see also
         401(k) plans
      403(b), 140
      pension plans, 144–145

Return
   annualized, 252
   average, 254
   compound annual, 256
   on equity, 257
   expected, 259
   on investment (ROI), 267
   nominal, 264
   rate of, 266
      time-weighted, 269
   real, 266
   relative, 266
   risk-free rate of, 267
   total, 269–270
Risk, 246, 267
   of bond market, 82–85
   currency, 257
   lowering of, 100–102
   mistakes related to, 93
   monitoring and controlling, 125–126
   prospectus and, 234
   as related to time, 97–98
   systematic, 267
   unsystematic, 6, 267
Risk-free rate of return, 119, 267
Risk level, of mutual funds, 51
Risk level flexibility, of mutual funds, 51
Risk objectives and rate of return, 66, 72
Risk profile questionnaire, 36–39
Risk tolerance, 267
Roth IRAs, 138–139
Rule of 72, 267

S

Sales charges (loads)
   for annuities, 168–169
   for mutual funds, 45–48, 168–169
Salomon Smith Barney, 210
S&P 500, 59, 69, 70, 267
Schwab 1000 Index, 59
Securities and Exchange Commission (SEC),
       76–77, 235, 268
Securities Investor Protection Corporation
       (SIPC), 268
Security selection, 268
Security selection criteria, 120